I0819227

REDEEM A NATION

REDEEM A NATION

THE CENTURY-LONG BATTLE TO RESTORE THE SOUL OF AMERICA

DAMARIO SOLOMON-SIMMONS, ESQ., M.ED.

NEW YORK

STOREHOUSE VOICES
An imprint of the Crown Publishing Group
A division of Penguin Random House LLC
1745 Broadway
New York, NY 10019
storehousevoices.com
penguinrandomhouse.com

Library of Congress Cataloging-in-Publication Data

Names: Solomon-Simmons, Damario, 1976– author
Title: Redeem a nation : the century-long battle to restore the soul of America / Damario Solomon-Simmons, Esq., M.Ed.
Other titles: Century-long battle to restore the soul of America
Description: First edition. | New York : Storehouse Voices, [2026] | Includes bibliographical references and index.
Identifiers: LCCN 2025055073 (print) | LCCN 2025055074 (ebook) | ISBN 9780593874585 hardcover | ISBN 9780593874592 ebook
Subjects: LCSH: Tulsa Race Massacre, Tulsa, Okla., 1921 | African Americans—Reparations—Oklahoma—Tulsa—History—21st century | Solomon-Simmons, Damario, 1976– | African American lawyers—Oklahoma—Tulsa | Lawyers—Oklahoma—Tulsa | African Americans—Violence against—Oklahoma—Tulsa—History—20th century | Greenwood (Tulsa, Okla.)—Race relations—History—20th century | Greenwood (Tulsa, Okla.)—History—20th century | Tulsa (Okla.)—Race relations—History—20th century | LCGFT: Autobiographies
Classification: LCC F704.T92 S65 2026 (print) | LCC F704.T92 (ebook)
LC record available at https://lccn.loc.gov/2025055073
LC ebook record available at https://lccn.loc.gov/2025055074

Hardcover ISBN 978-0-593-87458-5
Ebook ISBN 978-0-593-87459-2

Editor: Chelcee Johns
Production editor: Abby Oladipo
Text designer: Andrea Lau
Production: Chris Andrus
Copy editor: Maureen Clark
Proofreaders: Sigi Nacson, Sibylle Kazeroid, and Nicole Ramirez
Indexer: Jane Farnol
Publicist: Jennifer Valentin
Marketer: Mason Eng
Publisher: Tamira Chapman
Associate Publisher: Porscha Burke
Editorial Director: Jennifer Baker
Publishing Associate: Isabela Alcantara
Editorial assistant: Camryn Johnson

Manufactured in the United States of America

2nd Printing

First Edition

The authorized representative in the EU for product safety and compliance is Penguin Random House Ireland, Morrison Chambers, 32 Nassau Street, Dublin D02 YH68, Ireland, https://eu-contact.penguin.ie.

For the people of Greenwood—founders, survivors, descendants, those who were lost, and those who stand together as one today—may this book help deliver justice long denied.

To "Mother" Viola Ford Fletcher (1914–2025), who passed before this work reached the public. You endured unspeakable hardship with grace and courage. You spoke truth to power when power refused to listen. And you never stopped believing in love, community, and justice. Representing you was one of the great honors of my life.

CONTENTS

PART FOUR
WEALTH CIRCULATION 201

PART FIVE
WILLFUL RESILIENCE 273

AUTHOR'S NOTE

ON REPAIR AND SOUL

When I speak of repairing America's soul, I do not mean restoring something that was once whole. America has never had a soul. From its beginning, this nation was built on genocide, slavery, and racial exploitation. There was no moral center to recover.

Repair, as I use it, means something different. It is not just healing a wound but creating what has never existed by confronting the truth, delivering reparations, and making justice real. Repair is not nostalgia. It is construction. It is laying the foundation that was denied at the beginning, insisting that integrity and dignity be established where none existed before.

I also mean the Black community as a nation within a nation, formed not by borders but by history, culture, and shared subjugation. This book is written from that truth. It is a blueprint for repair that refuses to choose between redeeming America and repairing the Black Nation, because the future of each is bound to the other.

That is why Greenwood matters. The struggle for justice in Greenwood is not about returning to a mythical past. It is about proving whether America can build a soul at all through truth, through justice, through repair.

PREFACE

When I arrived at the Tulsa County Courthouse on the morning of May 2, 2022, for the motion to dismiss hearing, the weight of my community sat heavily on my shoulders.

In 2020, my legal team and I had filed a lawsuit on behalf of the last living survivors of the Tulsa Race Massacre of 1921, accusing the defendants of deliberately perpetuating the harm of the Massacre over more than a century. The City of Tulsa and other entities had created an ongoing public nuisance that negatively affected the health, prosperity, and security of the Black population of North Tulsa . . . my people. That public nuisance, we argued, demanded reparatory justice.

The defendants hated our lawsuit and used every procedural tactic they could to delay and hinder it, including motions to dismiss. Finally, after nearly two years, I was about to go before Judge Caroline Wall to argue that our case was just and should proceed to discovery. No one had ever filed a suit like ours or gotten this far, which is why the courtroom was buzzing with descendants of the Massacre, news crews, and people from the community and all over the country who had come out to show their support. The courtroom itself was about half full when I walked in.

My three survivor clients—107-year-old Lessie Benningfield "Mother" Randle, 107-year-old Viola "Mother" Fletcher, and 101-year-old Hughes Van Ellis (known to everybody as "Uncle Redd" and who had flown in from Denver for the hearing)—were seated at the front of the courtroom, behind the short wall that separates the counsel tables from the spectators. The defense attorneys were seated at the left-hand table. My legal team and the staff of Justice for Greenwood totaled about twenty people, with six of us seated at the right-hand table. But while I appreciated all the support, I was so focused on getting our technology set up and making sure our presentation was working correctly that I could barely take it all in.

Once everything was in order, I excused myself to the restroom, where I could have a quiet moment to do my pretrial ritual of affirmations, prayers, and enunciation and pronunciation drills, to get my mind and spirit right. As I prayed, I was talking to God, my ancestors—including my grandmother Mama Brown; my grandfather Daddy Brown; and my Uncle Don Simmons—and lawyer role models like Buck Colbert "B. C." Franklin, Johnnie Cochran, and Thurgood Marshall, asking them to speak through me and give me guidance. *I am standing on your shoulders.*

After maybe seven minutes, I came out of the restroom, and the crowd had tripled in size. I could feel its energy coursing through me. The moment brought back memories of playing football at the University of Oklahoma (OU), when I would run out of the shadows of the tunnel and emerge in the blinding sunshine to the roar of the crowd to take our positions on the field. I could feel electricity in the air. As I walked back to the courtroom, the hallway was packed with people standing shoulder to shoulder. I went through the door at the back of the room, which meant I had to walk through the gallery. I couldn't believe how many people were there; it was standing room only. As I crossed the gallery, I heard my good friend Terry Bradford shout, "It's the people's champ!" The entire courtroom gave me a standing ovation.

This *never* happens. There are strict rules of decorum in every courtroom. Everyone, from attorneys to spectators, is expected to sit quietly and respectfully. Yet hundreds of people from my community were whooping and hollering like it was a Saturday afternoon in Norman and the OU Sooners were playing the Oklahoma State Cowboys! It was an incredible show of support and enthusiasm, a Friday night lights energy I had never experienced in a courtroom.

As I walked to the counsel table, I also noticed some high-profile supporters. There was Representative Sheila Jackson Lee, the leading sponsor in Congress of H.R. 40, the bill to establish the Commission to Study and Develop Reparation Proposals for African Americans. She was a racial justice warrior who had supported the reparations fight for twenty years and knew Tulsa was the tip of the spear for the national reparations movement. I saw Barbara Arnwine, a legendary civil rights attorney. I saw Seth Bryant, the great-grandson of A. J. Smitherman (one of the leaders of the Greenwood community in 1921) and a successful lawyer in New York.

As the ovation died down, I was surprised to see my in-laws seated in the gallery. My mother-in-law was seventy-eight years old; my father-in-law was eighty-six. They had never been in a courtroom, but they had come to support me and our movement. I started to get emotional. This felt like a moment when history would be made. All the work I had put in and the lifetime of hope I had invested in obtaining justice for my people could finally pay off.

Judge Wall came in and took her seat on the bench. I had been in front of Judge Wall many times, but today, her appearance was different. She was wearing makeup, and she'd had her hair professional styled instead of pulling it back in a casual ponytail. I believe she understood, as we all did, how momentous this day was. She addressed the overflow crowd standing at the back of the gallery and told them they could stay as long as the fire marshal didn't make them leave.

The bailiff stepped forward and gave everyone the usual warning: "No phones, no recording. If I see your phone, I'm going to confiscate it." Then, with the preliminaries out of the way, my team and I started our argument against dismissal.

Where did the road to that courtroom begin? There's a short answer and a long answer. The short answer is that it began in January 2020, when I stood on Mother Randle's front porch in the winter chill, debating whether to ring her doorbell.

At the time, Mother Randle was 105 years old. She had survived the Dust Bowl, two world wars, the Great Depression, and Jim Crow segregation. She had raised five children and outlived two husbands. Yet, despite all this, she was living in bitter poverty.

Nearly a century earlier, her home in North Tulsa was burned by a white mob, her family's hard-earned savings reduced to ashes along with it. Her family had rebuilt that home, only to have it taken by the city and bulldozed nearly fifty years later in the name of urban renewal.

This second destruction was an act of economic violence from which she, like countless Black people in cities and communities across the United States, would never recover. Mother Randle had worked hard, lived an honorable life, and suffered almost unimaginably. And she was still here, deep in the heart of North Tulsa, surviving in an urban desert where there were no grocery stores or hospitals, and few community resources of any kind.

Standing on her doorstep just after sunset on that cold, windy January evening, I took in the neighborhood that had defined much of Mother Randle's life. There were few streetlights on this block, but I could make out the network of potholes and cracks spiderwebbing across the worn-out concrete of an urban street beat down by decades of municipal neglect and disrepair. Weeds sprouting up on property lines were the only hints of green. A group of neighborhood kids kicked a ball around on the uneven sidewalk and into the crumbling street. I had played on those same neglected streets growing up.

Reaching out to press Mother Randle's doorbell, I hesitated. I was built for the battle I was about to take on in the Oklahoma courts on behalf of victims of a crime that had occurred in Tulsa nearly a century before. I went to law school to become an attorney, but in my heart, I have always been a warrior. But I wasn't sure I should be dragging Mother Randle into this fight.

I knew how the wheels of the American justice system could grind down even the strongest. Also, I knew that Mother Randle still suffered from the trauma she had experienced so long ago. She had trouble sleeping, her family told me, and sometimes woke up with night terrors. She deserved to live out her final days in peace.

But could she really have peace? Could her family, or the thousands of families whose lives had been blighted by racist policies and generations of harm in North Tulsa, ever really know peace without justice? This gnawed at me. I had to ask Mother Randle herself if she wanted to fight alongside me.

I rang the bell.

Mother Randle's granddaughter LaDonna Penny swung the door open and greeted me with a warm hello. I stepped into the living room, where Mother Randle was seated on a worn leather couch, a handsewn quilt tucked across her tiny frame. She looked small and frail but also alert and present. When I sat down beside her, she took my hand and held it in her own. Her grip was surprisingly strong.

"I heard you had a birthday not so long ago," I said.

"Yes, November tenth." She smiled. "This year I will be a hundred and . . ." She covered her mouth. "Not doing too bad for an old girl."

"I spoke with your granddaughter this morning," I began. "She told me you were living in Tulsa in 1921 during the Massacre."

"Oh, yes. I was staying with my grandmother and my auntie. She was a schoolteacher."

"Mother Randle, can I ask if you remember what took place in Tulsa on May thirty-first of that year?" I asked, pulling out my yellow legal pad to take notes.

"Yes, I can recall some things that happened in that . . ." She paused for a moment and closed her eyes. "Well, I remember it as a war. Of course, I was very, very young. Maybe five or six years old. What I remember most is just running. Waking up and people running us out of our house. We had to get out of the house. We had to leave. I was just running right alongside, tagging along. And I remember the fires. Buildings burning."

"Mother Randle, do you know why I'm here?"

"LaDonna told me you're a lawyer." She looked over at her granddaughter and smiled.

"She said to me, 'Grandma, you got a whole lot more to do. God is not through with you yet.' I told her, 'Well, if the Lord just give me strength, I'll do it. Just give me health and strength and I'll do it.'"

She paused and looked at me for a moment. It was a look I'd seen my mother and grandmother give me many times before. She was peering into my soul and sizing me up.

"You think we can win?" she asked.

"I can't make any guarantees." I hesitated. Then, understanding the gravity of the moment, I said, "But yes, ma'am, I believe we can win."

At the core of the so-called American dream is a promise that every citizen has an equal opportunity to achieve prosperity. This is a myth, but the story goes that those who work hard can own a home, start a business, and accumulate the kind of wealth that can be passed down to the next generation. Yet for centuries, African Americans have lived the American nightmare. Again and again, we have been stripped of our property, labor, dignity, and wealth, and with those things, the promise of prosperity. Property stolen and turned into universities, highways, or parking lots. Wealth taken that would have preserved a legacy for an entire family, community, and bloodline.

The American legal system was not built to stand up to these kinds of injustices, and every time Black people have sought justice in the courts for verifiable historical trauma, the goalposts have been moved and justice has been denied. Even today, decades after the most violent criminal acts against Black generational wealth building were committed, the effects of these crimes reverberate throughout American society, and they impact everyone, Black and white alike.

Whether you live in a house by the coast in San Francisco, in a New York City high-rise, on a family farm in Georgia, or deep in the desert of the American Southwest, the horrific crimes against Black citizens and freed and former enslaved people and their families affect you. They stunt the American economy, create a permanent underclass, lead to blight in our cities, and perpetuate inequality throughout the nation. They mark America as a cruel, uncivilized, and unjust country.

Wealth accumulation is a generational pursuit. It takes decades (if not centuries) of ownership and investment to secure prosperity and opportunity for future generations. To protect this kind of sound decision-making, citizens need good public policy and the help of courts, law enforcement, and insurance companies. They need reliable institutions working on their behalf to safeguard and guarantee the money that pays for healthcare, college tuition, home maintenance, investing in a 401(k), or moving to a great school district.

But what happens when these safeguards fail? Worse, what happens if the very institutions that should protect you on your journey of building wealth and security for your family deliberately act against you? What if the government fails you so completely that it becomes a party to crimes that destroy your health, freedom, and opportunity?

The only way to counter such malice is through *reparatory justice.*

I have spent decades fighting for reparations in courtrooms, legislative hearing rooms, and city halls, but I prefer to think of the word *reparations* beyond its legal context. At their core, reparations are a social contract between individuals or groups that have failed each other in some profound and deliberate way. Sometimes justice can be as simple as returning a stolen package to a doorstep with a note reading, "Sorry."

However, some large-scale harms, which destroy the lives, livelihoods, and wealth of entire swaths of the population, rise to the level of a gross violation of human rights. Because these cases require comprehensive redress, reparations should mean money allocated to fairly compensate victims for their losses. But that's not all. Public apologies are issued. Stolen land is returned. Guilty parties are punished. New laws are passed to keep the harm from happening again.

That sounds great in theory. But African Americans, victims of hundreds of years of racial violence, theft, arson, and murder by gun, knife, and rope, have never gained a tangible foothold in the U.S. legal system. To many in the white power structure, reparations for Black people are simply unacceptable. Japanese Americans received multiple payments from the federal government as compensation for their internment during World War II, but Black people have never received a penny.

To answer the question of why reparations are necessary, I could point to how a wealthier, more prosperous Black community confers economic benefits on everyone, and that would be valid, but it wouldn't be the main reason reparations are a duty. The true reasons are as follows: First, the evidence is ironclad. White society has taken from Black people on an unimaginable scale, and that's a debt that must be settled. Second, without reparations and reform to close the racial wealth gap, Black people will never be more than second-class citizens. Third, without repairing the injustice done to Black people, America will *never* achieve greatness.

We live in a time when millions proudly shout the slogan "Make America great again," but America has never been great. Rich? Yes. Powerful? Yes. Influential? No question. But great? No. True greatness is not about armed might. It's about a country's willingness to live up to its values, stand on principle, and do what's right by all its people. The United States, a country built on the genocide of Indigenous peoples and Africans, has never even accepted that reality, much less acted to repair the great harm done. Until we do so, we cannot and *will not* be a great country.

Given the current administration and the overt anti-Black and anti-justice trend of the country, this will be an uphill battle, but it's a battle worth fighting. Debts must be paid. It is to this belief that I have devoted my life.

I'm a child of North Tulsa, Oklahoma. The event that makes the clearest case for reparations post-enslavement occurred blocks from the house where I grew up, not even two generations before I was born. Yet I was a young man in college before I even knew about the Tulsa Race Massacre of 1921 and heard the word *reparations*.

North Tulsa was once home to the greatest, best-organized, and most vibrant Black community in the history of this country. Deep Greenwood, as it was known, was the beating heart of Black Tulsa. It was a bustling promenade more than a mile long, lined with Black-owned grocery stores, physicians' offices, pharmacies, real estate agencies, hotels, movie theaters, newspaper headquarters, juke joints, barbershops, billiard halls, and beauty salons. Black families at the turn of the twentieth century had invested in themselves and one another with what little they had and found huge success in doing so. They built a community with their sweat, love, and ingenuity, and they built it to last. Greenwood in the early 1900s was a booming mecca of Black Community Love, Freedom Mind State, Ownership, Wealth Circulation, and Willful Resilience—what I today call "the Think-Greenwood principles."

However, in today's North Tulsa, there are no major shopping centers or movie theaters, no sit-down restaurants or supermarkets, and not a single hospital. You can drive south for miles on Martin Luther King Jr. Boulevard, one of two main arteries running through the neighborhoods where I grew up, and pass a dozen churches, a few tire shops, car washes, bootleg convenience stores, liquor stores and medical cannabis dispensaries, dilapidated houses, and vacant lots overrun by trash and waist-high weeds, until you reach the highway. There, MLK runs into six lanes of concrete that cut a dividing line between North and South Tulsa.

South of that highway is a humming metropolis. On summer evenings, the city's arts district bathes in a warm glow coming off the minor-league stadium lights at ONEOK Field. BOK Tower and more than a dozen other skyscrapers rise like fireworks against the light of the setting sun. But in the part of North Tulsa where Mother Randle lived when I met her, where I grew up, the darkness is a reminder of all that was lost.

The explosion of violence and destruction that shook Tulsa over a thirty-six-hour period in 1921 was a horrific event. But the damage didn't end when the last fires were extinguished; it has continued unabated for more than a century. Billions of dollars in property, businesses, investments, and more—wealth that should have helped the children and grandchildren of Greenwood prosper and keep North Tulsa a vibrant, vital place—were stolen or destroyed and never passed on to the rightful owners. Worse, the lives of more than ten thousand Greenwood residents were thrown into chaos forever.

In this book, I will reveal what happened to North Tulsa and its residents, explain the centuries of history behind it, and discuss why it matters to all of us, even those of you who have never been to Tulsa and will never visit. I will talk about the factors that led to Greenwood's rise, and the racism and greed that brought about its destruction. I will show how the devastation of the Massacre is still happening, trapping the Black community of North Tulsa in a cycle of poverty, poor health, urban decay, and hopelessness. You'll see that Tulsa is a microcosm of cities and towns all over the United States, each with its own history of state violence and racism, slavery and continued harm, theft and corruption meant to keep Black people from wealth and opportunity—a fact that led directly to the fascism of MAGA 2.0.

I will show you why and how reparations work and explain why we need apologies to forgive, compensation to be whole, restitution to truly be equal under the law, and new laws (plus the enforcement of laws already on the books) to ensure our safety. I will tell the inside story of the legal fight for reparatory justice that began immediately after the Massacre; continued with the work of towering lawyers and scholars, courageous community activists and leaders; and passed to me and my team in 2018, leading to both devastating setbacks and landmark victories. I've learned hard-won lessons and gained fresh insight and wisdom on how to approach social justice fights today and in the future, and I'll share that as well.

I will introduce you to some survivors of the Massacre whom I have had the pleasure to represent—both those who have passed away and those who are still with us—and share some details of their extraordinary lives, as well as a national community of passionate descendants who continue to this day to work for justice.

Finally, I will teach you about the ThinkGreenwood principles—the five powerful, fundamental ideas that were the foundation of Greenwood at its peak—and show you how Black communities throughout the nation can employ them to build coalitions, create strategies, gather resources, and pursue reparatory justice suited to specific harms and people's specific needs. These are the ThinkGreenwood principles:

1. Community Love
2. Freedom Mind State
3. Ownership
4. Wealth Circulation
5. Willful Resilience

But these five principles are more than an organizing philosophy: They have also been the heart and soul of my journey even before I knew them by name. That's why I've threaded them through this book. Each has shaped a different stage of my story.

The long answer to where the road to that courtroom began? That story begins in Tulsa. It must. Nowhere else has such a violent historic act of racial terrorism been so well documented, with page after page of evidence, pictures, video, and eyewitness testimony. Nowhere else are there still living Black victims of a racist crime of this magnitude. I focus on Tulsa because I am from Tulsa. This place has my heart, sweat, blood, and attention, and its pain, the pain of justice denied, is my pain. However, Tulsa is just the tip of the spear. Just as the Massacre reverberated across the nation back in 1921, the hopeful message of reparations and justice finally won for its victims would reverberate across the world, too.

We are living in an era where too many Americans define "greatness" based on who holds the power to harm, terrorize, impoverish, or imprison someone weaker than they are. But that is not greatness. Great nations are not built on anger, oppression, or the thirst for revenge. If more than twenty years of working within the legal system on behalf of some of the most brave and remarkable people I've ever met has taught me anything, it's this: There is a deep longing for healing, equity, and justice in this country. People want to be heard, respected, and treated with fairness and dignity.

Are we, at long last, ready to do that? Are we ready to be great—for real? Read on and decide for yourself.

Damario Solomon-Simmons, Esq., M.Ed.
Tulsa, Oklahoma
Summer 2025

PART ONE

COMMUNITY LOVE

Greenwood wasn't a utopia. It had its problems just like any other community. But it was also a sacred space where Black people expressed their love for one another and their community in many ways: worship, raising and educating their children, and lending a hand to those who needed help. Today, the Greenwood diaspora—the descendants of Massacre survivors—maintains that same love, devotion, and dedication to the cause of justice. They've grounded me in family and community and taught me that oftentimes loving something means fighting for it. This story begins with community love, and with the people who would destroy that love in the name of greed and hate.

The Mann brothers had a store there on Greenwood Avenue. They had ransacked it and set it on fire, too. They'd set all the stores on fire. They just went in and took everything they wanted and then burned them all down. Eventually, the soldiers came along in a bus, picked us up, and took us down to the Fairgrounds. But I remember seeing a truck, a flatbed truck. They had loaded it with bodies. They just threw dead bodies on that truck, stacked them up like livestock after a slaughter. They said they were going to take them to the morgue, but we heard later they took those bodies down and threw them in the river.*

—Lessie Benningfield "Mother" Randle

A cabinet card featuring an aerial view of Greenwood as it burns in the background during the Tulsa Race Massacre. A Group of African Americans stand on a dirt road in the foreground. June 1, 1921. Courtesy of Museum of Tulsa History.

CHAPTER 1

CROSSING THE TRACKS

When May 30, 1921, dawned, the City of Tulsa was really two cities: one Black, one white, both prosperous. The discovery of the Glenn Pool Oil Reserve in 1905 (on land owned by a Black Creek woman, Ida Glenn) had in a few short years transformed northeastern Oklahoma from rural Indian Territory into the world's largest crude oil producer and Tulsa from a small railroad stop into a cash-rich boomtown of more than one hundred thousand residents known as "the Oil Capital of the World."

The city was home to more than four hundred oil and gas companies and numerous other businesses that served the petroleum industry: tank manufacturers, pipeline suppliers, and refineries. Oil money had funded the construction of new schools and parks, a civic auditorium, a new bridge across the Arkansas River, and even an airport. Tulsa was served by four rail lines, had two daily newspapers—the *Tulsa World* and *The Tulsa Tribune*—and was home to dozens of thriving medical, legal, financial, and insurance offices. The city skyline revealed what passed for skyscrapers in that age of brick buildings, with hotels, theaters, restaurants, and saloons.

In 1921, about 90 percent of the residents of Tulsa were white. The other ten thousand or so people, nearly all of the city's Black population, lived in the four-square-mile city within a city (larger than Harlem, New York) known as the Greenwood District. Bordered on the south by the Frisco railroad tracks, on the west by Detroit Street, and on the east by Lansing Street, Greenwood was a vibrant North Tulsa community that included more than 1,250 homes, numerous churches, a library branch, two newspapers of its own (*The Tulsa Star* and *The Oklahoma Sun*), and a bustling business district featuring grocery stores, barbershops, hotels, schools, pharmacies, bus companies, airplane taxi services, movie theaters, concert halls, doctors' offices, and legal practices, nearly all of them Black owned.

Most of the neighborhood's residential blocks were tucked into the area west of the main commercial artery, Greenwood Avenue, and were filled with rows of colorful, well-kept bungalows. Few homes had electricity or phones, and there was no city water or sanitation. Light came mostly from candles and lanterns, while residents got their water from wells and cisterns and relied on outhouses. Despite this, the mostly working-class folks enjoyed days that were close-knit and neighborly. On weekdays, the streets were buzzing with the activity of residents headed to work and children going off to school; the weekends would often be marked by good-natured chatter, music, and mouthwatering smells of backyard cookouts and fish fries and front porch conversations.

Most of Tulsa's Black population didn't participate directly in the regional oil boom that was minting new millionaires each year, but Greenwood had a remarkably vigorous, mostly self-contained economy. Many of its residents who did not own businesses worked in South Tulsa as custodians, porters, oil field workers, and domestics for wealthy white Tulsans, and then returned home to spend their money in the restaurants, businesses, and shops along the Greenwood Avenue and North Lansing Avenue business districts. The dime that bought a root beer at the Kyle's Sundry soda fountain might find its way into the collection plate at the Vernon AME Church and might then be used to help pay a local Black carpenter to make repairs to the church building. That economic independence gave Greenwood power.

By 1921, Greenwood had become a forty-square-block oasis of entrepreneurship, freedom, and apparent safety where Black people could live their lives mostly set apart from the widespread racial oppression of Jim Crow America. This voluntary, purposeful self-segregation and self-determination allowed residents to properly nurture their mental and physical well-being, build a social fabric around love and respect for everyone, and exercise their right to "pursue happiness" as promised in the Declaration of Independence. After a while, Greenwood became so successful and prosperous that when the great educator and founder of the Tuskegee Institute, Booker T. Washington,[1] visited in 1913 on his way to a speaking engagement, he called the area "the Negro Wall Street of America." (Later, as that "n-word" passed into disuse during the civil rights movement, the sobriquet became "Black Wall Street.")

However, you may have noticed that I used the phrase "apparent safety" in describing Greenwood. That's because the district and white Tulsa existed in a fragile racial equilibrium. Beneath its wealthy facade, Tulsa was seething with crime, racism, and the resentments and poisonous beliefs of white supremacy. Upon statehood in 1907, Oklahoma had embraced racist Jim Crow laws, and Tulsa was a deeply segregated city. For example, the city passed an ordinance prohibiting anyone from living on a city block if 75 percent of the other residents of that block belonged to the other race.

White vigilantism was a growing threat, and not just against Black people. On August 21, 1920, a white mob had forcibly taken a nineteen-year-old white man, Roy Belton, who had been arrested for shooting a white taxi driver, Homer Nida, from the county jail and lynched him, hanging him from the Federal Tire Company advertising sign in front of a crowd thought to number as many as two thousand.[2]

Following that incident, the great A. J. Smitherman, the activist lawyer who owned *The Tulsa Star,* said privately that if a lynch mob could abduct and kill a white man with no resistance from police, no Black man accused of a crime would be safe. Smitherman had already earned the respect of Black leaders—and the animosity of the white community—for intervening in Black-white conflicts. In 1917, after a white mob burned twenty Black homes in Dewey, Oklahoma, forty miles north of Tulsa, his outreach to Governor R. L. Williams resulted in thirty-six members of the mob, including the town's mayor, being arrested. He prevented a lynching in 1918 by leading an armed group of

Black men thirty miles southwest of Greenwood into Bristow to protect Edgar Bohanan, a Black man charged with robbing and shooting a white man.[3]

But the most serious threat to Greenwood was white Tulsa's deep resentment of the economic successes, self-confidence, and landholdings of the community's residents. Throughout the United States, Black economic empowerment was seen as a threat to established racial hierarchies, and in Tulsa a dangerous stew of jealousy, entitlement, and hate had been stoked to a boil by the racist headlines and violent rhetoric that appeared daily on the pages of *The Tulsa Tribune,* the city's largest evening daily newspaper.

In his book *The Burning: Massacre, Destruction, and the Tulsa Race Riot of 1921,* journalist Tim Madigan described Richard Lloyd Jones, the owner of the *Tribune,* as Tulsa's "most vocal racist"[4]: "Jones's paper published what amounted to a press release for the new KKK, a story that lauded the secret order's ambitions to add chapters in Oklahoma. The new Klan, the story said, was to be a living, lasting memorial to the original Klan members who had saved the South from a 'Negro empire [built] upon the ruins of southern homes and institutions.'" This same sort of toxic revisionist history is still found throughout the South and is common in today's MAGA movement.

Greenwood's southern border was the Frisco rail yards, a set of Burlington Northern Santa Fe train tracks that snaked from St. Louis, Missouri, to Floydada, Texas, and marked the dividing line between Black and white Tulsa. Beyond that line was a white community that resented the very existence of Greenwood, with people in positions of power who wanted to eradicate the mostly self-sustaining Black community—the stereotypical "uppity niggers"—to the north and seize their valuable land. All they needed was a spark, something that would let them blaze a path into Greenwood so they could violently take what didn't belong to them.

Not long after the lynching of Roy Belton, A. J. Smitherman warned that the next time a Black Tulsan was arrested and threatened with lynching, Black leaders had better be ready to intervene. Unfortunately, he would prove prophetic.

Dick Rowland had grown up in Greenwood and played football at Booker T. Washington High School[5] before leaving to take a job as a "bootblack"[6] at a shine parlor in downtown Tulsa for five dollars a week. On the afternoon of May 30, Rowland reportedly took a break from his work and stepped into the elevator of the Drexel Building on Main Street, home of Renberg's[7] department store, intending to use the "Colored" restroom on the fourth floor.

No one knows exactly what happened next, although there is no shortage of speculation. Most believe that Rowland tripped on his way into the elevator and either stepped on the foot of or grabbed the arm of the only other person inside: seventeen-year-old white elevator operator Sarah Page. Page may have thought she was being assaulted; according to some accounts, she hit Rowland with her purse and even showed the damaged bag to her neighbor Anna Green later in the day. What is widely believed is that Page screamed, and witnesses saw Rowland running out of the elevator.

Those who would ask, "If he hadn't done anything wrong, why did he run?" are not considering the tenor of the times or the racial animus that was approaching a boiling point in Tulsa.[8] Sure enough, the next day, after Page told her story to Clarence Poulton, a clerk and tailor at Renberg's, and despite the fact that Poulton later told an investigator that Page "was not bruised nor her clothing disarranged in any way,"[9] Tulsa police arrested Rowland and charged him with sexual assault on a white woman—tantamount to a death sentence in Jim Crow America. By three o'clock that afternoon, the racist *Tulsa Tribune* hit newsstands with a front-page article headlined "Nab Negro for Attacking Girl in Elevator"[10] and an editorial calling for Rowland's murder titled "To Lynch Negro Tonight."[11]

Within an hour, hundreds of white Tulsans began gathering outside the County Courthouse—a churning, murmuring mass of men in dark trousers, work boots, and white shirts, sweat staining their collars and armpits, demanding that Dick Rowland be handed over to them to be lynched. Sheriff Willard McCullough refused, telling the men to go home. Meanwhile, on the top floor of the four-story limestone courthouse, the terrified teenage boy sat on the cold concrete floor of a cramped jail cell, alone in the darkness as bloodthirsty shouts of "Let us have the nigger!" echoed from the street below.

A white man smoking a cigar poses with his weapons in front of the Dreamland Theatre during the 1921 Tulsa Race Massacre. Courtesy of Museum of Tulsa History.

As the abduction and death of Roy Belton had proved, the threat of lynching was not an idle one. Throughout much of the country, "mob justice" was the norm, particularly when white supremacists were presented with the chance to vent their bottomless fury against Blacks. According to one of my mentors, the great human and civil rights attorney and author Bryan Stevenson, and his Equal Justice Initiative, more than four thousand Black men and women[12] were lynched across twenty states between 1877 and 1950.[13] Lynchings were a brutal tool of white supremacist terror intended not only to torture and kill but also to break the spirit of the Black communities where they occurred.

For example, in 1898, when Blacks were elected to political office in Wilmington, North Carolina, the city's white power structure exploded with rage and conspired to break what they called "Negro rule."

A call to arms appeared in *The Wilmington Messenger*: "There will be a meeting of the White Men of Wilmington this morning at 11 o'clock at the Court House. A full attendance is desired, as business in the furtherance of White Supremacy will be transacted." In the racist violence that followed, as many as three hundred Black men were killed, with an unknown number lynched, in what historians have called the nation's only violent coup d'état against a duly elected government.[14]

Lynchings were horrifying extralegal executions that often—but not always—followed a Black person being charged with a crime. However, Black victims were lynched for offenses as minor as bumping into a white person or not addressing a white person with the right amount of deference. When we picture a lynching, we may visualize someone hanging from a tree or lamppost, but often victims were mutilated, decapitated, or burned alive. After L. D. Nelson was accused of shooting and killing Okfuskee County Deputy Sheriff George H. Loney, he and his mother, Laura, were taken from their cells in the Okemah County Jail by a group of forty white men and lynched on May 25, 1911, near Okemah. According to some reports, Laura was raped before both were hanged from a bridge over the North Canadian River.[15]

One of the most notorious, gut-wrenching lynchings of the time took place on May 19, 1918, when a white mob in Brooks County, Georgia, lynched Mary Turner, who was eight months pregnant, for the crime of publicly speaking out against the lynching of her husband, Hayes, one day earlier. The mob took Mary to Folsom's Bridge near Valdosta, hanged her from a tree by her feet, soaked her in gasoline, then set her on fire. While she was still alive, a member of the mob sliced her belly open with a butcher knife, spilling her unborn baby to the ground. Another member of the mob crushed the still-living baby's skull under his boot. No member of the mob ever faced justice for the brutal slaughter of Mary and her child.[16]

But lynchings were not simply about murdering someone for the unforgivable "crime" of being Black. They were about terrorizing and demoralizing every Black man, woman, and child in the United States. While they could be shadowy, secretive affairs, lynchings were often public spectacles held before picnicking white crowds that could number in the thousands. Photographs of the torture and murder were often turned into postcards and sold as souvenirs. Lynchings were tools to rally the white supremacists of the day. It is hard to imagine anything more evil.

As word of the lynch mob gathering downtown spread, the people of Greenwood determined to act. At about 6:30 P.M., a group of some of the district's most prominent businessmen and community leaders assembled at the headquarters of *The Tulsa Star* to talk about what to do. Among them were real estate tycoon Ottawa W. Gurley, who, in 1905, had purchased the first dusty acres of land from which Greenwood had sprung; attorney John the Baptist "J. B." Stradford, whose fifty-four-room luxury boardinghouse, the Stradford Hotel, was the largest, finest Black-owned and -operated hotel in the country; World War I veteran O. B. Mann, co-owner with his brothers of a luncheonette and three of Greenwood's two dozen grocery stores; and entrepreneur John Williams, proprietor of several businesses on Greenwood Avenue, including an auto repair shop, a confectionery, and the world-famous 750-seat Dreamland Theatre.

Stradford was especially ready. Many times, he had warned, "The day a member of our group was mobbed in Tulsa, the streets will be bathed in blood."[17] That night he stated (regarding going to the courthouse to protect Rowland), "If I can't get anyone to go with me, I will go single-handed and empty my automatic into the mob and then resign myself to that fate."[18]

I still find this astonishing. Those men were outnumbered twenty to one, but they went anyway, each of them aware that tomorrow they could be the one sitting in a jail cell, falsely accused and waiting to be handed over to a chanting mob hungry to see their bodies hanging from a tree or bridge. Why would the most powerful men in Greenwood, who had so much to lose, put everything on the line to protect a shoeshine boy?

The answer is simple. Dick Rowland was one of Greenwood's own. Much of the country knows Greenwood as Black Wall Street, but the community was much more than a commercial center. It was a community bound together by faith, pride in what they had built together, and love for one another and for a place where they could live as they had a *right* to live, freely and without fear. In the face of reckless, violent hatred, these men chose to stand up for their own humanity by loving one of their own—no matter the cost. To them, wrong was wrong. If they didn't do something to defend Dick Rowland, they would have as much blood on their hands as the mob chanting for the boy's death. If they wanted change, they had to make it happen.

The men marched up the courthouse steps and offered to help defend the jail from the angry white mob—which was, according to reports, now some two thousand strong, many of them armed—now spilling out into the surrounding streets. By this time, the tension of barely suppressed violence was palpable. Sheriff McCullough assured Stradford, Gurley, and the rest of the Greenwood men that Dick Rowland was safe and turned them away. As they descended to the street, an old white man broke through the crowd. "What are you gonna do with that gun, nigger?" he shouted in O. B. Mann's face.

"I'm going to use it if I need to," Mann replied.

"No, you give it to me," the white man demanded.

"Like hell I will," Mann said.[19]

When the man reached out to snatch Mann's army-issued revolver, the gun went off. For a moment, the only sound was the crack of a single gunshot ricocheting off the stone walls of the courthouse. Then all hell broke loose.

"On May 31st, 1921, I went to bed in my family's home in the Greenwood neighborhood of Tulsa. The neighborhood I fell asleep in that night was rich—not just in terms of wealth, but in culture, community, and heritage. My family had a beautiful home. We had great neighbors and I had friends to play with. I felt safe. I had everything a child could need. I had a bright future ahead of me. Greenwood could have given me the chance to truly make it in this country.

"Within a few hours, all of that was gone. The night of the Massacre I was woken up by my family. My parents and five siblings were there. I was told we had to leave. And that was it.

"I will never forget the violence of the white mob when we left our house. I still see Black men being shot, and Black bodies lying in the street. I still smell smoke and see fire. I still see Black businesses being burned. I still hear airplanes flying overhead. I hear the screams. I live through the Massacre every day."[20]

Those were the words of my client Viola "Mother" Fletcher, sitting next to me and testifying before the U.S. House of Representatives Subcommittee on the Constitution, Civil Rights, and Civil Liberties on Wednesday, May 19, 2021. Despite being 107 years old, she bravely traveled to Washington, D.C., in the middle of the Covid-19 pandemic and the shadow of the January 6 insurrection, to read her testimony into the *Congressional Record*—a living witness to history. But even her words cannot capture the rage and savagery of what took place after the white mob crossed the Frisco railroad tracks into Greenwood.

After Mann's gun went off, members of the mob began firing their own guns on the men who had come down from Greenwood, who returned fire even as they began retreating north, badly outnumbered. As many as a dozen people died in that initial exchange of gunfire, and gun battles erupted between the Black and white groups at various points between the courthouse and the boundaries of the Greenwood District. The remaining Black men were able to make it across the Frisco tracks into friendly territory, but men of both races lay dead in the streets of downtown Tulsa, which now filled with thousands of angry, vengeful white men, most armed, some inebriated, and all looking for a reason to commit mayhem.

For many decades, the events that followed were regarded as a "riot," a spur-of-the-moment eruption of violence. They were not. What happened next was deliberate and had long been planned. After the Greenwood group's retreat, around five hundred white men gathered outside the Second Street headquarters of the Tulsa Police Department as officers swore them all in as "special deputies," complete with temporary badges. Laurel Buck, a bricklayer who was part of this group, later testified that a police officer had told him to "get a gun and get a nigger."

Correction: Five hundred white men and one *Black* man gathered at the police HQ. Walter White, a national NAACP officer in Tulsa to investigate lynchings in Oklahoma, was a light-skinned Black man who could easily "pass"[21] as white. He went to the station to witness what was happening and incredibly ended up being deputized. Imagine being Walter, shoulder to shoulder with a mob of incensed white men hell-bent on killing the next Black person they laid eyes on. It must have been terrifying. Later, White told associates that a fellow posse member said excitedly, "Now you can go out and shoot any nigger you see and the law'll be behind you."[22]

The city government had officially sanctioned violent action against Greenwood. Random violence? No. This was premeditated war with the intent of killing Black citizens and stealing their property, and now the city had raised an army.

The white terrorists soon began looting downtown stores for guns and ammunition and attacking any Black residents they found. As rumors flew that a "Negro uprising" had begun in North Tulsa, thousands of armed white men headed toward Greenwood. Cars filled with terrorists began driving through Greenwood neighborhoods, shooting indiscriminately at homes and at anyone who happened to be outside. Some of the butchers went further, invading homes and murdering the Black residents. One horrifying account provided by Walter White told of an elderly couple quietly saying their evening prayers in their Greenwood Avenue home when terrorists broke in, shot them both in the head execution-style, looted the modest house, and then set it on fire, leaving the still-warm bodies inside to burn.

By one o'clock on the morning of June 1, fires could be seen burning around the perimeter of the Greenwood District. When Tulsa Fire Department crews arrived to fight the fires, gunmen chased them away. Meanwhile, the two sides started exchanging gunfire along the

Frisco railroad tracks, turning the unofficial boundary into a military front.

Around this time, John A. Gustafson, the Tulsa chief of police, sent a telegram to Governor James B. A. Robertson, asking that he call up the Oklahoma National Guard to quell the violence: "Race riot developed here. Several killed. Unable handle situation. Request that National Guard forces be sent by special train. Situation serious."[23] Note the use of the loaded term *race riot,* as though both Black and white forces were equally responsible for the carnage. In fact, Black Tulsans were acting in self-defense, and it was lawless white Tulsans who were now rampaging through the streets and setting buildings ablaze. This false equivalence contributed to the narrative that the city's Black residents were somehow culpable—a kind of "permission slip" for the atrocities to come.

As the long night wore on, while fires burned and armed groups stood in stalemate at the railroad tracks, other important events occurred. A small group of white men gathered at the courthouse shouting, "Bring the rope!" and "Get the nigger!" But their efforts to lynch Dick Rowland never went further than that, and they eventually dispersed. Ironically, all the charges against Rowland were ultimately dismissed. For white Tulsa, he had played his role, that of the match to dry kindling.

While this was happening, National Guardsmen (all white) began arriving in the city, and it quickly became evident that they were not neutral peacekeepers. Instead, some guardsmen began leading armed "patrols" of white vigilantes through the streets, eventually capturing Black Tulsans and handing them over to the police as prisoners. Meanwhile, some residents of Greenwood had started to move stealthily among the streets and houses, informing residents of what was happening. Alerted to the danger, residents divided themselves into two camps. Some were determined to defend their property and community. Dreamland Theatre owner John Williams stood watch in the window of his family's apartment at the corner of Greenwood and Archer, armed with a rifle and shotgun.

Many others decided to flee to the countryside for the safety of their families. Groups of Black residents began driving cars, riding horses, and walking out of Greenwood under cover of darkness, hoping to escape to nearby towns. Even then, there was no guarantee of safety; some were shot dead by the side of the road as they walked with their children and grandchildren.

At about 2:00 A.M., the fighting at the Frisco rail yards ended with neither side victorious. This led some in Greenwood to conclude that the violence was over. However, thousands of angry, armed white men still milled about the streets of downtown Tulsa, intent on violence. Fighting broke out between Blacks and whites in an area known as Sunset Hill, with reports that a white woman had been shot and killed. Wild rumors spread, including the claim that five hundred armed Black men would be arriving at the Third Street railway station, ready to participate in the alleged "Negro uprising." The report was false, but when law enforcement officials heard the rumor, they dispatched police to defend white neighborhoods. Meanwhile, a train carrying one hundred additional National Guard troops was set to arrive in Tulsa at 5:00 A.M.

In the hours before dawn on June 1, thousands of armed white men had gathered on the edges of Greenwood, exchanging ammunition and planning their assault. One group of National Guardsmen carried a machine gun to the top of the five-story Middle States Milling Company grain elevator, where they would have an unobstructed field of fire along Greenwood Avenue.

At sunrise, what sounded like a factory whistle raised a clear signal, and several thousand armed white men organized into regiments charged into Greenwood. As the white men manning the machine gun opened fire on panicked Black residents, the mob spread through the commercial district—screaming with lust and rage, riddling the buildings with gunfire, shooting or beating any Black resident they could find, and using torches and oil-soaked rags to set fire to every building along Greenwood Avenue. Numerous Black citizens were gunned down in cold blood, including A. C. Jackson,[24] a renowned surgeon who surrendered to a group of whites only to be shot where he stood. From Greenwood Avenue, the mob quickly fanned out into the residential streets of the district.

Most of the Black men attempted to fight back and protect their families, homes, and businesses, but the ferocity and sheer numbers of the white terrorists quickly overwhelmed them. Desperate, they attempted to escape with their families, but the machine gun sweeping the surrounding streets with bullets made flight nearly impossible. Men, women, and children were running and screaming, trying to find safety.

Obviously, I was not in Greenwood on those terrible days, so I have done my best to re-create the events of the Massacre. (For an extremely detailed retelling of the events leading up to, during, and after the Massacre, read the indispensable *Tulsa Race Riot: A Report by the Oklahoma Commission to Study the Tulsa Race Riot of 1921.*) However, other people who *were* there have shared their recollections, and they serve to better complete this terrible picture.

Like Viola Fletcher, Mother Randle was a small child in 1921, but she shared many of her memories of the terrible event with me.

> I remember the people coming to our house and pushing us out of the house. We had to get out of the house. We had to leave. We walked on out to Mohawk [Park]. I'm right alongside them, tagging along. On our way out there, the soldiers came along in a bus and picked us up. They had to call in the soldiers it was so bad.
>
> What they [the white savages] would do, they would go into the stores and pick all the food and everything out of the store they wanted. Then, they'd set the stores on fire and burn the stores down. . . . I just call them hoodlums. That's what

they would do, so they had to call the soldiers in, the authorities of the town called the soldiers in. They came in and chased them out of here. . . . They took us out to the Fairgrounds. They had cots and hot soups and what have you, out there for the people.

It was quite a day. I never want to see that again. No no, no, that was awful. The thing of it was, I don't know why they were looking for all the men, but they were looking for all the men. They were— I don't know, but they killed a lot of men. They had a flatbed truck. They tell me that they killed those men and stacked them on the truck like you would sardines, and took them down to the river and threw them in the deepest part of the river. That's what they told us they did with them. I didn't see them do that. That is what they said they did with them. It was terrible. It was terrible. They killed all the men.

They came out to our house, and we had a loft up there. They had a cover, you know, pulled back, and they looked up in the loft. . . . But they were afraid to take the cover off because they didn't know what was up there, looking for men. They thought they were hiding in the loft. . . . I never did learn why they wanted to kill the men, but they did. It was senseless to me. . . . It was something else. Really something. I never want to see that again. It was so foolish. I don't know what in the world the riot was all about anyway. It just sounds so foolish to me. I just never could make any sense out of it. That's what they did.

In her series of powerful oral histories with Massacre survivors, Greenwood historian Eddie Faye Gates shared Juanita McGowan Burnett Arnold's eyewitness account of the events before and during the bloodshed:

The day before the riot there was an incident right in front of our house. A group of angry white men were roaming up and

> down our street. They were so full of anger, jealousy, and rage. They were using the "N" word in every sentence they spoke. It was "Nigger this," and "Nigger that!" They were especially jealous of men like my father and grandfather, who had nice homes and businesses. My dad got his gun and went out into the yard and ordered the men off his property. He told them to respect his wife and children. All the men left, except one man who was obviously intoxicated. Dad drew his gun on him and told him to leave. The angry, defiant man finally did reluctantly leave. The next day, when the riot was on, and after we had fled to safety farther north, a person who was in the area described an armed, angry white mobster who stood in front of our house and snarled, "Where is that uppity Nigger who was so bold yesterday?" If my father had still been in our house, he would surely have been killed by that hate-filled man.[25]

One of the most gripping pieces of historical testimony comes from one of my heroes, Black attorney B. C. Franklin, whose ten-page typewritten account of the Massacre survives to this day. He wrote of his experience:

> From my office window, I could see planes circling in mid-air. They grew in number and hummed, darted and dipped low. I could hear something like hail falling upon the top of my office building. Down East Archer, I saw the old Mid-Way hotel on fire, burning from its top, and then another and another and another building began to burn from the top. "What, an attack from the air too?" I asked myself.[26]

As Franklin described, airplanes appeared shortly after the white mob entered Greenwood and began dropping bombs on the district and shooting Black people from the air. Respected physician Robert Tyler Bridgewater said of the air assault: "Shortly after we left a whistle blew . . . and aeroplanes began to fly over us, in some instances very low to the ground. A cry was heard from the women saying, 'Look out for the aeroplanes, they are shooting upon us.' "[27]

The entire Greenwood District was soon engulfed in flames, with pillars of black smoke visible twenty miles into the countryside. At this point, white murderers freely broke into any remaining homes. Black occupants who were armed or who resisted were shot, their blood and brains splattering the walls. The gunmen lined up the rest and led them away to hastily erected "internment centers." (What kind of "spontaneous" riot includes the foresight to set up internment camps?) After murdering or imprisoning the property owners, the terrorists stole what they wished and then set each building ablaze before moving on to the next. Tulsa police officers in plain clothes participated in the violence as well.

Despite fierce fighting in the neighborhood's Standpipe Hill district, the Black residents of Greenwood had no chance against superior numbers, superior firepower, and the complicity of both Tulsa police and the Oklahoma National Guard. By 11:00 A.M. on June 1, when Governor Robertson declared martial law and additional National Guard troops arrived in Tulsa, nearly the entire forty square blocks of Greenwood—hotels and stores, churches and theaters, the pride and heart of Black Tulsa and Black Americans everywhere—lay in ashes.

The photographs of the time show smoldering, skeletal ruins that resemble the remains of bombed-out villages from World War I. On June 10, *The Black Dispatch*, the leading Black newspaper in Oklahoma City, ran a photograph of the destruction headlined "Not Belgium, but Greenwood Street in Tulsa, Oklahoma."[28]

At the time, city officials estimated that one hundred to three hundred Black residents had been killed in the violence, but those numbers are painfully imprecise. Adjutant General of Oklahoma Charles Barrett refused to allow funerals for the Black victims, making it even more

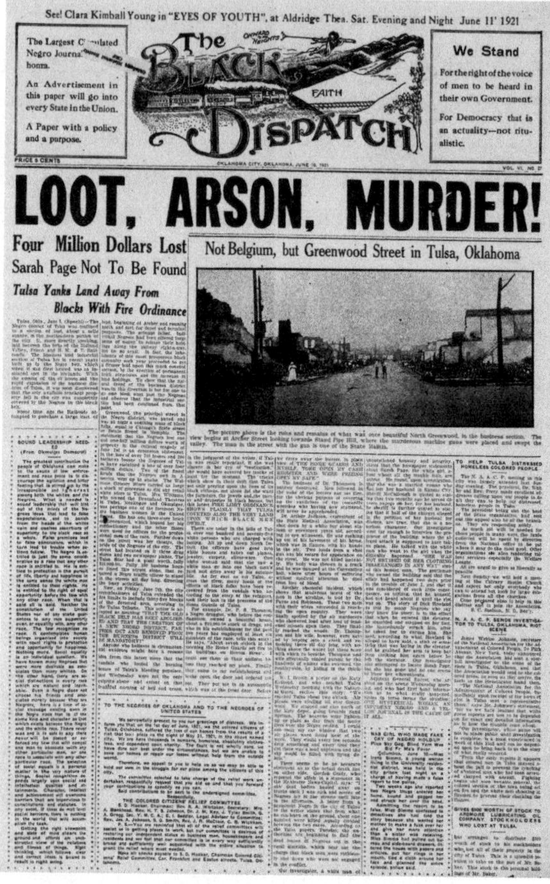

See! Clara Kimball Young in "EYES OF YOUTH", at Aldridge Thea. Sat. Evening and Night June 11' 1921

The Largest C[illegible]ulated Negro Journa[illegible] homa.

An Advertisement in this paper will go into every State in the Union.

A Paper with a policy and a purpose.

The Black Dispatch

We Stand

For the right of the voice of men to be heard in their own Government.

For Democracy that is an actuality—not ritualistic.

PRICE 5 CENTS

LOOT, ARSON, MURDER!

Four Million Dollars Lost

Sarah Page Not To Be Found

Tulsa Yanks Land Away From Blacks With Fire Ordinance

Not Belgium, but Greenwood Street in Tulsa, Oklahoma

On June 10, 1921, *The Black Dispatch*, the leading Black newspaper in Oklahoma City, ran a photograph of the destruction headlined "Not Belgium, but Greenwood Street in Tulsa, Oklahoma." Courtesy of the Oklahoma Historical Society.

difficult to identify and count the dead. According to some accounts, many of the dead were piled like cordwood onto trucks and carted to anonymous mass graves, dumped into coal mines, or thrown into incinerators. In a 2021 affidavit given to the Department of Justice, Lolita Buckner Inniss, dean of the University of Colorado Law School, described the work of her ancestors, who ran a Greenwood funeral home that was burned in the Massacre:

> Because they were undertakers, they took on an especially grim task—recovering and burying the bodies of many murdered Black Tulsans. Members of my family shared accounts of being asked to retrieve bodies that had been thrown into the Arkan-

> sas River over a several day period. Some of the bodies recovered had been badly beaten, burned, and/or shot. Some families were able to claim their deceased loved ones, and funerals were arranged at Oaklawn Cemetery in Tulsa, and at least a few at Agency Cemetery in Muscogee. Many of the bodies were so damaged that open casket funerals were not possible. Some bodies from the river were never claimed. These were taken to mass grave sites in Tulsa.[29]

We may never know the actual number of Black Tulsans who died. We do know that overnight, more than ten thousand people were left homeless and destitute. About three thousand of Greenwood's people simply disappeared. Whether they died, fled to neighboring towns or distant cities, or simply dropped off the community's radar is difficult to say. What we do know is that in about thirty-six hours over two days, the greatest community in the history of Black America, along with untold millions of dollars in wealth, businesses, and real estate, was wiped out.

But property damage was only the beginning of the toll. In reducing more than fifteen hundred homes, churches, schools, businesses, and hospitals to ash and rubble, the terrorists also destroyed future wealth—real estate equity, business value, compounding investment income, professional expertise, and earning power—that would have been passed along to the children, grandchildren, and great-grandchildren of Greenwood's residents. Had it survived, that wealth would have become the foundation of prosperous Black families and communities throughout the nation today.

But the impact was much more than economic. Thousands of Greenwood residents fled their homes or were placed in internment camps and only allowed to go to their jobs if a white person was accountable for their whereabouts. The trauma and despair were overwhelming, the mental health effects devastating.

According to research by Harvard's Dr. Nathan Nunn and others at the National Bureau of Economic Research,[30] before the Massacre, Black leaders had largely believed the federal and state governments would intervene on their behalf to prevent or repair the harm done to their communities by white racism. The nonresponse to Greenwood proved that belief false. Nunn and his colleagues also found that in other Black communities that saw extensive news coverage of Greenwood, the shadow of the Massacre depressed homeownership rates as Blacks in these areas became too frightened and discouraged to risk building prosperous communities of their own. Why invest in the future when everything could be wiped out in a matter of hours based on the impulses of white supremacists who would never face consequences?

The Massacre was intended to be an extinction event for Black pride, aspiration, and economic achievement, and to a great degree, it was. Economist Lisa Cook (who, as I write this, is fighting President Trump's unlawful efforts to fire her from the Federal Reserve's Board of Governors) learned as much when she researched Black innovation and found that after 1921, patent filings by Black entrepreneurs fell off a cliff throughout the United States.

"Tulsa demonstrated that no one would help them—no one. The local government failed. The state government failed. The U.S. government failed at every single level," said Cook in an interview with NPR. "If I'm a Black inventor, why would I ever invent anything if I thought the intellectual property was never going to be defended? You don't feel safe anywhere, but also, my livelihood might be in jeopardy."[31]

Even though I grew up in greater Greenwood, I knew nothing about the Tulsa Race Massacre or the prosperous Black community of Greenwood that was reduced to a smoldering wasteland overnight.[32] I went to George Washington Carver Middle School on Greenwood Avenue and played football at Booker T. Washington High School, just like Dick Rowland. But I never learned his name or those of the men who put their lives on the line to protect him, and I certainly never heard the story of the violence and death that rained down on my home back in 1921 or the white supremacist rage that sparked it. Few in my generation did.

It wasn't until my junior year of college that I discovered that some people I had known my whole life were survivors of the bloodiest race massacre in the history of the United States—a crime systematically covered up by the powers that be in Oklahoma for close to a century. I remember sitting in my Introduction to African American Studies class, taught by one of my greatest mentors, the late Dr. Khepra NuRa Khem, and hearing him talk about Tulsa and Greenwood, how North Tulsa had all these successful Black-owned businesses, and how white Tulsans swept in back in 1921 and laid it all to waste, murdering hundreds of innocent Black people.

What? I had never heard anything about this from my parents or anyone else. This *couldn't* be true. Such horrible events couldn't possibly be kept secret for more than seventy years . . . could they? I was tempted to speak up, but Dr. NuRa Khem was intimidating. He was a big man—about six foot five and three hundred pounds—with long locs and his hair shaved on the sides Mohawk style, and he spoke with a big, booming James Earl Jones voice. He was a no-nonsense professor who didn't care if you were an athlete, which I was. I enjoyed his class, but I hadn't engaged with him. However, when he talked about the Massacre, I said to myself, "Nah, this cannot be true."

Reluctantly, I raised my hand and said, "I'm from North Tulsa, and that's not true." Dr. NuRa Khem told me that it was, and that if I asked my older relatives and elders from the community about the Greenwood Massacre, they would confirm that it had happened. I did talk to my elders, and they backed up what Dr. NuRa Khem told me. It was a shock and an embarrassment to discover that I did not know my own community's past—its real, secret past—especially since I had just earned my associate's degree in history from Tulsa Junior College the semester before!

It wasn't until the late 1990s that the community began to talk freely about Greenwood and opened the eyes of people like me. That was when I became obsessed with Greenwood's hidden history. Many of the survivors of the Massacre and their descendants were people I knew, people I had grown up with, people I had attended church with. My wife, Mia, my high school sweetheart, is a descendant of one of the survivors. But we never knew about any of it because nobody talked about it. Even our elders had internalized silence as an essential mechanism of survival.

I became consumed with getting justice for my people who had lost everything in the worst act of domestic terrorism ever to occur on American soil. That's what makes Greenwood important and unique. Black towns and communities throughout the country had been razed by white rage and greed for a century, but what set Greenwood apart was the size, scope, and scale of the destruction and the quantity and quality of the body of evidence. The Massacre and its aftermath were documented, photographed, filmed, and accounted for by hundreds of hours of testimony from witnesses. Insurance claims were filed, and paperwork was amassed.

The perpetrators and instigators of the Massacre—the City of Tulsa, the Tulsa Chamber of Commerce, Tulsa County, *The Tulsa Tribune,* and others within the white power structure that had been in place in Oklahoma since 1907—tried to erase Greenwood from history. They believed they had run out the clock on the last survivors and that the only way to bring a reparations case to trial would be with a living victim. They believed they could create a narrative that relegated the Massacre to a half-imagined past and whitewashed its atrocity.

They were wrong in many ways. However, before we can explore the long, arduous battle for justice for Greenwood, let's take a closer look at what made the district and its people so precious and celebrated—and their loss so excruciating.

I saw two sights that will live in my memory to my dying days. One was a woman on the opposite side of the street. She was traveling south—hair disentangled and disheveled—in the very path of whizzing bullets. She was calling wildly to a little tot that, a few moments before, had dashed in panic before her and turned off Greenwood on Archer at the corner. I hollered to her, "Turn back woman, for God's sake turn back. You will be mown down." Never turning her head, she answered, as she hurried on, "I must follow my child." And so she did follow her child and not a bullet touched her although they literally rained down the street. This brave self-denying mother lives today here in Tulsa and with her that tot—now a splendid young lady—whom she risked her life to save.*

—B. C. Franklin, attorney-at-law

Pictured are members of the Colored Citizens Relief Committee and East End Welfare Board. Standing are *(left to right)*: Williams, Phillips, Esta "Essie" A. Loupe, Reverend E. N. Bryant, Horace T. Hughes, and McLean. Kneeling are *(left to right)*: Perry R. Russell, Ottawa W. Gurley, Bush, and Tucker Gilmer. Courtesy of Museum of Tulsa History.

CHAPTER 2

THE GREATEST BLACK TOWN IN AMERICA

For the entirety of this country's history, African Americans have had to struggle for basic human rights and the necessities of life. Following the Civil War, and with the enactments of the Thirteenth Amendment in 1865, the Fourteenth Amendment in 1868, and the Fifteenth Amendment in 1870 (which abolished slavery, guaranteed the rights of citizenship to Blacks, and guaranteed Black men the right to vote), African Americans, in theory, gained the opportunity to obtain some degree of freedom.[1]

From the end of the Civil War in 1865 through the end of Reconstruction in 1877, Black citizens enjoyed a brief but significant period of newfound freedoms and opportunities, despite resistance from many parts of Southern society. They began participating in elections, and many were elected to public office. There were many Black legislators in Southern state governments, and even African American members of Congress, such as Mississippi Senators Hiram Revels and Blanche K. Bruce, and a Black governor of Louisiana, P.B.S. Pinchback.

There was a strong push for land reform, with many formerly enslaved people advocating for the redistribution of land, famously summed up by the phrase "40 acres and a mule." This view became clear when, on January 12, 1865, at a historic gathering in Savannah, Georgia, often called "the Savannah Colloquy," General William Tecumseh Sherman asked a group of Black faith leaders about the prospects for Black progress amid white supremacy, oppression, and racial violence. The leaders told Sherman that only in separate enclaves could Black people achieve their full educational, political, social, and economic potential as free people.[2]

This meeting led to the issuing of Special Field Order No. 15 on January 16, 1865, which famously set aside some four hundred thousand acres of confiscated Confederate lands in Georgia, South Carolina, and Florida for the settlement of formerly enslaved people. In March 1865, Congress created the Bureau of Refugees, Freedmen, and Abandoned Lands, commonly called the Freedmen's Bureau,[3] headed by Civil War hero General Oliver O. Howard, the namesake of Howard University. It extended the force and effect of Special Field Order No. 15 across the entire Confederacy under the jurisdiction of the postwar civil system. This allowed many Black families to acquire land and work it.

Unfortunately, after President Lincoln was assassinated and replaced by Southerner Andrew Johnson, former plantation owners and enslavers were granted amnesty and their lands were returned. Still, from 1865 to 1876, schools were established for Black children and many of the country's top historically Black colleges and universities (HBCUs) were founded. Blacks were also able to form churches, businesses, social organizations, civic societies, and newspapers.

However, forces with a deep-seated interest in continuing white supremacy had other plans. Beginning in the late 1870s, racist governments put in place a new system designed to restrict and oppress African Americans that was built around segregation, racist laws, Black codes,[4] lynching, sharecropping,[5] and other barriers against the progress of African Americans.

Hungry for *genuine* freedom—from fear, injustice, and hatred, along with freedom to determine their own economic and cultural futures—African Americans began a frantic search for an environment where they could live in peace and safety, where they could prosper and be duly rewarded for their hard work, and where they could build healthy families and tightly knit communities based on cooperative economics and mutual aid.

To understand how Greenwood came to be, fulfilling the dreams of those post-Reconstruction Black leaders, you must understand Oklahoma's Black history, the most distinctive yet unknown Black historical account in the country.

Some people know that before the turn of the century, Oklahoma was Indian Territory, part of a vast expanse of land west of the Mississippi where the U.S. government forcibly sent tens of thousands of Native Americans: most notably the formerly called "Five Civilized Tribes"—Creek, Cherokee, Seminole, Choctaw, and Chickasaw. They were called this because many of their citizens had adopted European customs and religion, along with plantation-style economies that included the enslavement of Black people. The government forcibly removed these people from their stolen traditional homelands in Alabama, Georgia, and Florida and from 1831 to 1850 sent them on "the Trail of Tears" to be resettled in what is now Oklahoma.[6] However, what most people don't realize is that a substantial percentage of the members of these Five Tribes would be labeled as Black today, including many of my ancestors on my father's side of the family, who were Muscogee (Creek).

Some of these Black people were Africans enslaved by the tribes to work their plantations. Others were runaway enslaved Africans. Others were "Native Blacks," descendants of African explorers to America hundreds of years before Europeans or simply indigenous to North America, free independent people who had never been enslaved.

The Creek Treaty of 1866 was signed on June 14. One of the five individuals who negotiated and signed on behalf of the Muscogee (Creek) Nation (MCN) was a wealthy, well-known Creek of African descent who became a chief: Cow Tom, aka Cow Mikko, my paternal great-great-great-great-grandfather.[7] The treaty became the foundational legal document between the United States and the Muscogee (Creek) and established the modern MCN in northeastern Oklahoma, including what is now Tulsa, as well as their citizenship, protection under the law, and right to settle on tribal lands.

In 1866, in the aftermath of the Civil War, each of the Five Civilized Tribes signed Reconstruction treaties with the U.S. government (due to siding with the Confederacy) that included provisions mirroring the protections of the Thirteenth, Fourteenth, and Fifteenth Amendments. Creeks of African descent became even more essential parts of the MCN and served in important positions.[8] In fact, according to an 1894 U.S. Department of the Interior Census Bulletin, "The Creek nation is an alert and active one . . . largely due to the negro element which fairly controls it."[9] Moreover, the report states that "the Creek Nation affords the best example of negro progress. The principal chief, virtually a negro, comes of a famous family in Creek annals. His name is Lequest Choteau Perryman."[10]

But some provisions of the treaty were punitive. Article 3 specified the territory the Creeks had to surrender as compensation for some members having fought on the side of the Confederacy. This effectively reduced MCN territory by half.[11] However, in return, the treaty gave the MCN ownership rights to its remaining lands forever . . . in theory. As has so often happened, the government broke its promises.

The Dawes Act of 1887 introduced "allotment" policies for Indian Territory in which the federal government divided communally owned tribal lands into individual plots, allowing non-Native (mostly white) settlers to acquire large portions of land through land runs, effectively breaking up reservations. In 1893, an act of Congress created the Dawes Commission, which attempted to "negotiate" with the Five Tribes to give up tribal title of their lands. When tribal leaders resisted, Congress passed the Curtis Act in 1898, dissolving tribal governments and allowing the federal government to seize the land. Between 1898 and 1907, the federal government distributed the land to each MCN citizen as a 160-acre allotment, creating millions of acres available for "settlement" in northeastern Oklahoma, including the land that later became Greenwood.

So, ironically, the glory of Greenwood was made possible by the destruction of the Creek way of life. Given that my father's side of the family wanted to remain free and separate from the white man in Indian Territory, but some of my mother's side of the family came to Oklahoma because of the seizure of Creek land (which opened up work opportunities), I am the living embodiment of that contradictory reality.

What was a catastrophe for the MCN sparked opportunities for thousands of freedom-seeking Black people from across the nation. In Indian Territory, Black people could now be free and independent. They could control their own educational and economic destiny. This was sweet music to the ears of newly "free" African Americans throughout the United States. As Michael Eric Dyson writes, "Black folk were always on the move, throwing off oppression like stifling clothes and inhabiting new lands with old hopes of freedom."[12] African Americans even lobbied the U.S. government for a place where they could live their lives away from the hell of oppression. The search took them to Kansas, Liberia, Canada, and even the British West Indies.[13] Yet at the conclusion of the Civil War and the ending of chattel slavery, many freedom-starved Africans[14] viewed Oklahoma as the ideal place to start their new lives.

By the 1880s, thousands of Black families (including my wife's) had migrated to Oklahoma from Mississippi, Tennessee, Georgia, Alabama, and all over the Deep South, where Jim Crow laws sought to undo the rights granted to them by the Thirteenth and Fourteenth Amendments. They came seeking freedom, landownership, and prosperity. As a result, Oklahoma became—and remains—home to the greatest number of all-Black towns in this nation's history, islands of freedom and safety in a deeply racist, violently oppressive state.

Black settlers rushed in to claim homesteads, and as a result, from the 1880s through the early 1900s, more than twenty Black towns—Langston, Boley, Clearview, Brooksville, and Tullahassee, to name a few—started popping up. These were communities living in a "freedom mind state" because they had access to three essential ingredients: landownership, education, and economic wealth. All-Black settlements offered the advantage of cooperative economics, safety from white violence, culturally relevant schooling, the freedom to be a "person," and the ability to access markets for crops. According to historian Arthur Tolson, many Blacks in Oklahoma turned to "ideologies of economic advancement, self-help, and racial solidarity."[15]

How did all this migration, Native dispossession, and town building lead to Greenwood? In 1905, two years before Oklahoma statehood, Black entrepreneur and educator Ottawa W. Gurley used money he'd made selling property in Perry, a small town eighty miles northwest of Tulsa, to purchase forty acres of land in Tulsa, north of the Frisco railroad tracks. Gurley built a boardinghouse at the end of a trail that, importantly, did not run through any white neighborhoods. He then built a grocery store, where he sold meat and produce from his eighty-acre farm a few miles away. A hotel, barbershop, café, and cigar store soon followed. Gurley also divided the land into residential and commercial lots and partnered with another Black businessman, J. B. Stradford, to develop a community. Later, he would rename the dusty trail Greenwood Avenue.

It's also important here to mention Gurley's wife, Emma. Unlike many women of the time who were forced to stay in the background, Emma was a powerful and public player in Greenwood's founding. She was a full partner in the Gurleys' interests, managing land purchases, running their businesses, and building a respected reputation in Greenwood. In 1905, Emma purchased two pieces of undeveloped land and had the title put in her name, something unusual for a woman in that period. She further expanded her family's holdings in 1906 by purchasing additional land from a white local, Giuseppe "Joe" Piro. Emma was as important to Greenwood's rise as her husband.[16]

While Emma was running things, Gurley and Stradford laid out streets, alleys, and housing plots, and Gurley reportedly named the new community Greenwood after a Black district in Mississippi whose residents were fleeing to escape Jim Crow violence.[17] Stradford built the Stradford Hotel, which soon became the country's largest, most luxurious Black-owned hotel.

Greenwood grew quickly. The discovery of oil in the region and the resulting increase in Tulsa's wealth and population had made in-migration to Oklahoma even more attractive to Blacks looking for safety and economic opportunity, and thousands of individuals and families poured into the district between 1906 and 1920. Some came from Oklahoma's other all-Black towns;[18] others came to the territory as part of the migration of Native people. Some found employment serving wealthy whites as domestics, cooks, shoeshines, and landscapers; others launched small businesses such as restaurants and beauty salons along bustling Greenwood Avenue. By 1920, the district's population had grown to about eleven thousand.

Although Greenwood was not its own municipality, for all intents and purposes it functioned as an independent city because state laws prevented Greenwood residents from participating in the City of Tulsa government or receiving municipal services. Undeterred, the residents governed their part of town as a separate entity, and when asked, many identified their hometown as Greenwood, not Tulsa.

Greenwood was unlike any other Black community in the country: affluent, self-sufficient, and flourishing, nourished by more than fifty years of Black Power and progress. Much of the land and the structures in Greenwood were owned by its residents. Black people from around the country visited, and many relocated so that they could be part of its peace and prosperity. It was a hub of Black achievement and entrepreneurship, featuring luxurious shops and homes, more than twenty restaurants, nearly thirty grocery stores, a hospital, hotels, a library, a bus and cab service, and much more. In the documentary *Before They Die!*, Massacre survivor and former client of mine Otis Granville "Dad" Clark said, "We lived like we were Wall Street. A lot of folks would come in from New York and Chicago. We had a big time here on Greenwood. This was oil country."[19]

Greenwood thrived in every way possible. If a Black family moved there with children, they would attend the Dunbar School[20] and learn all about livestock and agriculture, helping them develop sustainable, employable skills. Mary Parrish, who survived the Massacre and published the first book about it in 1922, started her own private school. Children who didn't take to school would be mentored by elders, who would help them figure out their natural interests.

If you needed a home, Greenwood was bursting with real estate agents, construction workers, plumbers, and electricians. The Midland Valley and Frisco railroad tracks provided the infrastructure to bring in whatever you needed, from brick to sand to lumber.

What if your kids got sick? You had dozens of doctors to choose from, including Dr. A. C. Jackson, whom William James Mayo and Charles Horace Mayo (co-founders of the Mayo Clinic) called "the most able Negro surgeon in America."[21]

Simon Berry embodied Greenwood's entrepreneurial spirit. He ran an airplane charter service that did entertainment rides and took people all over Oklahoma. He also ran Berry Jitney Service, a fleet of drop-top Model T Fords that would take you anywhere in the city, making him Uber before Uber was Uber! In 1921, he made $500 a day, or about $9,000 in 2026 dollars (which adds up to an annual income of about $2.25 million for someone working Monday to Friday, fifty weeks a year).

But Greenwood was about more than its economic activity. Most people were working-class and lived simply, but this was a community in every sense of the word. People cared about and for one another. The district was safe and peaceful. Everyone knew everyone, which meant they knew your mother, father, and grandparents, so you behaved yourself. "This [was] like having Detroit, Harlem, D.C., Atlanta, Beale Street, and Bourbon Street, all in one place," says Chief Egunwale Amusan, author of *America's Black Wall Street,* a descendant of three Massacre survivors, and one of the most knowledgeable people alive about Greenwood.

In his book *Built from the Fire,* Victor Luckerson described Greenwood as a "fairyland." But it wasn't a fairyland. It was real. And for many people south of the Frisco tracks, that was a big problem.

You cannot talk about Tulsa in the early twentieth century without talking about the Ku Klux Klan. Despite how it is often portrayed in today's mass media, the Klan, founded by the former Confederate general Nathan Bedford Forrest in Tennessee on December 24, 1865, was not a comical boys' club for blundering rednecks. It was a well-funded, militaristic, racist, terrorist organization and a deadly tool of white supremacy.

One of the most notorious, bloodiest acts of Klan violence in its early years was the Colfax Massacre in Colfax, Louisiana, on April 13–14, 1873. Following a disputed 1872 election marked by anti-Black violence, two factions—the legitimate, Black-led administration and the white-led insurgent militia—fought for control of the local government. The white supremacist militia (which included many Klansmen) targeted Black residents who had sought refuge in the courthouse, with militia members firing wildly into the building and eventually setting it on fire, leading to a massacre that lasted for two days. The death toll remains uncertain but is estimated to be as high as 150 Black victims, compared to only three white casualties.[22]

The Colfax Massacre exemplified how the KKK used violence to intimidate and suppress Black political participation and civil rights. It set the tone for decades of anti-Black racial violence and discrimination, especially as the federal government began pulling back its support for Reconstruction in the South.

However, four years before Colfax, in 1869, dismayed by the group's lack of military-style discipline, Forrest had officially dissolved the Klan and publicly repudiated its ideas and methods.[23] Two years later, Congress passed the Enforcement Act of 1871, also known as the Ku Klux Klan Act, which made it a federal offense to conspire to deprive citizens of their right to hold office, serve on a jury, or enjoy the equal protection of law. (This was an example of robust enforcement essential for lasting change.) The intent was to bring an end to the Klan. But by this time the group had more than five hundred thousand members, and as the events in Colfax showed, its ideology was too strong to die out.

In 1910, the Oklahoma legislature passed the infamous "grandfather clause" amendment to the state constitution, affirming that only residents who could read and write any section of the Oklahoma Constitution could vote, unless their grandfathers had voted before January 1, 1866. Since virtually no Black man had been allowed to vote prior to Emancipation, this effectively disenfranchised Black Oklahomans. This law was later challenged before the U.S. Supreme Court.

My friend Shayla Moon is a Massacre descendant, and the plaintiff in the grandfather clause case that went before the Supreme Court was her great-great-grandfather. She posted about the case on LinkedIn:

> My great-great grandfather, Green Irving Currin . . . was the first African American elected to serve in the Oklahoma territorial legislature in 1890.
>
> Despite having held one of the state's highest political offices, in 1910 he was denied the right to vote. When Oklahoma had been admitted to the United States as a state in 1907, it had adopted a constitution which allowed men of all races to vote consistent with the Fifteenth Amendment to the United States Constitution. . . .
>
> However, state legislators soon passed an amendment to the Oklahoma Constitution that required voters to satisfy a literacy test and a so-called "grandfather clause." The "Grandfather Clause" stipulated that men could only vote if their lineal ancestors could vote before 1866; this effectively barred anyone whose ancestors had been enslaved. . . .
>
> The [Supreme Court's] decision handed down on June 21, 1915 (two years after oral arguments—when G.I. Currin was 67 years old) ruled the Oklahoma grandfather clause "to be repugnant to the Fifteenth Amendment and therefore null and void."[24]

The state legislature kept trying, passing a variety of segregationist laws, including making Oklahoma the first state in the country to seg-

A Caucasian man armed with a shotgun stands in front of railroad tracks with other men in the background. The back of the physical photograph contains this handwritten note: "Sir Galahad 'Where our cause is just.' A white hope." June 1, 1921. Tulsa Race Riot. Courtesy of Museum of Tulsa History.

regate public telephone booths with a law passed in 1915.[25] God forbid a white person might have to put their mouth or ear near where a Black person's mouth or ear had been!

In 1915, the KKK was reborn under the leadership of William Joseph Simmons (no relation, in case you weren't sure), and membership quickly grew to at least one hundred thousand men. Shortly thereafter, the revitalized Klan began making overtures to whites in Oklahoma. Early in 1919, Klan members were part of a public parade in the town of Skiatook, just thirteen miles north of Greenwood. According to historian Scott Ellsworth, the Klan made its official presence known in Oklahoma in the summer of 1920, when George Kimbro, Jr., and George C. McCarron arrived in Oklahoma City, set up an office in the downtown Baltimore Building, and began recruiting potential Klansmen from fraternal orders such as the Masons, Knights of Pythias, Elks, and Odd Fellows.

According to Ellsworth, by the fall of 1921, the Tulsa chapter of the Klan had at least 3,200 members.[26] By targeting civic, business, and religious leaders, the organization had acquired a great deal of power and influence. In 1922, the KKK formed the Tulsa Benevolent

Association, a holding company for the Knights of the Ku Klux Klan, Incorporated, which helped raise the $200,000 needed to build Beno Hall, the Klan's temple, or Klavern, in Tulsa. It was an enormous whitewashed building, hatefully and deliberately located at the foot of Standpipe Hill (where many Black residents had lost their lives defending their homes during the Massacre) at the edge of Greenwood. Local racists liked to joke that the hall's name stood for "Be No Nigger, Be No Jew, Be No Catholic, Be No Immigrant."[27]

One of the city's most prominent confirmed Klan members was politician, developer, entrepreneur, and Tulsa booster Tate Brady, who owned the land on which Beno Hall stood and after whom the city's Brady Theater, Brady Arts District, and Brady Heights neighborhood were named (the theater and arts district have since dropped the Brady name). In 1918, amid rising racial and labor-related violence, Brady and the Tulsa Chamber of Commerce brought the Sons of Confederate Veterans to Tulsa for their annual reunion, including the group's future commander in chief, Nathan Bedford Forrest II. As the late historian and journalist Lee Roy Chapman wrote, the event "demonstrated that Tulsa's most powerful and influential leaders at the very least tolerated—and at the most promulgated—the beliefs and biases that primed Tulsa for its most violent display of racial tension, the Tulsa Race Riot of 1921."[28]

At the time, Tulsa was a mostly lawless, fast-growing oil boomtown whose leaders—among them Brady, who owned property in Greenwood—craved land where they could build railroad depots and other industrial properties. Their plan was to move the Black population of Greenwood farther north, seize the land crisscrossed by four railroad lines, and expand the city's rail network to better serve the oil and gas industry.

By stoking the city's inherent racial hatred and white supremacist anger, and by recruiting members in positions of wealth and power greedy for the land rightfully owned by the law-abiding citizens of Greenwood, the Klan amplified Tulsa's racial animus. There's little question that this led to the terrorist violence of those two terrible days. In the words of *The Black Wall Street Times*'s editorial board:

"The Tulsa Race Massacre didn't start because a Black teenage boy bumped into a White teenage girl on an elevator. The seeds for the massacre and destruction of the Greenwood community also known as Black Wall Street had been brewing long before."[29]

The Klan didn't hide its approval of the destruction, either. Two months after the Massacre, Caleb Ridley, a national KKK official, spoke at the Tulsa Convention Hall and said that the Massacre "was the best thing to ever happen to Tulsa and judging from the way strange Negroes were coming to Tulsa we might have to do it all over again."[30]

We had a little pet bulldog named Bob that everybody just loved. Bob was so protective of our house. He was never seen again. I just know that Bob fought bravely to protect our house. I do believe he was a victim of that mob, too. When things cooled down in Tulsa and it was safe to return, I went to our home site. There was nothing there but ashes. I raked through the ashes trying to find something to cherish from the past. But I couldn't find nothing. Absolutely nothing. I believe Bob's remains were in those ashes.*

—Otis Granville "Dad" Clark, as told to Eddie Faye Gates

This postcard shows African Americans being led to the Tulsa Convention Hall during the Massacre. Black-and-white postcard measuring 3.4375 x 5.4375 inches. Courtesy of Museum of Tulsa History.

CHAPTER 3

URBAN REMOVAL

Even after Dr. Khepra NuRa Khem opened my eyes, I wasn't fully aware of the scope of the violence against my people in Greenwood. It would be years until I really grasped the scale of what happened—as well as the depths of Tulsa's vengeful racism—and how the Massacre had not been the end but the beginning of the ongoing campaign to destroy Greenwood.

In the immediate aftermath of the Massacre, Tulsa was under martial law, and the Tulsa Chamber of Commerce was put in charge. Led by chamber president Alva J. Niles, the chamber formed the Public Welfare Board, all the members of which were white. Under the authority of this board, Oklahoma National Guardsmen and some of the white terrorists marched as many as eight thousand Greenwood residents at gunpoint through the streets like prisoners of war, past their still-smoldering homes and businesses, to be detained in what the *Tulsa Daily World* called "concentration camps."[1]

One camp was located at the Brady Theater at the corner of what was then known as West Brady Street (and today as West Reconciliation Way) and North Boulder Avenue, but more were opened to take in all the Greenwood refugees, including at the National Guard armory, the Tulsa County Fairgrounds, and the McNulty Park baseball stadium, home to the Minor League Baseball Tulsa Oilers of the Class A Western League.

Some Greenwood residents were held captive in these detention centers for days while the bodies of their loved ones were carted away to be dumped in unmarked graves, the Arkansas River, or worse. Most were only allowed to leave these camps if a white person "sponsored" them and vouched for their good character, and they were required to wear or carry a green card bearing their sponsor's name while out of the camp.

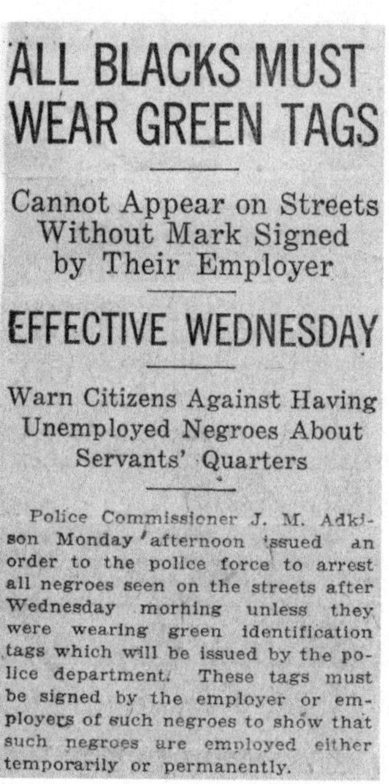

ALL BLACKS MUST WEAR GREEN TAGS

Cannot Appear on Streets Without Mark Signed by Their Employer

EFFECTIVE WEDNESDAY

Warn Citizens Against Having Unemployed Negroes About Servants' Quarters

Police Commissioner J. M. Adkison Monday afternoon issued an order to the police force to arrest all negroes seen on the streets after Wednesday morning unless they were wearing green identification tags which will be issued by the police department. These tags must be signed by the employer or employers of such negroes to show that such negroes are employed either temporarily or permanently.

According to this June 7, 1921, article from the *Tulsa Daily World,* African Americans were required to wear or carry a green card bearing their sponsor's name while on city streets. After June 8, the article states, "Negroes who are not supplied with identification tags will be arrested and taken to the fairgrounds for permanent identification." This order, which was issued by the Tulsa police commissioner, James Adkison, remained in effect until July 7. Courtesy of Museum of Tulsa History.

Piling humiliation on top of genocidal outrage, many of these Greenwood residents were forced to work for their sponsors or for the city under threat of violence and without pay. (There's another term for that: *enslavement.*) The cards featured the words "Police Protection" printed on one side, and information such as the individual's name, address, and employer on the other side. Any Black person found on the street without a properly completed green card was immediately arrested and sent back to their camp.

IDENTIFICATION CARD

Name........*Mary E. Jones Parrish*........

Sex........*Female*........ Age........

Where Living........*535 E. Dunbar St.*........

Employed by........*Mr. Hooker & Gregg*........

Address........*Y. M. C. A.*........ Phone........

Kind of Work........*Y. M. C. A.*........

Employer's Signature........*G. G. Gregg*........

Card Approved........*E. J. Austin*........

Date........*6/13/1921*........

This reproduction of an identification card issued to Mary Elizabeth (Jones) Parrish on June 13, 1921, shows that her employers are Mr. Hooker and Mr. G. G. Gregg of the YMCA. Courtesy of Museum of Tulsa History.

The camps were miserable places, particularly for those who had been wounded or injured in the Massacre. The only Tulsa hospital that would care for Blacks, Frissell Memorial Hospital, had burned, so the refugees—injured, sick, exhausted, and in shock—had to make do with makeshift first aid stations; however, these were not sufficient to care for the seriously wounded. For example, according to the 2001 *Tulsa Race Riot* report produced by the Oklahoma state legislature, Black victims like Dr. A. C. Jackson bled to death in a detention center instead of being transported to a hospital. In the words of the report, "Compared to white victims, those who were black victims were treated with what would today be considered cavalier, if not criminal, carelessness."[2]

Many Black detainees had to work their way out of custody in the most degrading way imaginable: cleaning up the debris left on the streets of Greenwood. On June 2, Charles Barrett, the adjutant general of Oklahoma, issued Field Order No. 4, which decreed that "all able-bodied Negro men remaining in detention camp at the Fairgrounds and other places in the City of Tulsa are required to render such service and perform such labor as is required by the military commission."[3]

Photographs from the time show a handful of Black men on the shattered streets of Greenwood, picking their way through the rubble and ash of what had been their home.

In short, the residents of Greenwood were treated like chattel. In forcing humiliation after humiliation on innocent people who simply wanted to live in peace but who had just been violently dispossessed of everything—and who often had no idea if their loved ones were alive or dead—the racist power brokers of Tulsa had (temporarily) achieved one of their chief goals. They had resurrected slavery.

But there's a deeper, even more sinister dimension to the Massacre and its aftermath. The events bore many similarities to violent European ethnic cleansing terror campaigns called pogroms that targeted a specific ethnic group, most commonly Jews. In fact, the Museum of Jewish Heritage has called the Massacre "an American pogrom" that attacked Black people, homes, and businesses.[4]

My friend and former client Dr. Olivia Hooker was six years old when the Massacre left her homeless. Despite experiencing lifelong effects from this trauma, she lived an extraordinary story. In 1945, she became the first Black woman to join the U.S. Coast Guard, serving during World War II and reaching the rank of yeoman second class. Later, she earned her Ph.D. in psychology from the University of Rochester and became a professor at Fordham University. She was active in the civil rights movement and testified in front of Congress in 2007 in support of the John Hope Franklin Tulsa-Greenwood Race Riot Claims Accountability Act. She passed in 2018 at the age of 103.

When she was interviewed at age ninety-five about her experiences during the Massacre, Dr. Hooker said that her innocence and belief in the goodness of people left her devastated by the violence. "My family had not told me about prejudice and hate," she said. "I thought everything in the Preamble to the Constitution referred to me."[5]

Willfully resilient, Greenwood's survivors wanted to begin rebuilding right away, but the city and the chamber of commerce, along with white developers, real estate magnates, and other business allies, placed barrier after barrier in their path. Tulsa Mayor T. D. Evans blamed the violence on a "Negro uprising"[6] and proposed that the district be redeveloped as an industrial park and railroad station—effectively stealing the land from the rightful owners through murder and mayhem.

To grease the wheels for such wholesale theft, the city illegally passed a fire ordinance that prohibited the construction of "frame structures" (buildings framed with wood) in the Greenwood area. Black residents would have to construct the foundations of their rebuilt homes and businesses out of masonry or stone, something city officials knew was prohibitively expensive. Fortunately, attorney B. C. Franklin, together with his partners I. H. Spears and P. A. Chappelle, challenged the city's ordinance on the grounds that Tulsa was conspiring to deny Greenwood's survivors their legal property rights without due process.

Franklin and his partners filed Tulsa County Case No. 15730, *Joe Lockard v. T.D. Evans*, against the Tulsa mayor and the city commission, and the building code was found to be unlawful. The city appealed, but on September 2, 1921, a three-judge panel from Tulsa County ruled that the city had indeed attempted to deny Greenwood's residents the right to their lawful property—a transparent attempt to confiscate property without due process.[7] Massacre survivors were now free to rebuild, but finding the resources to do so was challenging for people who had lost literally everything.

While they struggled to begin rebuilding, Greenwood's survivors erected whatever makeshift shelters they could: hundreds of Red Cross tents pitched in vacant lots, and shanties and shacks built from scavenged materials and scrap, sometimes put up right on the ashes of once-beautiful houses. For years after the Massacre, Greenwood was reminiscent of a refugee camp after a natural disaster or an occupied city during wartime. B. C. Franklin wrote that "not a Negro dwelling-house or place of business" remained, and that "Negroes who yesterday were wealthy, living in beautiful homes and in ease and comfort, were now beggars, public charges, living off alms."[8]

Many of the survivors had insured their homes and businesses, but

After the Tulsa Race Massacre, victims search through rubble on June 1, 1921. Courtesy of the Oklahoma Historical Society.

how could you confirm someone's claim to a plot of land when all that remained was a shattered wall or charred timbers? In 2009, survivor Wess Young, then ninety-three years old, recorded an interview for the Oklahoma Historical Society and spoke about the difficulty that survivors had trying to prove ownership of their gutted homes.

"They stayed in these what you call internment camp[s] until they could clean off the debris where the houses burned down," he said. "And the way they could tell who owned this piece of property, the insurance companies when they sold a policy, they had a map of where all their policies was in this area. Back on Greenwood they had ten or fifteen policies there. Well, they had that whole block where those policies was. That's the way the peoples could claim their property. They had an insurance agent come in and the policies were like five cents a week or twenty-five cents a month or something like that. But that was the onliest way that they could claim that they had a legitimate claim, that was their property."[9]

However, collecting on these insurance and legal claims would prove impossible. Between June 14, 1921, and June 6, 1922, survivors filed nearly two hundred lawsuits for damages totaling about $4 million ($72.5 million today), naming a wide range of defendants. The survivors also sought damages from the more than thirty insurance companies that had insured property and lives in Greenwood.

One of the most famous photographs taken in the aftermath of the Massacre (and an image that has inspired me since the start of my legal career) shows B. C. Franklin and I. H. Spears sitting in a tent erected as a makeshift law office, surrounded by stacks of law books, reviewing statements from survivors and flanked by a legal secretary typing up complaints and pleadings. Lawsuits had to be filed within one year, and Franklin knew there was no time to wait for a proper office.

This temporary law office was set up in a Red Cross tent following the 1921 Tulsa Race Massacre. Pictured in this photograph taken on June 6, 1921, are attorneys Isaiah H. Spears and Buck Colbert Franklin with their secretary, Effie Thompson. By the next year, the law firm Spears, Franklin & Chappelle was open for business on North Greenwood Avenue. Courtesy of Museum of Tulsa History.

Franklin's determination to give Greenwood residents the protection of the law made him a hero. But shortly after the violence, Tulsa County convened an all-white grand jury to determine legal responsibility for the destruction, and unsurprisingly, the grand jury absolved the City of Tulsa of any legal responsibility and directed the blame at the Black community. On June 6, 1921, this jury indicted fifty of the most prominent leaders of Greenwood, including J. B. Stradford, for inciting a riot. A Black man named Garfield Thompson was sentenced to thirty days in the county jail for carrying a concealed weapon.[10] And that was it. No white man was ever charged with a crime or spent a day behind bars for the Massacre.

More relevant to the survivors, the bogus "official" finding that cleared Tulsa of responsibility meant the damage complaints against the city were dismissed, the last one in 1937. Franklin and Spears had also sued dozens of insurance companies seeking payment for specific claims such as "broom factory stock and fixtures,"[11] "2 feather beds and 2 mattresses,"[12] and "6-room house, modern and sanitary."[13]

However, most of the insurance policies included a clause that released the companies from paying claims for damage due to "riot, civil commotion, and the like." By charging Blacks like Stradford with "inciting a riot," the grand jury had legally designated the events of May 31 to June 1 as a riot. Great American Insurance Group (still in business under the same name) sold Hope Watson a $1,400 policy for property she owned on Greenwood Avenue. Hartford Financial Services Group (also still in business as the Hartford Insurance Group, Inc.) wrote a $1,500 policy for Emma Gurley to cover one of the three properties she owned at 116 North Greenwood Avenue, not far from what is now the Greenwood Rising Black Wall Street History Center.[14]

But the companies denied Gurley's and Watson's claims, and subsequent lawsuits were also dismissed on the same grounds: that the Massacre had actually been a riot.[15] With the city government refusal to provide reparations or assistance, destitute survivors were now responsible for the full cost of rebuilding.

To add insult to injury, 198 of the case files containing the lawsuits filed against the city and the insurance companies disappeared from the courthouse shortly after the cases were dismissed. A comprehensive search by attorneys, law clerks, and private investigators over more than sixty years found nothing. Finally, one of my colleagues, attorney Jim Lloyd (who also served on the Oklahoma Commission to Study the Tulsa Race Riot of 1921), found the case files in the state's decennial index in 1999. He made copies of all the files; the originals are now in the custody of the Oklahoma Historical Society. The files contain all the pleadings—including accusations that Sinclair Oil dropped aerial firebombs on Greenwood—along with the insurer denials of responsibility. Here is an example:

> Defendant further alleges and states; that during the night of May 31, 1921 and the morning and day of June 1, 1921, there was a race riot between the white and colored races, engaged in by persons of both said races . . . joined and met together of unlawfully with common intent creating a great commotion, riot, and tumultuous disturbance of the peace by engaging in fighting, shouting, the discharge of fire arms [*sic*], assault, burglary, robbery, larceny, theft, murder, arson and incendiarism, by the use of force and violence.[16]

In plain English, this response from Westchester Fire Insurance Company (still operating as Westchester, a Chubb Company) characterizes the events of the Massacre as a riot and claims that both the white terrorists and the Black victims were equally responsible for the mayhem. Jim's discovery of the buried case files confirmed that no one was coming to the aid of the Massacre survivors.

While insurers were denying survivor claims, the city and white power brokers were moving on their plans to steal Greenwood's land. On June 2, 1921, the Tulsa Real Estate Exchange, run by Klan member Merritt Glass, rolled out its plan via an article in *The Tulsa Tribune*. The exchange would appraise all the land in the area where Greenwood had stood, free of charge, out of the goodness of their heart, naturally. The exchange and its shareholders would then buy the land from its owners at those appraised values. The city would build a railroad depot and industrial complex on the land, while the Black survivors would be granted a parcel of partially developed land northeast of Greenwood, where they would receive assistance in building a new neighborhood. Of course, the truth was that once the survivors were relocated, they would have been abandoned on the site of their "new home."

The *Tribune* even published this description of the exchange's proposal, which lays bare the city's segregationist position:

> We believe that the vacant lots with proper railroad facilities will bring enough money to enable the negroes to build in a more removed section. We further believe that the two races being divided by an industrial section will draw more distinctive lines and thereby eliminate the inter-mingling of the lower elements of the two races, which in our opinion is the root of the evil which should not exist.[17]

Some whites decried this blatant land grab, including Maurice Willows, the Tulsa director of the American Red Cross, who said that the city and chamber of commerce had conspired to create "public sentiment which would force the negros to rebuild in a section somewhere outside the city limits."[18] According to the *Tribune,* the exchange set up a headquarters in a tent at the corner of Brady Street and Greenwood Avenue and invited property owners to come and report their losses. (Later, another makeshift office would open at Booker T. Washington High School.) According to the *Tribune* article, landowners and renters were "urged by the exchange not to consult attorneys or make claims for insurance independent of the exchange, which will furnish this service and advice free of charge."[19]

Because I am an attorney, such language makes my blood boil. The exchange's offer was insulting, manipulative, unethical, and exploitative. Their intention was to convince Greenwood's Black property owners to forgo independent legal counsel and swindle them out of their land by valuing it for a mere $500 per lot. Exchange investors would then build industrial facilities that would increase the value to about $1,750 per lot.

Furthermore, exchange leaders discouraged Black churches and Black residents in other cities from sending donations to help the survivors rebuild, insisting that rebuilding was "a Tulsa affair."[20]

Fortunately, many of Greenwood's Black landowners weren't fooled and sought their own lawyers anyway. As a result, this attempt to cheat brutalized, traumatized people out of their homes and property largely failed. When the survivors were finally released from detention, they got about the task of building temporary shelters against an already sweltering summer and the coming winter and began making plans to, against all odds, rebuild their paradise.

Some Black families accepted Red Cross offers of free rail tickets to leave the area, but most stayed. These were proud men and women whose ancestors had built Oklahoma. Having endured Jim Crow inequality and Klan violence, they had no intention of yielding their home to thieves and murderers. Even as B. C. Franklin was suing Tulsa over its racist zoning code, displaced Greenwood residents were laying new foundations and reconstructing homes, stores, and offices, often working at night to avoid being seen and fined by police for violating the new zoning law.

But where did the Massacre survivors get the money to rebuild? Most had lost everything in the devastation, including bank deposit records. They had no assets and no ability to borrow, and their insurance claims had been denied. However, some had family members who had built wealth since the end of enslavement and who were more than willing to lend to relatives they knew to be in need.

A few lucky Greenwood residents also had business interests outside of Tulsa that were untouched, and those provided revenue for construction. Others were Native Blacks who made money through oil or crops produced on land that they owned. Still others cashed in war bonds (if they had been fortunate enough to survive the fires and looting), while Black churches in Tulsa and around the country donated money to the rebuilding effort. (A partial record of those donations can still be seen in a membership book kept by my former client the Vernon AME Church, housed in the only Massacre-era structure still standing on Greenwood Avenue.)

Tulsa, ever vindictive, interfered with fundraising efforts as much as it could, deliberately rejecting some monetary aid flowing into the region to assist displaced Greenwood residents. For example, the city and the Tulsa Chamber of Commerce returned a $1,000 (about $18,000 today) contribution sent by the *Chicago Tribune*.[21]

Other Black people didn't trust white-owned banks, which were often run by Klan members. Instead, they hid their money in the one place they knew to be fireproof: their chimneys. After the Massacre, those people went back to the wreckage of their homes and found their money safe and sound. With this patchwork of savings, other income, loans or gifts from family, and investments, some of the more fortunate people in Greenwood pulled together the funds they needed with astonishing speed.

The Williams family, which had owned the Dreamland Theatre, still had income from two other theaters in the nearby towns of Okmulgee and Muskogee, and they used that and money from other sources to raise $75,000 for initial construction and quickly resurrected the Dreamland. The September 14, 1922, issue of civil rights leader Roscoe Dunjee's *Black Dispatch,*[22] the leading Black newspaper in Oklahoma City, ran a story announcing the reopening of John and Loula Williams's businesses, including their confectionery and suite of offices at the corner of Greenwood Avenue and Archer Street.[23] "It is a pleasing sight for the visitor who knows Tulsa as it stood in ashes one year ago to return to the same spot and view two blocks of solid business blocks," the piece read. "The rugged faith and courage of the black man were never better expressed than in the re-erection of the homes and business property of the Negroes of Tulsa."[24]

According to journalist and author Carlos Moreno, by December 1921 there were 738 Greenwood homes in the process of rebuilding.[25] In some ways, post-Massacre Greenwood became more prosperous and beautiful than the district that existed before the terrorist attack. Many people don't know that while the area was nicknamed "Negro Wall Street" in 1913, the name "Black Wall Street" came into the popular consciousness *after* the Massacre.

By the end of World War II, as Moreno writes in his book *The Victory of Greenwood,* the district had experienced a renaissance, rebuilding in many ways bigger and better than it had been before the Massacre. Of course, it could never fully recover because some of its original leaders and top businesses didn't survive. Still, by the early 1940s, the district's population had nearly doubled to more than twenty thousand people. Juanita Alexander Lewis Hopkins, a survivor, shared her thoughts with Eddie Faye Gates as part of Gates's book *They Came Searching*: "North Tulsa after the [Massacre] was even more impressive than before. . . . That is when Greenwood became known as 'The Black Wall Street of America.'"[26]

Indeed, the spirit of Greenwood's residents proved far more resilient than any efforts the Klan-backed city or chamber of commerce could muster to stop them. As Eunice Jackson told Gates: "They just were not going to be kept down. They were determined not to give up. So, they rebuilt Greenwood, and it was just wonderful."

How was it possible for a catastrophe of this scope to be kept quiet for all those years, so that even boys and girls like me who grew up where it happened didn't know anything about it? Immediately after the Massacre, a conspiracy of blame started playing out in the form of inflammatory articles and editorials in the Tulsa newspapers that laid the responsibility for the Massacre at the feet of the city's Black community. The *Tulsa World* began writing its revisionist history immediately, running a June 4 editorial titled "Bad Niggers":

> There are those of the colored race who boast of being "bad niggers." These it was, seizing the merest semblance of an excuse, who armed themselves and invading the business district of the city defiantly sought to take the law into their hands. If possible harmony between the races is to be restored in Tulsa these "bad niggers" must be controlled by their own kind.[27]

Later, on June 14, the *World* ran a story in which Mayor Evans blamed "bad" Black people, who refused to submit to their white superiors, for the Massacre:

> Let the blame for this negro uprising lie right where it belongs—on those armed negroes and their followers who started this

> trouble and who instigated it and any persons who seek to put half the blame on the white people are wrong and should be told so in no uncertain language. . . . It is the judgment of many wise heads in Tulsa, based upon observation of a number of years, that this uprising was inevitable. If that be true and this judgment had to come upon us, then I say it was good generalship to let the destruction come to that section where the trouble was hatched up, put in motion and where it had its inception.[28]

Richard Lloyd Jones, publisher of the *Tribune,* initially held the city and county responsible for the destruction, even urging his readers to donate food and clothing to the Red Cross to help the victims. But his racism quickly reasserted itself and on June 4, he published a repulsive editorial called "It Must Not Be Again": "Such a district as the old 'Niggertown' must never be allowed in Tulsa again. It was a cesspool of iniquity and corruption. . . . Anybody could go down there and buy all the booze they wanted. Anybody could go into the most unspeakable dance halls and base joints of prostitution."[29]

This editorial, along with condemnations from civic organizations like the Kiwanis, revealed the true motives of the Massacre. The destruction of Greenwood was a *good* thing, the powers that be said, a *service* to the white residents of Tulsa, because it eliminated a den of vice and potential Black rebellion. Never mind that the real Greenwood had been a haven for families, educated professionals, and hardworking, God-fearing folk. Greenwood was an affront to white supremacy, and it *deserved* to be burned to the ground just for existing.

To reinforce this narrative, criminal charges were filed against some brave Greenwood brothers. A. J. Smitherman and many other Greenwood leaders had to flee the state for their own safety. Smitherman and his family first moved to Boston but then had to resettle in Buffalo, New York, in case he needed to flee to Canada to escape extradition. He opened two newspapers there, one was the *Buffalo Star* (later renamed the *Empire Star),* and died in 1961 while sitting at his desk working on his autobiography.

As time passed, the conspiracy of blame became a conspiracy of silence. No one in Tulsa spoke about the events of May 31–June 1, 1921. Afraid of a costly PR backlash that might negatively affect business activity in "the Oil Capital of the World," the leaders of Tulsa did everything they could to bury the truth about Greenwood. By mutual consent, nothing was written about the Massacre in local newspapers or historical books about the city for years. Few people, including the survivors, talked about what had happened.

In a 2022 scholarly paper, Suzette Malveaux, Roger D. Groot Professor of Law at Washington and Lee University School of Law, wrote, "The Massacre was excluded from Oklahoma history textbooks and historical accounts. This 'conspiracy of silence' was so effective that even Tulsa County District Attorney Bill LaFortune had never heard of the Massacre when asked in 1996. The Massacre was a 'public relations nightmare' for a city and state that wanted to continue to 'attract new businesses and settlers.' Moreover, with a government populated with the Klan from top to bottom . . . it is unsurprising that a massive effort would be made to hide its perpetrators, some of whom were government officials themselves."[30]

The information blackout even extended to researchers, scholars, and the press. In an interview for the *CounterSpin* podcast, journalist Joseph Torres described the atmosphere of secrecy. "There was this white reporter, back in 1971, who was asked—unbelievably, by the Tulsa Chamber of Commerce—to write something and commemorate what happened on the 50th anniversary," he said. "And he started researching this story. And he started getting basically threatened by strangers that would approach him on the street and tell him not to write the story; calls to his house; someone wrote on his car windshield with a bar of soap, 'Better look under your hood.' "[31]

As the proud people of Greenwood worked to rebuild, the white leaders of Tulsa did everything they could to sabotage their efforts. As highlighted in my public nuisance lawsuit, city leaders supported the ongoing terrorist activity by the local members of the Ku Klux Klan. In March 1922, Greenwood resident John Smitherman, brother of A.J., was kidnapped, beaten, and mutilated (his ear was cut off) by the members of the Tulsa KKK.

His crime? Registering Greenwood residents to vote. No one was charged or arrested for the attack.

However, the city was just getting started. In 1923, Tulsa again tried to use zoning laws to prevent Greenwood residents from legally developing their property. A new comprehensive zoning plan designated Greenwood for industrial use. Suddenly, neither developers nor Greenwood residents could build new housing in the district, causing a housing shortage and leading to decades-long overcrowding. As the years passed, the city also refused to provide essential public services, utilities, or municipal amenities—paved streets, running water, sewers, regular trash pickup, parks and playgrounds—to the rebuilt Greenwood.

Because of these forces, the homes of Greenwood residents lost almost all their value. No new buyer wanted to purchase a home located in a decaying industrial-only neighborhood, and no bank would lend money to a homeowner offering a worthless house as collateral. So, as the years passed, as Greenwood's public spaces and services decayed and fell apart, so did its homes, as their owners lost their ability to borrow to renovate or simply perform needed maintenance. Because of the city's malicious efforts, in the 1940s and beyond, many of the Black residents of Greenwood lived in ghetto-like conditions.[32]

Resident Dr. Charles Bate, a Black physician who moved to Tulsa in 1940, recalled that during the 1940s, "There were about 20,000 blacks in an area about less than four square miles. I had never seen living conditions in a city like they were in Tulsa. [There were] 25-foot lots with 3 houses on one lot. And you'd have to go through the first two houses to get into the last house. There were outdoor privies everywhere. And none of the streets were paved in the Negro area of Tulsa. . . . They didn't get paved up until the late 40s or 50s. Just mud streets everywhere. And very narrow."[33]

In 1958, the Tulsa Urban League published a report titled "A Concise Review of Housing Problems Affecting Negroes in Tulsa" that documented the shocking neglect of Greenwood and its people:

> Since the race riot of 1921, a critical shortage of this type [suitable] housing, almost to the point of non-existence, forced Negroes who desired better housing but could not afford new houses to remain in shacks or in blighted old houses . . . for Negro Tulsans, the slums . . . where at least 65% of the Tulsa Negroes still live, cannot be ignored. Much of the housing in the Negro slum areas is substandard and inadequate in basic structure and sanitary facilities. Shacks constructed from building material scraps and tarpaper serve as shelter to many Tulsa Negro families. Old buses have been parked and converted to resident uses. Unscreened windows provide easy access for flies and vermin. In dilapidated apartment buildings and rooming houses, baths are often shared by the occupants of as many as five to twenty dwelling units. Many dwelling units have no running water and no sewer connections for sinks and water closets. . . . The 1950 census indicated that over-crowding was a big problem in Tulsa Negro localities and the situation has not improved to the present date.[34]

Why did Tulsa's leaders remain so fiercely dedicated to harming the Black residents of Greenwood? Greed and anger. The white power brokers still wanted that land, and its Black owners continued to defy them. Their strategy was to neglect Greenwood to the point where conditions became so squalid and decrepit that the only reasonable solution was demolition. That set the stage, in the late 1950s, for what folks in North Tulsa still call "the second massacre." You probably know it by its more innocent name: *urban renewal*. But the people of Greenwood, then and now, call it something different: *urban removal*. And it's not uncommon to hear someone bitterly refer to the effort as *Negro removal*.

In 1957, the Tulsa Metropolitan Area Planning Commission released a Comprehensive Plan that included a new ring road around downtown called the Inner Dispersal Loop, or IDL. All over the country, urban planners were scheming to bulldoze historic, walkable, dense, diverse, working-class Black neighborhoods in favor of high-speed expressways. The IDL plan called for two new highways—Interstate 244 and U.S. 75—to be constructed and aimed directly at the heart of the rebuilt Greenwood.

The intended route of the I-244 loop was horrifying. It barreled across the 100 block of Greenwood Avenue, the core of Black Wall Street and the business district, and its construction would obliterate many of the most important businesses—hotels, offices, theaters—that had been built as part of Greenwood's reconstruction. It would leave Greenwood Avenue a forlorn landscape of missing buildings and vacant lots, "a lonely, forgotten lane ducking under the shadows of a big overpass" noted *The Tulsa Tribune*.[35]

This was a common strategy of white city leaders nationwide in the 1950s: lay waste to "undesirable" Black neighborhoods under the guise of building more efficient transit systems. The result was devastation in Black neighborhoods all over the United States. In New Orleans, an extension of Interstate 10 ruined beautiful Claiborne Avenue, once the center of daily life in the city's mostly Black Tremé neighborhood. In San Francisco, urban renewal projects forced nearly five thousand families, most of them Black, to abandon the Western Addition neighborhood. When James Baldwin visited the area, a Black teenager who had just lost his home and his neighborhood told him, "I've got no country. I've got no flag."[36]

Despite protests, the IDL was completed in 1971, and Greenwood was never the same. With its twenty-foot elevated grades, dim sixty-foot-wide overpasses, and endless traffic noise, the new highway tore the heart out of Greenwood's street life. Speaking to Eddie Faye Gates for *They Came Searching,* Massacre survivor and elementary school teacher Jobie Holderness said, "Urban renewal not only took away our property, but something else more important—our black unity, our pride, our sense of achievement and history. We need to regain that. Our youth missed that and that is why they are lost today, that is why they are in 'limbo' now."[37]

What remains of Greenwood is a sad ghost of its former glory. There is only one block remaining of Black Wall Street's sprawling business district, lined with a scattering of small storefronts, while new, modern high-rise apartments, glittering office buildings, and trendy hotels south of the old business district are owned by white business interests, not Black locals or original Greenwood families. To the west, where neat rows of proud Black-owned homes once stood, now stands a new, modern minor league baseball stadium. To paraphrase Nehemiah Frank, founder of *The Black Wall Street Times*, gentrification had succeeded in doing what physical violence couldn't.

Greenwood legend Mabel Little was a typical casualty. She was just twenty-five years old when the Massacre destroyed the Greenwood beauty parlor, restaurant, and rental properties she and her husband, Pressley, worked for years to acquire and grow. Gradually, she rebuilt, only to lose her home and salon again to the construction of I-244. For her loss, the city paid her a paltry $16,000. She bitterly told city officials, "You destroyed everything we had. I was here in it, and the people are suffering more now than they did then."[38]

"Urban removal" did what the terror of the Massacre couldn't. It broke the spirit of Greenwood and left the district fragmented and barren. As horrific as the terrorism of 1921 had been, when the ashes cooled, rebuilding began. But an interstate highway is a permanent scar. It was violence by public policy, an effort to crush Greenwood's future in a way that mob violence could not, and it worked.

The first three chapters of this book are table stakes for grasping some of what happened to Greenwood and why. They're also essential for understanding the story to come. But before we can go back to that courtroom in May 2022, I want to show you why Greenwood's story is also the story of me and my family, and how the mission to pursue justice for Greenwood helped me mature from an angry, out-of-control young man on a path of self-destruction to a nationally recognized advocate called to give everything for my people.

PART TWO

FREEDOM MIND STATE

A freedom mind state is an ethos of self-determination within the Black community that focuses on achieving liberation, peace, and security by depending on ourselves and building solutions that do not rely on the largesse of a racist political and social system. It encompasses Black cultural pride, fostering a self-sufficient economic system, teaching our history and narratives without outside influence, and creating our vision of the future without waiting for permission or approval.

But as I came of age in Greenwood in the grim "white flight" 1970s and 1980s, those fundamental pieces of a freedom mind state were difficult to find. As I found myself drawn to the law and the cause of justice, I would also discover my own version of this way of being.

The Tulsa Race Massacre isn't a footnote in a history book for us. We live with it every day, and the thought of what Greenwood was and what it could have been. We aren't just black-and-white pictures on a screen. We are flesh and blood. I was there when it happened. I'm still here.*

—Hughes "Uncle Redd" Van Ellis

African Americans with their hands up are transported on a wagon on June 1, 1921. The original photograph by Francis Schmidt is in the Department of Special Collections, McFarlin Library, the University of Tulsa.

CHAPTER 4

THEY'LL KILL YOU IN THIS TOWN

I was born in North Tulsa in 1976, five years after the completion of Interstate 244 and the devastation of the heart of Greenwood. Still, my family, as did many who held generational ties to Greenwood, fought to remain and find some semblance of life, liberty, and happiness. But as I grew up, I heard nothing about the Tulsa Race Massacre or the prosperous Black community that Greenwood had been. No one in my family nor the people I knew ever talked about it.

My mama, Kathy L. Brown-Banks, was a wonderful mother to me and my brother Damen. Mama was born with cerebral palsy, did not walk until she was five, and had to endure nearly ten surgeries before she was ten years old. Her grit and determination to live a good life despite her challenges always inspired me. She has always been my biggest cheerleader and advocate. What made her even more remarkable was that she never let her physical challenges stop her from being there for us. Even while on SSI, Mama worked wherever she could—babysitting, cleaning houses, helping my grandma cook at her restaurant—whatever it took to make sure we had what we needed.

My parents never married, and my father moved to Florida when I was twelve, so money was always tight. My saving grace was spending a lot of time at the home of my maternal grandparents, Mama and Daddy Brown, at 243 East Woodrow Place. I basically lived there off and on throughout my childhood and became very close with my cousins Deon (who we all called Dre) and Chris, who lived with my grandparents full-time. The three of us, along with Damen and my other cousins—Stevie, James, Misty, and Nett Nett—saw each other practically every day and thought of ourselves as siblings.

When we moved into our neighborhood in 1978, North Tulsa was a mixture of everything—working-class, middle-class, and poor folks—and still a nice place to be a kid. We had lots of businesses in my neighborhood and even a few white residents who had resisted white flight. I later learned that our house abutted the same railroad tracks people had used to escape from the Massacre. About twenty years ago, those tracks were pulled up to make room for a walking trail.

My family was working-class poor and extremely close. My mother, her siblings, most of my cousins, and my grandparents all lived within a seven-minute drive of one another, so we hung out all the time. But while our entire community was tight and loving, I was especially close to Mama and Daddy Brown.

My grandfather's name was William Lee Brown, Sr., but most people called him Daddy (except for me, who called him Papa). He was passionate about family, sports, and nature, and I wanted to be just like him. He had been a pretty darned good Negro League pitcher and second baseman for the semipro T-Town Clowns and even got a tryout with the St. Louis Cardinals. To this day, some Tulsa old-timers still talk about the time Papa hurdled a man to complete a double play, or the no-hitter he pitched. He also worked for the City of Tulsa as a trashman for thirty years, rising to the position of head supervisor before health problems forced him to take an early retirement.

Papa was an expert hunter, fisherman, and outdoorsman who served for years as the secretary-treasurer of the North Tulsa Fish and Wildlife Club. Even if you had never laid eyes on his house, you could find it by looking for the line of twenty-foot-long cane fishing poles stacked against the outside wall. I still remember the big "wild game" holiday dinners the club would put on at the W.L. Hutcherson YMCA in the winter, featuring dishes like goat, rabbit, squirrel, turtle, frog legs, quail, pheasant, deer, and duck, not to mention the huge summer fish fry at North Tulsa's O'Brien Park with all the fried catfish, crappie, buffalo, and perch you could eat.

But to me, nothing was better than all the time Papa and I spent just hanging out together—watching baseball, making homemade bullets and lures, training dogs, and taking our early morning trips to fishing holes all over northeastern Oklahoma. You never knew what you were going to find when you walked into Papa's house. He was pure country, and he brought the country to the city. I adored him.

In the 1950s, he and my grandma were the first Black family to own a home on their street, which was in an all-white North Tulsa neighborhood. Being Black in a white neighborhood meant that no matter how hard he worked, Papa had to fight every day of his life. He fought to get his job with the city, and then he fought for equal pay. Because of the racist lending policies of the time, he had to fight with the bank to get a mortgage and then to protect that home from racists who didn't want Black people moving into their neighborhood.

After working all day as a trash collector for lower pay than the white guys on his shift, Papa moonlighted as a janitor at a bank. When he came home, he sat at his window most nights, a shotgun by his side, to stop vandals from throwing eggs, rocks, and bricks at the house. These life experiences forged his belief that Black men must always be mentally and physically tough.

My grandmother Vernice "Mama" Brown was her own brand of pioneer—a world-class cook, pastry chef, and entrepreneur. Over the years, she owned and ran several food businesses in North Tulsa, but the one I remember most vividly was Mama Brown's Barbecue, a takeout restaurant inside the Apache Discount grocery store in the heart of North Tulsa. She was famous throughout the state for her cooking (especially her sweet potato pie), compassion, and caring nature. Anybody who knew Mama Brown knew that if anyone came into her restaurant hungry, no matter how down on their luck they were, she would make sure they got a plate of food.

I loved spending time with my grandmother. When I was young, my mama and Damen would go on trips, but I would always say that I didn't want to go because I didn't like traveling. The truth was, I wanted to stay at home with Mama Brown so I could have her to myself. She was the kindest, sweetest, most loving, most dedicated, most influential person I have ever known. She was an angel. That's why one of my favorite songs of all time is the great Bill Withers's "Grandma's Hands."

I was a sickly child, with severe asthma that put me in the ICU multiple times. I also spent years in speech therapy to correct an impediment that I still struggle with from time to time. Despite this, I had one goal as a young boy: make it to the NFL and play for the Dallas Cowboys. To me, that meant going to the University of Oklahoma, which has one of the greatest Division 1 football programs of all time, and playing for the Sooners.[1] But I knew the only way my family could afford to send me to OU was if I got a scholarship, and my best chance of earning one was playing for Carver Middle School and then attending the great Booker T. Washington High School and playing for the mighty Hornets. That became my obsession.

When I wasn't playing football, I was reading, devouring information about the world like it was my grandma's sweet potato pie. By the time I had finished fourth grade, I had read every book in the *World Book Encyclopedia* set my mother had saved up all year to buy me for Christmas. The only thing I enjoyed more than knowing random facts like the life cycle of the North American bullfrog was sharing that information with everyone around me.

But my favorite passages, the ones I read over and over until I knew them by heart, were the histories of courageous people. Joan of Arc, Frederick Douglass, Sojourner Truth, Harriet Tubman, Martin Luther King, Jr., and Malcolm X were all heroic figures who had dedicated their lives to fighting for justice for their people. I wanted to be like them.

But despite our close-knit community and the hard work of people like Mama Brown and many other Black business owners and entrepreneurs I came to know, by the time I was ten years old North Tulsa (which was about 35 percent Black, compared with the rest of Tulsa, which was about 10 percent Black) was becoming the place of vacant storefronts, cracked sidewalks, and empty parking lots that it still is today.

While the IDL had destroyed what remained of Black Wall Street in the name of urban renewal, some pockets of Black-owned businesses in North Tulsa clung stubbornly to life. A few even thrived with Black Tulsa's support. I remember a vibrant, prosperous North Tulsa from my early childhood. Within a one-block radius from my house there was a Dillard's department store, the Northland Shopping Center (with national brands like Firestone Tire and Service Center, J. C. Penney, and TG&Y), Skate Town Tulsa (where the kids would go to hang out before we learned to drive), and the Skyline Shopping Center, which featured the famous Skyline Barber Shop, where I got my hair cut.

But Greenwood's pride and joy was the historically Black Booker T. Washington High School. With its deep tradition of academic excellence, social consciousness, and athletic prowess, Booker T. has been one of the greatest high schools in America since it opened in 1913 at the corner of Elgin Avenue and Easton Street. Its founding principal, the great E. W. Woods,[2] oversaw a class of fourteen students and two teachers. He and his staff encouraged students to attend college and then come back to the community to inspire the next generation. Students were also required to participate in sports, and that early effort led to the school's stellar athletics programs.

My middle school, Carver, which opened in 1928, has its own rich history. It was built just seven years after the Massacre on the ashes of what had been the north end of Greenwood Avenue. Carver has always been regarded as one of the best middle schools in the country. Most everyone in my family went there.

However, in the late 1960s and into the early 1970s, the Tulsa Board of Education responded to federally mandated school desegregation by taking the best Black teachers from the city's predominantly Black public schools and reassigning them to white schools in South Tulsa, while transferring less qualified, less skilled white teachers to all-Black schools on the north side.

This was the era of white flight, and as white people moved out of North Tulsa, they did their banking elsewhere; by 2007, all the banks in Greenwood had closed. Westview Pharmacy, where I still get all our prescriptions, is the only Black-owned pharmacy left in all of Oklahoma; all the other Greenwood pharmacies shut down. Stores like Apache Discount, where my grandmother had her restaurant, closed.

Eventually, Tulsa's disinvestment and its open contempt for the Black community and the needs of its people bred decay in North Tulsa. The racist lending practice known as "redlining" accelerated the slide and the flight of capital to areas seen as "safer." By the time I started middle school at Carver in 1987, most of all the local businesses I had grown up around were gone, except for the Skyline Barber Shop, and the area was in terminal decline. After that, when we needed to go shopping or see a doctor or dentist, we had to go "out south," across the Frisco tracks into white Tulsa.

I was too young to understand it, but I was seeing one of the long-term impacts of the Massacre on Greenwood. The violence destroyed Black wealth and property, preventing it from being passed down to the people of my parents' generation, and drove down the value of homes and land in North Tulsa. As urban renewal forced thousands of Black families out of Greenwood and into other neighborhoods in North Tulsa, the area became like a ghost town. After it passed under I-244, Greenwood Avenue became a forlorn, mostly empty road lined with vacant storefronts. In the late 1970s and early 1980s, the Tulsa Development Authority tore down numerous buildings in Greenwood to build new cul-de-sac roads and install stormwater management systems.[3]

By 1994, when my family bought my high school class ring from Holman's Jewelry, it was the last remaining Black-owned jewelry store in Tulsa. Holman's opened in 1946 at 1204 North Greenwood Avenue, but in 1971 urban renewal forced them to move to Springdale Shopping Center on Pine and Lewis in North Tulsa. But things were never the same. In an interview with *The Oklahoma Eagle*, founder Leonard Holman described what doing business in the heart of Greenwood before urban renewal had been like: "Customers would leave the barbershop, come by my place, buy some jewelry or have a watch fixed, stop at the drug store for a malt or medicine, then buy their groceries at the store down the street before they returned home."[4]

But years before I learned about the Massacre, the vital, mercantile Greenwood, with its vibrant street life and prosperous bustle, lived only in the memories of people like my parents and grandparents. In early 2002, Holman's Jewelry closed for good.

I might not have known about Greenwood's former glory as a child, but I was still proud of my family, my community, and my people. When I got older, I learned that I have an incredible family legacy of activism and the pursuit of justice.

As I've said, my great-great-great-great-grandfather on my father's side, Cow Tom (aka Cow Mikko), was one of five Muskogee (Creek) Nation citizens who negotiated and signed the 1866 treaty between the United States and the MCN that ended the enslavement of African/Black Creeks.[5] But Cow Tom was a legend before he got involved in politics. He came to Oklahoma on the Trail of Tears and fought in the Seminole Wars. Cow Tom has been featured in several books, including *Citizens Creek* by Lalita Tademy and *Staking a Claim: Jake Simmons, Jr., and the Making of an African-American Oil Dynasty* by Jonathan Greenberg. In 1867, he traveled to D.C. to testify in front of the U.S. Senate and lobby on behalf of Black Creeks whose treaty payments were illegally withheld. He got the payments released.

My great-great-grandfather on my father's side, a half Creek named Jake Simmons, Sr., was a major financial supporter of Booker T. Washington's Tuskegee Institute and sent three sons there, including my great-grandfather John W. Simmons. My paternal great-great-uncle, Jake Simmons, Jr., was the longtime president of the Oklahoma NAACP and used his oil wealth to finance some of the most important civil rights court cases in history.

My father's side of the family didn't get all the glory, either. My maternal great-uncle, Lloyd Ransom, helped integrate Oklahoma State

University in 1956 and was the first Black person to purchase a house in Torrance, California, back in 1964, after a long court battle and thirteen months of demonstrations by the Congress of Racial Equality.

My father and my Aunt Edna, my mother's oldest sister, were in the first class of Black students at their schools, enduring trauma, violence, and racism.[6] That was the age of *Brown v. Board of Education,* which provoked Alabama Governor George Wallace to declare, "Segregation today . . . segregation tomorrow . . . segregation forever,"[7] and saw Arkansas Governor Orval Faubus deploy the National Guard to block Black students from entering Little Rock Central High School.[8]

Even Daddy Brown, whom I saw as a loving, easygoing grandfather who knew all about hunting and fishing, had fought for equality every day of his life. Once, he successfully staged a one-man protest by walking from North Tulsa to downtown because his paycheck was half that of the white sanitation workers.

My family had endured prejudice, hardships, violence, and disability to get where we were, and I was proud of my heritage and my people. And on one fall day in 1988, I got the first hint that I might follow in their footsteps. My seventh-grade social studies teacher, a white woman who didn't live in my community and didn't know the struggles my people had faced or the sacrifices they had made, suddenly said, "Black men can't wear normal-sized condoms."

She was laughing as she said this, clearly meaning it as a joke. But I didn't think it was funny at all. I didn't even realize I had stood up at my desk until I saw the entire class looking at me in startled silence. I didn't know what I was going to say or do, but I knew I couldn't just sit there in silence.

I told my teacher that what she had said was racist, and then I walked proudly out of the classroom. After that, some people started calling me "the Martin Luther King, Jr., of Carver Middle School." I also got called into the principal's office.

Principal Bobbie Johnson, a graduate in the Booker T. class of 1962, and a classmate of my mother-in-law's, was a stern, educated, dignified Black woman with glasses perched on the end of her nose. She said she understood my position but gave me an in-school suspension anyway for disrupting the class. I knew I was also going to be in trouble when I got home, but I didn't care. What my social studies teacher had said to the class about Black men was inappropriate.

When I got home, Mama Brown came out of the kitchen to talk to me. She stood in the doorway for a moment, just looking at me. She wasn't angry like I thought she would be, but there was something about the way she was looking at me that I had never seen before. Years later, I would come to understand that she was afraid for me.

"A Black man can't be that strong in Tulsa," she had said finally, shaking her head. "They'll kill you in this town."

I didn't know it yet, but Tulsa and I were a perfect match: a community that needed someone to fight for it, and a young man down to fight.

I have never had any faith in the justice system of the United States, when it comes to be about "black" people. You just need to watch what is going on without letting fake news or wrong analysis twist your judgement. . . . This has been going for so long. As a musician, I have been on the road in the States since 1938 and travelling through the World since 1964. America is not fair toward its black citizens. You are certainly aware of a study done by one of your colleague [*sic*], Mr. Orlando Patterson, sociology teacher at Harvard and the author of "The Ordeal of Integration: Progress and Resentment in America's 'Racial' Crisis." The situation did not change from the one I experienced as a very young kid. You know that I am at your disposal for any testimony or contribution; because we can lose a battle but we have to fight for our rights and for our dignity.*

—Hal Singer

After being detained, African American men and women are marched through town. The original photograph by Francis Schmidt is in the Department of Special Collections, McFarlin Library, the University of Tulsa.

CHAPTER 5

LAW IS MY MINISTRY AND JUSTICE IS MY PASSION

I don't like the idea of y'all driving all the way to Langston at this time of night," my mama said, following me out the door as I was heading to my car with my cousin Homer. "Hold on. Where's my purse?" she said. "I got something I want to give you."

I was already running late, but I knew there was no point arguing, so I waited patiently as she disappeared back into the house. It was 1997 and we were driving down to Langston University, the only HBCU in Oklahoma (located in one of the last remaining historically Black towns in the state) to pick up my girlfriend, Mia Fleming, who was studying broadcast journalism there, for the weekend.

Mama came out of the house. "Here, take this," she said, handing me her cellphone. "In case you break down or there's an emergency." It was one of those mid-nineties boxy "baby-brick" prepaid cellphones that she never used because it cost like fifty cents a minute to make a call. But in her mind, it would help keep me safe. Although I didn't dwell on it, the prospect of danger from racist violence was ever-present in Oklahoma, and it was always on every Black parent's mind when their children went out into the world.

Homer and I climbed into my black 1995 Honda Accord, I tossed the cellphone in the glove compartment, and then we headed west on Highway 51, toward Stillwater, the lights of Tulsa's skyline receding in the rearview mirror.

After about an hour, we turned south onto Coyle Road, a dark, two-lane country road, Tupac and Public Enemy blasting through my speakers so loud I could feel the bass in my chest, nothing but cows and farmland out each window for miles. There were hardly any streetlights, so the only light came from a full moon poking through the clouds. After about ten minutes, we saw the red glow of taillights ahead. As we got closer, the car in front of us slowed down until it was driving about twenty miles an hour right in front of us. We were the only two vehicles on the road, so I figured I'd just go around. But every time I tried to pass, the other car sped up. This game of chicken went on for maybe half a mile. Eventually, getting more and more annoyed, I started blowing the horn and flashing my lights.

We had pulled up to the intersection where the road merged with Highway 33, and I finally got a good look inside the car in front of us. It was full of white boys, drinking beer, pointing at us, flipping us off, and laughing. After taking a call from Mia, I still had the cellphone in my hand when one of them leaned out the window of the back seat and threw his bottle at my car. Then they tore off down the highway.

I should have known better than to get baited by a bunch of country boys looking for a fight, but when I heard that bottle shatter against the side of my car, the linebacker in me took over. I gunned the engine and flew down the highway after them. We must have been doing one hundred miles an hour for two or three miles before I saw their headlights suddenly turn right off the highway and disappear down a dark dirt road. I slowed down just in time to make the right turn and raced about a hundred yards before catching up to the car, which had pulled over in a clearing. When they saw we had followed them, one of them jumped out of their car and started running toward us. In a rage, I gunned my engine and tried to run him over. Fortunately, he dove out of the way.

I slammed on the brakes and told Homer, "Let's beat their ass." Before I even put the car in park, Homer had jumped out and I started to get out, too, ready to fight. That's when I noticed that the white guys had pulled over in front of an old farmhouse, and all these white people had started piling onto the porch. Our testosterone-poisoned, dumb asses had followed these boys back to their family's house! When an old man in overalls stepped out on the porch, looking like Jed Clampett from *The Beverly Hillbillies,* and aimed his double-barreled shotgun at us, I called out to Homer, "Man, we gotta go! That motherfucker got a shotgun!"

The two of us jumped back in my car and I didn't even try to turn around. I just shifted into reverse and punched the gas, backing all the way up that dirt road to the highway, tires squealing and kicking up dirt and gravel. We drove for about a mile in silence, adrenaline still pumping. Then Homer said something about the crazy grandpa with the shotgun, and we both busted out laughing. It was a close call, but we had gotten ourselves into and out of much worse situations.

A few miles later, we were passing through Coyle, a rural white town with a population of three hundred, almost to Langston, when we heard police sirens in the distance and saw flashing lights coming toward us from the east. I thought they were going to pass us, but the two patrol cars boxed us in and forced me to pull over by the side of the road. Suddenly there were five or six cops surrounding my car, weapons drawn and shouting, "Get out of the car! Get out of the fucking car!"

We stepped out onto the road, arms raised. The officers patted us down, threw us up against a barbed wire fence facing a cow pasture, then started searching my car. One of them kept shouting, "Where's the gun? Where's the gun?" Homer and I just kept looking at each other like, *What gun?* While this was happening, a truck pulled up, and the country boys and their grandpa got out. They started pointing at us and telling the cops, "That's them. That's the niggers who pulled a gun on us!"

Homer and I looked at each other. We were standing side by side against the fence with our backs to the road. A big brown cow had wandered over and was just standing there, a few inches away from our faces, staring at us. "We have to fight," I said. I was so scared that it came out as a whisper. "We can't let them take us anywhere." He nodded like a young soldier who had just been ordered to charge an armed position, knowing he was likely to be gunned down. But if these cops were going to kill us, they were going to have to do it right here on this road.

Just then, we heard more police sirens approaching in the distance, this time coming from the west. Two more black-and-whites pulled over about fifty feet down the road, and all of a sudden, it was like we were in a scene from the 1995 movie *The Tuskegee Airmen*. Black cadets Lee, Roberts, Cappy, and their commander, Lieutenant Glenn, make an emergency landing on a country road in Alabama during a training mission. A Black prison chain gang is working in a field, and the prison guards force the prisoners out of the way to make room for the planes to land. But when the aviators exit the planes, the guards are appalled to see that they're Black, while the prisoners are surprised and delighted.

When we saw these other police cars coming, we felt sheer terror. Then out stepped four Black men in Langston University PD uniforms, and I was never more relieved to see anyone in my life! Never mind that we were in custody; we ran to them like they were our daddies. It turned out they had heard the call go out on the police scanner: Police were looking for two Black men in their early twenties heading west on Highway 33. They had driven out here to make sure the cops from Coyle weren't messing with students from Langston. Now the white cops became less combative. Of course, they found no weapon in my car, and we explained that the country boys had probably seen me holding my mom's cellphone and mistaken it for a gun. Reluctantly, the white cops agreed to release us to the Langston officers.

But as they were getting back in their patrol cars, the oldest of the white cops called out, "You boys didn't have nothing to worry about out here." He smirked. "When we get the rope and take you behind the barn, *that's* when you should worry."

Mia was relieved to see me, and I was relieved that my anger and foolishness had not ended with me in jail or worse.

I learned about Mia when we were both thirteen. One of her friends told me that Mia had seen my eighth-grade yearbook photo and wanted me to call her. But when I did, I mispronounced her name, got embarrassed, and hung up. Smooth, right? That was it until we started high school at Booker T. the next year.

On the first day of our freshman year, I saw Mia in person for the first time and was like, "Damn!" Even back then she was tall, beautiful, poised, and elegant, and so talented that even a blind man—or a clueless teenage boy like me—couldn't have missed her glow. It was love at first sight.

Mia didn't aspire to be a broadcast journalist then, but she was in the Booker T. High School band, which was a big deal. She even had a cute band uniform, even if she was embarrassed for me to see her in it. Mia didn't have any sisters, but her three cousins all went to Booker T., and they were like her sisters. They were all beautiful "band queens," and everybody called them "the Harris girls." Eventually I got up the courage to ask her out, and we were on-again, off-again all through high school. But by the end of 1994, we were forever.

But before I got my life together, I let myself get caught in the same trap as many other young Black men who are told that their only value is as an athlete or an entertainer. As far as I was concerned, I was the next great NFL linebacker, and high school and college were just vehicles to take me to my destined greatness.

Looking back, the common thread between all my youthful foolish, self-destructive behavior was a lack of self-esteem, self-knowledge, and self-respect. Like many young Black men at that time, I was internalizing white society's misrepresentations of Black men and the corporate, commercialized hip-hop that glorified gang life, drugs, and being hard. I had no idea about the history of Greenwood. All I saw of North Tulsa was a dying community trying to maintain its dignity in the face of relentless white attacks. As a result, I did my best to live up to every negative stereotype of young, "urban" Black men.

I had been struggling to stay on the right path since middle school, but I started to spiral out of control after losing my beloved grandfather, Daddy Brown, right before my sophomore year of high school in 1991. He had a seizure and died in my grandmother's arms. Papa had been a towering figure in my family, and no one was the same after his death, especially me, who worshipped him. Before long, I was smoking weed, shooting dice, getting arrested, fighting, and skipping class. All I cared about was football, getting high, and hanging out with my homeboys and "dimes" (beautiful women). My nonchalant attitude toward school was so bad that I got a C in driver's ed during my junior year, and I didn't even deserve that.

Senior year, it all caught up with me. As the term started, the administration said, "Solomon, we just realized you never made up your algebra credit you failed as a freshman, and you can't graduate without Algebra One." I had to sit through freshman algebra (with my freshman brother), and I graduated by the skin of my teeth, mostly by cheating and getting special favors because I was a football player.

Then I found out that some of my Booker T. coaches were telling college coaches that I was a troublemaker and someone they didn't want in their programs. Things got real. Because of my bad reputation, my grades, and an injury to my right knee I suffered during senior year, there was no way I was going to get into OU or any other major Division 1 (D1) football school. But I didn't want to believe that, so I didn't take it seriously when small school powerhouse Northeastern State University (NSU) in Tahlequah started recruiting me.

I ended up accepting their scholarship offer anyway. I didn't have any other choice. No other schools wanted me. It was humiliating. Here I was, a future NFL star (in my own mind) and I was going to be stuck at an NAIA School! I was so embarrassed that when the school district held its all-school signing ceremony, where players revealed where they were going to college, I didn't even show up. I felt like a failure. I went to NSU with a huge chip on my shoulder and acted like a damned fool.

Then one day, everything changed.

On October 31, 1994, my roommate Shan Jordan (I had played football with him since sixth grade) and I were in the dorm room of a senior star linebacker from Tulsa, Kelby Farley. Shan started going on about Halloween and how it was the devil's day, and we started talking about the Bible and Revelation. All of a sudden, out of nowhere, I had a religious experience, like Saul on the road to Damascus. In that moment, I honestly thought I was about to die and go to hell because of all the bad stuff I had been doing. It was terrifying.

When I got back to my dorm room, shaking, my heart pounding, I called Mama Brown and said, "Grandma, I need you to pray for me. I've been a sinner. I'm sorry, I knew better. I want to give my life back to God." I was completely serious. I'd had a real conversion. I quit smoking weed and all my other self-destructive behavior. I stopped eating red meat and started taking better care of myself.

Then I thought, *I need a woman who will help keep me on the straight and narrow*. There was only one woman I knew who I respected, who was always a lady, and who had the character I needed. *Mia*. She had always believed in me, but we were not together, and it took me a couple of months to convince her that I truly had changed into the kind of man she needed me to be. Now I was determined that I would never let her down again.

My mind wasn't all that was changing. Unbeknownst to me, the story of Greenwood and the Massacre was starting to come to light. On October 9, 1995, the Greenwood Cultural Center (GCC) was dedicated at a site along Greenwood Avenue. At a cost of $3 million, the center was designed to educate the public about the community's history, celebrate Black culture in Tulsa, and support the revitalization of North Tulsa. Through exhibits, programs, and events, the GCC has continued to serve as a vital connection between the events of the past and the efforts of today.

The intersection of my life and Greenwood was still a few years away, but after my conversion I saw that I had been given an undeserved blessing. NSU had taken a chance on an injured athlete with an attitude problem, and I decided it was time I rewarded their belief in me. I went to spring practice, and then in the summer I worked out hard at home and got in the best shape of my life.

I came back to NSU for two-a-days, ready to ball, but I was shocked to find out that I was fourth string behind guys I felt were inferior football players to me—especially the guys from small towns I had never heard of. I was like, *Man, I'm from Booker T., I'm a baller!* I had worked hard, but I wasn't getting an opportunity. I didn't want to sit on the bench at NSU. Then we played our first game of the year against Missouri Western State University, and they beat us 44–7. I didn't even play.

That was it for me. I decided I would leave NSU, go to a top junior college for a year, prove myself, and then go to a big D1 school. I went back home to live with my mama and enrolled at what was then called Tulsa Junior College (TJC). I started training hard, trying to get in shape and attract the attention of college coaches.

Then one day I came home from working out and sat down in a chair at my mama's house, and my right shoulder dislocated. I was devastated. I had been working so hard to play football, and it seemed like I couldn't catch a break. I was done. My attitude became, *Fuck this, I ain't going to worry about school anymore.*

To earn extra income during the time at home, I had been selling air fresheners at barbershops and beauty salons for my cousin, who ran an air freshener business in Dallas. I was making money, and I decided if I couldn't play college ball, I would become an air freshener mogul.

My cousin was like a big brother at the time. When I told him my plans, he said, "Man, just come to Dallas. You can be my regional sales manager. The company's growing." I told Mia, "I'm moving to Dallas. I'm going to go work for my cousin. I want you to come with me. We're going to get rich." My mama and grandma didn't want us to go, and I had to beg Mia's mama for her permission. But I guess they figured that we were "grown" and would learn some valuable lessons about life, so they let us go.

Boy, were they right about the lessons.

In Dallas, everything quickly went to hell. My cousin had told me he had a warehouse, but he was actually running everything out of his garage. He also wasn't paying me. Now we were stuck in Dallas, living with him and his family, and not making any money. So we hustled. I sold air fresheners at car washes and went door-to-door to Black barber and beauty shops to get customers, and Mia worked two jobs.

Then came the second Saturday in October 1996. One of my customers was Graham's Barber Shop, a Black-owned place located near the Cotton Bowl in South Dallas. I was in that area when suddenly I noticed all the white people walking around in OU gear. Then it hit me. OU was playing the University of Texas that day! I went into the barbershop and they were watching the game. All of a sudden I was watching De'Mond Parker, who grew up in North Tulsa and who had been my teammate at Booker T., take the field for OU and have a monster game.

I felt like such a buster (loser). I thought, *This is crazy. My guy from Booker T. is balling right down the street and my ass is in here selling air fresheners.* At that moment, I knew I had to do something different. This wasn't the life I wanted, and it wasn't the life I wanted for Mia. I had to get an education. I had to get serious about life. I call that time in Dallas "a semester of life," because I saw what life could be like as a Black person in America with no education.

A few weeks later, we drove back to Tulsa. Mia went back to Langston and I reenrolled at Tulsa Junior College for the spring 1997 semester and started working toward my associate's degree. Focused and motivated like never before, I got straight A's and made the President's Honor Roll. I also read every book about Black history and the Black experience I could get my hands on. Before long, I had been accepted to the University of Oklahoma for the fall semester, and I still had two years of eligibility left to play college football.

I was ready for OU and moved down to Norman early so I could work out with the team for summer. There was just one problem: NCAA rules required that a student coming from a junior college had to have an associate's degree to be eligible to play football at a D1 school. To get that, I had to pass one more class: algebra, which I had only passed in high school by cheating!

I found a nearby college where I could take the math course in the summer session. Trouble was, I was still a terrible math student. I was lost in the class (I got an F- on the first test), and I would have failed, but I got help from what can only be considered a miracle. One night I was home trying to study, panicked and near tears. I ordered a pizza, and about thirty minutes later, a white delivery guy knocked on the door. As I paid him for the pizza, I asked him for no reason in particular, "Do you know how to do math?"

He was a graduate student in mathematics.

Look at what God can do!

He agreed to tutor me in exchange for OU football tickets, and I passed the class with the sweetest D I ever got. The following Friday, I crisscrossed the Tulsa-Norman metro area, ignoring speed limits and driving to three college campuses to pick up documents, get transcripts updated, and deliver my associate's degree paperwork to the OU admissions office just before the five o'clock deadline. But it was worth it. I entered OU in the fall of 1997 as a junior with my AA in history. I intended to major in history, but that would change.

In football, I worked hard and had a "bring on the contact" mentality, and I made such an impression on the OU coaches that I made the team as a walk-on. It was amazing: One year after I had stood in that barbershop in South Dallas, burning with envy and embarrassment that I wasn't playing football, I was standing on the sideline at the Cotton Bowl in my OU uniform. I didn't play and we lost the game, but I was there. That's what mattered most to me.[1]

Even better, I was having an unexpectedly Black experience at a predominantly white institution (PWI).[2] When I was admitted into this huge white school with a mostly white faculty, and I had to pick my major, I happened to get the only Black academic adviser in the College of Arts and Sciences. He was also from North Tulsa and a graduate of Booker T. When I told him that I wanted to be a professor of Black history, he said, "Why don't you just major in African and African American studies?"

What? I had no idea I could major in my own people! I said, "Sign me up!" African and African American studies became my major, and that's why I had to take Introduction to African American Studies, where Dr. NuRa Khem turned my ignorance of Greenwood and the Massacre into knowledge and set the course of my future.

Dr. NuRa Khem was more than a professor to me. He was a mentor, a spiritual guide, and an inspiration. He spent hours teaching me how to improve my writing, critical thinking, and oratory skills. The first paper I got back from him was so covered in red ink that I couldn't even see what I had written, but he poured into me. He taught me how to project my voice and be a better speaker. I didn't have an athletic scholarship, so I didn't have much money, but he always made sure I had food and other necessities. He became a close family friend, even driving down to Tulsa to sing gospel songs to an ailing Mama Brown in his deep, resonant voice. When Mia and I got married, he sang at our wedding.

Dr. NuRa Khem didn't just give me Greenwood. He saw my gifts.

From 1997 to 2001, while I was pursuing my bachelor's degree in African and African American studies and my master's degree in adult and higher education at OU, the 1921 Tulsa Race Riot Commission (TRRC) was conducting the first-ever state-sanctioned investigation of the Massacre as well as the events leading up to it and their impact on the Black community.

A nine-member commission was empaneled and given a historic mandate to uncover the truth about the Tulsa Race Massacre, document its impacts, and make recommendations for reconciliation and reparations. Members included attorney Jim Lloyd (who found the 198 "lost" legal pleadings against Tulsa and the insurance companies) and historians Eddie Faye Gates, Dr. Scott Ellsworth, and the great Dr. John Hope Franklin.

The TRRC did extensive research, including interviews with survivors and descendants, examination of historical records, and archaeological studies to locate mass graves. The body was also charged with two critical tasks:

- Providing a list of people who could be verified as residents of Greenwood on or about May 31, 1921, or June 1, 1921
- Demonstrating that each person sustained an identifiable loss of personal relations, real property, or personal property, or another loss as a result of criminal conduct, whether or not the conduct was ever adjudicated in a court of law

In the end, the commission collected more than ten thousand pages of evidence, including public records, letters, photographs, news articles, and personal accounts, providing irrefutable proof that local officials had failed to contain the violence, and in some cases had participated in it. A team of historians, legal scholars, archaeologists, anthropologists, forensic scientists, geophysicists, and volunteers helped support the work.

The TRRC's final report, presented to the state on February 21, 2001, was the first comprehensive governmental accounting of the causes, events, participants, and damage of the Massacre, including

- a description of the racial environment in Tulsa, which featured the infiltration by the KKK into nearly every office of city leadership;
- a detailed timeline of the events leading up to the Massacre;
- a report by Richard Warner of the Tulsa Historical Society that found that airplanes dropped incendiary bombs on Greenwood;
- details on the investigation into alleged mass graves of Black victims, which would later be validated as mass grave sites were located, including one containing remains identified as World War I veteran C. L. Daniel;
- assessments by Larry O'Dell of the Oklahoma Historical Society and Alfred Brophy of Oklahoma City University of the monetary value of the property and wealth lost.

The final report also recommended reparations, including direct payments to survivors and their descendants. It led to the passage of the 1921 Tulsa Race Riot Reconciliation Act and the Greenwood Area Redevelopment Authority Act in 2001. However, the TRRC was unable to convince the Oklahoma legislature to fund its recommendations, and to many white people reparations in any form remained out of the question.

We see a resurgence of this thinking today. White privilege dies hard, and to white racists raised on hysteria and grievance, giving Black people even a tiny fraction of what we are owed equals white extinction. It's not hard to find the ridiculous phrase "white genocide" used in right-wing media today, whether the story is about crime and South African farmers or the removal of Confederate statues here at home.

Despite this reality, I was enjoying a golden era of Black equity at American colleges. All over the country, universities were still working to attract top Black students and celebrating Black scholarship. OU had an active Office of African American Affairs and the Henderson-Tolson Cultural Center, named after the school's first and second Black faculty members. I got involved with the Black Student Association and started attending meetings of the Big 12 Conference on Black Student Government.[3] I was presenting, speaking, and meeting people from all Big 12 schools. Things were going well.

Because I was an African American studies major, most of my classes were about Black people. Most of my professors were Black. Most of my classes were majority Black. I was on a football team that was majority Black, with a Black head coach. It was like I was attending my own private HBCU.

One of the high points of this time was meeting Pat Hall, the executive director of the Oklahoma Democratic Party. Hard as it might be to believe now, the Democrats ran Oklahoma until 2010, and every summer, they would hire one OU athlete as a summer intern. In 1998, that intern was me. I went to Oklahoma City to meet with Pat, we hit it off immediately, and he's been a mentor ever since.

Working with Pat, I fell in love with politics. He showed me how to write political memos, and I went with him when he delivered speeches, attended community events, and went to the state capitol to lobby. I soaked up everything I could. One of the best things about Pat was that he allowed me to be my full self. He was constantly explaining things and asking my opinion. If I wanted to wear a dashiki to the office or a kufi to an event, I was welcome to. During this time, I also embraced my African heritage, which included an eye-opening trip to Gambia and Senegal in the summer of 1999 (after graduating with my bachelor's degree in May) for postgraduate studies.

In the fall of 1999, I started graduate school at OU, pursuing my master's in adult and higher education. I was teaching, speaking, and loving my studies, but I was also starting to get involved with advocacy for the Black Creeks (aka Creek Freedmen). I had heard about my Creek heritage from my daddy growing up, but I didn't take it seriously. But then I learned that since 1979, the Muscogee (Creek) Nation had denied tribal citizenship to the descendants of Creeks of African descent who were listed on the "Creek Freedmen roll," one of the two definitive lists of tribal citizens created by the U.S. government between 1898 and 1906.

That's when I decided I would go to law school. But I didn't want to practice law. I was attracted to law school because I felt like the degree and the credential would help me be more persuasive and credible as a speaker, author, and professor. One thing I knew for sure: I did *not* want to go to law school in Oklahoma.

But life had some more surprises in store for me.

There's a power in awakening to who you are and where you come from; both can help you know where you want to go. My awakening began in Dr. Khepra NuRa Khem's class and culminated in graduate school, when I reconnected with my father, Ahmad Shadeed né Nehemiah Solomon, Jr., and the Simmons side of my family. That is when I met my great-uncle Don Simmons, an internationally renowned businessman who lived in Muskogee.[4]

One day in 2000, I went back to Tahlequah to speak to graduate students at NSU, the same college I attended for eighteen months right out of Booker T. Muskogee is near Tahlequah, so I told Uncle Don I would come by his home and meet him. I had planned on a short stay, but we wound up sitting up the whole night talking about the Creeks, Booker T. Washington, Muskogee, and the illustrious history of the Simmonses—including how Uncle Don's father, Jake Simmons, Jr., used his wealth to finance important civil rights cases and campaigns, including *Sipuel v. Board of Regents of the University of Oklahoma* and the nation's first lunch counter sit-in demonstration.

I have a connection to both of these historic events. In *Sipuel*, Thurgood Marshall successfully persuaded the U.S. Supreme Court in 1948 to order the University of Oklahoma to admit its first Black law student, paving the way for *Brown v. Board of Education*.[5] The parents of the student in question, Ada Lois Sipuel Fisher, had survived the Massacre, meaning Fisher was a descendant of survivors, like Mia. Later, I was able to attend the University of Oklahoma College of Law because I received the Ada Lois Sipuel Fisher Merit Scholarship.

The first documented lunch counter sit-ins in America started on August 19, 1958, at Katz Drug Store in downtown Oklahoma City.[6] The instigator of the campaign was NAACP Youth Council leader Clara Luper. Years later, Luper served as the director of the Miss Black Oklahoma pageant for many years, and Mia became a favorite of hers.

Jake Simmons III, Uncle Don's brother, worked at the U.S. Department of the Interior under President Kennedy, was undersecretary of the interior under Reagan, and in the 1980s and 1990s, sat on the Interstate Commerce Commission. His other brother, Kenneth Simmons, was professor emeritus of architecture at UC Berkeley and a professor at the University of the Witwatersrand in Johannesburg, South Africa. He was well-known for his work in equal rights, urban planning, and community development, was an Alpha Phi Alpha line brother to Dr. King, and also introduced Donald J. Harris and Shyamala Gopalan—the parents of Vice President Kamala Harris.

This was my illustrious Simmons family, and learning that I was a Simmons inspired me more than ever to strive for greatness. Now everywhere I looked I saw my connection to Greenwood, the Massacre, and Black Oklahoma's fight for justice. I finally began to understand the fire for freedom, justice, and equality that had been burning in me. The heritage of Greenwood was *my* heritage. This made me even more determined to attend law school, because that was a Simmons thing to do.

Inspired by Uncle Don, I was excited to pursue a legal education that would prepare me to be a person of global influence. To me, that meant getting to Washington, D.C.—specifically, George Washington University Law School, where I could pursue a dual degree in law and international affairs. Now that I knew my full family history, I felt destined to become a "race man" and fight for Black people's rights and dignity.

I applied to a handful of top twenty law schools and was accepted by George Washington, University of Southern California, and Emory in Atlanta. But how would I pay for law school? Then OU called me and said, *Please give us a shot*. I decided to apply, just to maintain good relationships with OU leadership.

Wouldn't you know it, OU Law School offered me the moon. I told them I wanted to do international work. They offered to pay for me to go to Oxford University for the summer and then to South Africa to stay with my uncle. I said I wanted to recruit other Black law students and faculty. "Great," they said, and I became a student ambassador at events around the country. I told them I wanted to spend time in Washington, D.C. They told me I could create my own externship in the nation's capital. Oh yeah, they also offered me the Ada Lois Sipuel Fisher Merit Scholarship that I mentioned. How could I say no?

I couldn't. In 2001, I finished my master's degree and entered OU Law School to begin my long quest to redeem my community and its people.

But before I became an L1, I got a taste of the legal profession. One of the biggest law firms in Oklahoma—Riggs, Abney, Neal, Turpen, Orbison and Lewis—hired me as a "runner." That's exactly what it sounds like: a glorified errand boy. If the firm needed a check hand-delivered across Tulsa, someone picked up at the airport, or a document filed at the courthouse, I did it.

It wasn't glamorous, but that didn't matter. I had never had any interaction with law firms, and now I was working for one of the most important practices in the state. Riggs Abney was started by the legendary David Riggs, a former state representative who narrowly lost the Democratic primary for governor in 1978, was number one in his law school class, is a tireless advocate for corrections reform, and is the only person in Oklahoma history to get his bar license without taking the bar exam, only to go back and take it anyway because he didn't think that was fair.

At Riggs Abney, I was a sponge, soaking up everything I could, building relationships, and learning how lawyers do what they do. It was the kind of education I never could've gotten in law school.

Then in the spring of 2003, the second semester of my second year, I got my externship approved and went to Washington, D.C., to work at the U.S. State Department. D.C. was wide open to me, and I owe that to my Uncle Don Simmons. Back in 1999, three years before his death, he and I had spent a lot of time together in Oklahoma. His health was failing, so I became his driver, and we went all over Oklahoma together. He knew everybody, and everybody knew him. Being with Uncle Don was a master class in networking and relationship building.

Then one day he said, "Damario, I wish I had known you earlier, but one thing I do know is that you are a Simmons. You need to change your last name to Simmons. The Simmonses are international. Everybody knows our name. It will open doors for you. You are a Simmons in every important way." Uncle Don died not long after that conversation, and out of respect for him, I changed my last name to Solomon-Simmons. It was one of the smartest things I ever did.

When I got to D.C., I found out that Uncle Don had been right. Everybody in the city knew the Simmons name. As I settled into life in Washington, I got to know the progressive, social justice–minded Black folks in D.C. But when I told them I was from Tulsa and told them about the Massacre, their minds were blown. Many had no idea what I was talking about, and most also had no idea of the rich legacy of Black people in Oklahoma. The erasure of Blackness in Oklahoma is a crime against humanity.

A few weeks after my arrival in D.C., things started to come together. On January 20, 2003—Martin Luther King Jr. Day—radio station WPFW broadcast coverage of a King Day rally held at Washington's Plymouth Congregational Church for about two thousand people. Ralph Nader and former U.S. Representative Cynthia McKinney gave the keynote address. But they also let me speak, and I tore it up. In the news coverage, everybody was asking, "Who is this law student?" Everybody wanted young people involved in the cause, and now I was in demand.

From there, it was a short step to becoming part of the reparations movement. I got involved with N'COBRA, the National Coalition of Blacks for Reparations in America. I also became aware of the Reparations Coordinating Committee, or RCC, a group of attorneys, academics, and advocates co-chaired by Charles Ogletree, Jesse Climenko Professor at Harvard Law School, and law professor Adjoa Aiyetoro, the former executive director of the National Conference of Black Lawyers. Getting involved with the RCC became my obsession.

Then came a rude awakening: The State of Oklahoma announced that even after the release of the 2001 report by the Tulsa Race Riot Commission, they would do nothing to bring justice to the survivors of the Massacre. Shortly after that story broke, I got a call from a friend, Changa Higgins. He and I had been grassroots organizers and once got pepper-sprayed and roughed up by Tulsa police while protesting a KKK rally downtown in the late 1990s.[7]

Now Changa was working at *The Oklahoma Eagle,* the Black-owned newspaper that succeeded *The Tulsa Star*. He told me that in response to the state's decision, the RCC was about to file *Alexander v. State of Oklahoma,* demanding reparations on behalf of 171 known living survivors of the Massacre (including Hal Singer). Professor Ogletree and Johnnie Cochran would be the lead attorneys, and they would be in Tulsa.

Changa said, "Man, you've got to get home. You need to be here."

But I had no money. I was living on public assistance and could not make it home. However, once the litigation was filed, D.C. turned out to be the perfect place for me to be. Everyone wanted to talk with me about Greenwood. I met Georgetown professor and reparations scholar Dr. Richard America, and before long I was having lunch with him and tagging along with him to his events. I met a reparations attorney named Nkechi Taifa, who is still collaborating with me today. I met the president of the National Black Law Students Association (NBLSA), Mishonda Baldwin-Tate, who appointed me the group's second national reparations director. Every day was filled with talk of reparations, the Massacre, and racial justice, and I knew that somehow I had to get involved in the lawsuit.

I wrapped up my externship and rushed home to be a witness to history.

On February 13, 2004, I was twenty-seven years old and in my final year of law school, and I found myself driving home to Tulsa from the University of Oklahoma campus to be with my community for a historic moment. More than eighty years after the destruction of Greenwood, attorney Johnnie Cochran (who had become a household name for his defense of O. J. Simpson) and Charles Ogletree had filed their federal civil rights reparations lawsuit—*Alexander v. State of Oklahoma*—against the State of Oklahoma and the City of Tulsa. The defendants had filed a motion to dismiss the case, and today was the hearing in the Northern District of Oklahoma where both sides would present their case before District Judge James O. Ellison.

The case represented the most high-profile attempt to legally hold the City of Tulsa, the Tulsa Police Department, and the State of Oklahoma accountable for the destruction of Greenwood and the murder and dispossession of its people. I wasn't about to miss it.

As I parked my car outside the courthouse in downtown Tulsa, I saw one of the survivors, World War II veteran John Alexander, walking up to the entrance. He had been just eighteen months old when his family was forced to flee their home. In an interview with Eddie Faye Gates, a member of the Oklahoma Commission to Study the Race Riot of 1921 and chair of the commission's Survivors Committee, John had testified about his family's attempted escape.

When they returned to Greenwood, the Alexander family found that while all the houses around their home had burned to the ground, theirs was miraculously still standing. "My kindhearted father," he said in his interview, "let people who had lost their homes come to our house, and he let them bring the things they had taken with them as they fled. He let as many as could fit in come to our house."[8]

Now in his eighties, John was moving slowly up the steps, shuffling his feet a little bit, so I caught up with him and asked if he needed any help (he declined), and we walked through security together. I had never been inside a federal courthouse. It was grand and huge, echoing every cough and footstep. I tucked myself into a seat in the back, spotted Professor Ogletree, and was instantly awestruck.

Remember the courtroom scene in *A Time to Kill,* where Matthew McConaughey defends Samuel L. Jackson? This was like that on a much grander scale. The room was crowded with survivors and descendants—Black faces, young and old—lined with hope and hurt. Judge James Ellison in his black robe sat elevated, an almost untouchable figure of authority. Then Professor Ogletree rose—trim and fit, dignified and deliberate, poised with glasses in hand, carrying himself with calm, unbreakable poise. Instantly, the huge courtroom fell silent. He had no notes that I could see (which is why to this day I don't like to have notes when I am presenting). He paused for a moment, then began his argument.

It was like hearing both a lawyer and a preacher speaking at once. Succinctly and forcefully, he traced the history of Greenwood with surgical precision, but he wasn't just making an argument—he was giving testimony and dropping truth. He recited the law . . . and he thundered to the heavens! At one point, he stopped, looked directly at the judge, and bluntly stated that the Massacre had been one of the worst episodes of domestic terrorism in our nation's history. The words landed like punches. I saw survivors grip each other's hands. Descendants leaned forward, breathless.

He argued that the survivors and descendants were entitled to "restitution and repair." He explained that the survivors had been physically or emotionally injured, that their relatives had been killed, and that they or their relatives had had businesses and personal property burned, looted, or otherwise destroyed. The defendants were responsible, he argued, because they "routinely under-investigated, under-responded, undercharged, mishandled and failed to protect Plaintiffs from a series of criminal acts or prosecute those responsible for such acts." It was thrilling to hear more than eighty years of outrage put into such eloquent words.

I couldn't hold back the tears. As I watched Professor Ogletree, everything changed for me. Up to that point, the law had been something to study, a degree that would give me more credibility as a speaker, an author, and a professor. But in that moment, I knew without a doubt that practicing law wasn't just something I wanted to do—it was who I wanted to be. It was my ministry. I wanted to be a lawyer like him—not just sharp but unshakable in the courtroom, scholarly but relatable, blending legal skill and moral conviction. I wanted to command the people in the courtroom—judges, jurors, the press, spectators—like he did, like a conductor directing an orchestra.

This was a man who won twenty-five straight jury trials as a Washington, D.C., public defender, stood with Anita Hill during the Clarence Thomas Supreme Court confirmation hearing, and was the most beloved and recognized Black law professor in the nation. I also knew that like Professor Ogletree, I didn't want to do "one-off" cases—standalone lawsuits—even though I could make a lot more money that way. No, I wanted to lead cases that would "move mountains" and advance the cause of justice for Black people everywhere.

Next, award-winning historian Dr. Leon Litwack of UC Berkeley and Massacre descendant and "Historian of the Century"[9] Dr. John Hope Franklin of Duke University gave their testimony. As they spoke, I thought about my own journey as a son of Tulsa. I had started out as a would-be history professor, found my way to D.C., connected with key people in the reparations movement because of my opposition to the Iraq War, met Mishonda Baldwin-Tate, and gotten involved in reparations work nationally . . . and now here I was, face-to-face with my destiny: fighting for Tulsa. I had come full circle. I still get chills thinking about it.

Finally, Professor Ogletree returned to the podium for his powerful summation. I thought, *There's no way we can lose this.*

When the hearing ended, I pressed through the crowded hallway until I finally reached him. My voice shook as I said, "Professor Ogletree, my name is Damario Solomon-Simmons. I'm a 3L at OU and the National Black Law Students Association's reparations director. I just want to thank you for what you did today, for filing this case, for coming to Tulsa. For the first time, it feels like our community has been seen, and I want to help fight for us."

He stopped, turned to face me, and looked me straight in the eye. "Thank you," he said with a warmth that cut through the weight of the day. Then he placed his hand on my shoulder and added, "Damario, we need all the help we can get, especially from young brothers like you." I felt like I grew a foot. It felt like he was tagging me into the fight, charging me with a responsibility I could not put down.

From that moment on, my path was set.

It's time to talk about reparations. Reparations are a well-established, long-standing principle of international law. *Alexander v. State of Oklahoma* was a civil rights lawsuit seeking monetary damages for each individual listed. The RCC brought the lawsuit using 42 U.S.C. section 1983 (a federal law that allows people to sue state and local government officials for violating their civil rights) and brought claims against the City of Tulsa and the State of Oklahoma. The goal of the suit was to obtain reparations according to the standards set by the United Nations. According to the Basic Principles and Guidelines on the Right to a Remedy and Reparation, adopted by the UN General

Assembly in 2005,[10] reparations must include five elements to be valid and effective:

1. **Restitution**: As much as possible, reparatory action restores the victim to the original situation enjoyed before the violation occurred. Restitution is a way to mend the relational and emotional damage inflicted upon the victim and is a moral duty that reflects an ethical commitment to righting a wrong.
2. **Compensation:** Repairs provable economic damages resulting from the violation, including the loss of property and loss of future earning power.
3. **Rehabilitation:** Includes medical, psychological, and social services to help the victim recover from the physical, mental, and emotional effects of the violation.
4. **Satisfaction:** Aims to provide a sense of justice and includes measures like public apologies and truth-seeking. In a reparatory justice context, this can include both an expression of regret, remorse, or sorrow and an admission of legal responsibility and liability.
5. **Guarantees of non-repetition:** Involves implementing reforms to prevent future violations, such as legislative remedies, judicial reform, human rights training, recognizing historical wrongs, holding responsible parties accountable, and engaging with and educating individuals, communities, and institutions.

Reparations occur every day in the justice system, such as when the driver of one car found to be at fault for colliding with another car pays for repairs to the second car as well as for the driver's medical expenses and pain and suffering. Things become many times more complex when you're talking about reparations for injustice against Black people, but the fundamental idea is still the same. You are returning injured people to their state before they suffered the harm you caused, compensating them for any additional damage inflicted on them by that harm, giving them the satisfaction of public acknowledgment and accountability, and promising that the harm will never recur.

Reparations are a bedrock of U.S. justice. The U.S. government actually paid reparations to Confederates during the Civil War. On April 16, 1862, the District of Columbia Compensated Emancipation Act[11] became law and paid Southern enslavers for what the law called "loss of property"—i.e., enslaved Black human beings. How much was paid to the generations of men, women, and children who endured imprisonment, forced labor, torture, rape, and murder? Not a damned thing.

The United States rightfully paid more than eighty thousand Japanese Americans reparations for their internment during World War II . . . several times. President Ford formally apologized in 1976.[12] Next, after ten years of lobbying and litigation, President Reagan signed the Civil Liberties Act of 1988,[13] which allocated $1.2 billion to compensate Japanese Americans for income, businesses, and property lost during internment. Finally, President George H. W. Bush signed the Civil Liberties Act Amendments of 1992, which appropriated an additional $400 million for compensation.[14]

The U.S. government knows how to do reparations. We recognize the validity of them both as a legal concept and as a necessity for a just society. And as Cornell William Brooks and Linda Blimes of the Harvard Kennedy School pointed out on the HKS *PolicyCast* podcast,[15] the United States pays reparations every day. We pay reparations to people who have had bad reactions to vaccines, to the families of veterans exposed to toxins like Agent Orange, and to coal miners with black lung disease. We just don't pay them to Black people.

Reparations are a moral obligation, but we don't even have to depend on the idea of "doing what's right" to make them worthwhile. Experts have demonstrated that large-scale reparations for enslavement will benefit society by closing the racial wealth gap and reducing poverty. The extreme income inequality found in the United States stems directly from enslavement, racial violence such as the Massacre, and 150 years of post-Reconstruction racist policies that have denied Black Americans jobs, loans, education, healthcare, equal justice in the legal system, and much more.

Shrinking that racial wealth gap, the experts argue, will reduce crime, improve "quality of life" outcomes, increase Black wealth, enhance the value of businesses and real estate, result in more Black students pursuing university educations, lead to more Black-owned businesses . . . the list could run for pages. The result would be greater prosperity, more economic opportunity, and the healing of a painful, shameful open wound on the American character.

There are small signs of progress. In November 2024, the city council of Palm Springs, California, approved a $5.91 million settlement to be paid to the former residents of a largely Black and Latino neighborhood called Section 14 who were evicted from their homes in 1959 to make room for new properties built by white developers. The city also set aside $21 million to be used for affordable housing programs, assistance for first-time homebuyers, and aid to entrepreneurs of color. The decision was the outcome of years of advocacy in the community and work by dedicated attorneys like my friend Areva Martin.[16]

Since 2022, the City of Evanston, Illinois, has given $25,000 and financial assistance to Black residents who had been victims of race-based housing discrimination.[17] And in 2022, the Los Angeles County Board of Supervisors voted to return Bruce's Beach, a parcel of valuable beachfront land that had been a resort for African Americans in the early 1900s before being seized through eminent domain, to the descendants of the Bruce family.[18] When pushed, city and county officials did what would change the narrative while serving the interests of the community. Reparatory justice is not an impossible goal.

A month after the district court hearing, the NBLSA hosted its thirty-sixth national convention in Boston—a stone's throw across the Charles River from Cambridge, where Harvard and Professor Ogletree were located. In fact, the professor was already set to be the keynote speaker for the NBLSA awards banquet.

After we met in Tulsa, Professor Ogletree had done his homework and learned all about the work I had been doing: organizing students, building momentum for reparations within the NBLSA, and trying to wake up a generation of young lawyers to the unfinished business of racial justice. He gave me his private email address and we started emailing regularly about reparations work in Tulsa and related issues. I found myself thinking, "I have Professor Charles Ogletree's email. I'm the *man*." I was becoming his mentee.

At the convention, I decided to stage the first-ever national reparations symposium run by a law student, in part to show my role model how committed I was to the cause. I titled it "Reparations Now: Getting Our 'Forty Acres and a Mule!'" Apart from impressing Professor Ogletree, the event gave me the chance to get to know other members of the RCC, including my now-colleague and brother Eric Miller.

Eric is important to this story, so introductions are in order. He worked for Professor Ogletree's Charles Hamilton Houston Institute for Race and Justice,[19] and I first met him when I invited him out to OU Law to present the RCC's Tulsa reparations case. His Scottish accent was even thicker in person than over the phone, so I said to him, "I have to know what makes a white dude from Europe so interested in reparations for Black people in Oklahoma." He laughed. While Eric looks white, his father is Jamaican and he is a Black man. We became and still are great friends.

That was an exciting time. Eric wrote an amicus brief in support of the RCC litigation on behalf of the NBLSA and Black law students, and I signed it. My Boston reparations symposium was well attended, and the law students were engaged and passionate, especially when I led the crunk call-and-response:

> "REPARATIONS! NOW!"
> "REPARATIONS! NOW!"
> "REPARATIONS! NOW!"

But the high point for me was Professor Ogletree's keynote. During his speech, he called me out by name, saying, "We need more Damario Solomon-Simmonses. We need every one of you to be a Damario Solomon-Simmons." By the time he finished, I felt like I was eight feet tall.

But he didn't just affirm what I had done at the symposium; he affirmed the years of preparation, persistence, and faith that had led me there. He affirmed my own belief that I wasn't just participating in history: I was being called to *make* history and to live up not only to the Simmons name but to the purpose that was my family's legacy. On that day, I decided on my motto: "Law is my ministry and justice is my passion."

As I progressed toward the end of law school in May 2004, I had grown from a football-obsessed kid, shaped as much by ESPN as by street culture, into a connected, crusading young attorney whose only objective was to do right by his people. I began clerking for the RCC and joined Professor Ogletree and Dr. Franklin as they took up B. C. Franklin's eighty-year-old battle for justice for Greenwood.

When my family was forced to leave Tulsa, I lost my chance at an education. I never finished school past the fourth grade. I have never made much money. My country, state, and city took a lot from me. Despite this, I spent time supporting the war effort in the shipyards of California. But for most of my life, I was a domestic worker serving white families. I never made much money. To this day, I can barely afford my everyday needs.*

—Viola "Mother" Fletcher, in her testimony to the U.S. Congress

Detainees are led into the Convention Center on June 1, 1921. The original photograph by Francis Schmidt is in the Department of Special Collections, McFarlin Library, the University of Tulsa.

CHAPTER 6

WE NEVER GOT AN EVEN PLAYING FIELD

On March 19, 2004, Judge Ellison issued his written decision on *Alexander v. State of Oklahoma*. He acknowledged that "despite duties to preserve order and to protect property, no government at any level offered adequate resistance, if any at all, to what amounted to the destruction of the neighborhood" and that "the root causes of the Tulsa Race Riot reside deep in the history of white supremacy in Oklahoma and Tulsa which included the enactment of Jim Crow laws, acts of racial violence (not the least of which was the 23 lynchings of Blacks versus only one white from 1911) against Blacks in Oklahoma, and other actions that had the effect of putting Blacks in Oklahoma in their place."[1]

Despite this, the judge ruled that Greenwood's survivors and descendants could not receive reparations from city and state governments because the suit came too long after the Massacre. "It is unbelievable and unconscionable that anyone would suggest that the City of Tulsa and the State of Oklahoma are not guilty of dereliction of duty and complicity in the riot itself," Dr. Franklin responded. "If [Ellison] thinks that a technicality is more important than justice, that's his view of the law but it's not my view of the law."[2]

The ruling was a painful event in an otherwise blessed period in my life. In May, I graduated from OU Law, becoming the first Black University of Oklahoma law student to be awarded the prestigious Joel Jankowsky "Most Outstanding Graduate" Award.[3] The award came with a stipend that freed me to study for the bar exam full-time, and in July, I passed it on the first try. Then in August, Mia and I got married, and I joined the OU African & African American Studies full-time faculty a week later. Finally, I had become the Tulsa liaison for the RCC, which earned me the opportunity to learn at Professor Ogletree's feet.

I sat in on calls and meetings about the *Alexander* case. I traveled with him, watched every move he made, and listened to every word he said, trying to absorb his wisdom not only about the law, justice, and civil rights but on how to be a great lawyer. Then in April 2005, I had the honor of accompanying Professor Ogletree and a group of Massacre survivors to Washington, D.C., where they would testify before the members of the Congressional Black Caucus and have their personal accounts of the Massacre included in the *Congressional Record*.

I was excited to be going on the trip, but there was also an undercurrent of tension and sadness in all of us. After the Ellison decision, Professor Ogletree, Johnnie Cochran, and Dr. Franklin had taken their case to the Tenth Circuit Court of Appeals, which upheld Ellison's decision and denied a rehearing.[4] On March 9, 2005, the case went to the U.S. Supreme Court. As we traveled to D.C. a few weeks later, we nervously awaited the court's decision. We also mourned the death of our colleague Johnnie Cochran from a brain tumor. I hadn't met Johnnie, but it still felt like we had lost one of our best generals while the war was still raging.

But once we arrived in Washington, I was too busy to grieve. Professor Ogletree had a busy schedule, so he handed me a wad of cash and told me, "Take the survivors to dinner. Get 'em whatever they want." I ended up responsible for this group of elders and loved every minute of it.

I spent the most time with Otis Granville "Dad" Clark, Dr. Olivia Hooker, and Wess Young.[5] Dad Clark was the oldest known living survivor at the time, and he was quite a character. When Mia was starting her career as a reporter for the local Fox affiliate, she had interviewed him when he was about one hundred, and he made sure to show her the big Cadillac that he drove between North Tulsa and Oklahoma

City (110 miles one way) to visit his girlfriend. Now he was 105 and as spry as ever. He did not wear glasses or contacts, still had most of his original teeth, and didn't even walk with a cane.

Dinners with Dad Clark were marathon affairs. He always ordered the biggest steak on the menu and ate it incredibly slowly, all the while saying, "Slow but steady, slow but steady." We all just sat there while everyone else finished their food and the waitstaff came and cleared away all the other dishes, watching Dad eat his steak like he didn't have a care in the world. He wouldn't move until he finished every bite.

Dad also loved to tell stories about growing up on Archer Street in Greenwood with his grandmother in a house built by his father, who worked as a Pullman porter on the Frisco rail line. As a boy, he had delivered groceries to the "sportin' women" who lived on First Street, across from the railroad tracks.[6] He was eighteen years old on the night of the Massacre and vividly described for Eddie Faye Gates how he and a friend were caught in the middle of a gun battle: "Some white mobsters were holed up in the upper floor of the Ray Rhee Flour Mill . . . and they were just gunning down black people, just picking them off like they were swatting flies," he said.[7]

The night of the violence, he hopped a freight train to Chicago and eventually landed in California, where he worked as a butler for Hollywood stars like Joan Crawford and Cary Grant.[8]

Dr. Hooker was just six years old on the night of the Massacre. Her father had owned a prominent clothing store on Greenwood Avenue, and more than eighty years later, she still recalled hiding under her family's kitchen table as white men invaded her home and "hacked up our furniture with axes and set fire to my grandmother's bed and sewing machine."[9]

She described the trauma of "hearing things hitting the house, 'bang, bang, bang, bang' like that, and thinking it was hail until my mother took me to the window and let me peer through the blinds and said, 'That thing up there on the stand with the American flag on top of it is a machine gun. And those are bullets hitting the house. And that means your country is shooting at you.' "[10]

During this time, I also got to know Dr. John Hope Franklin, who received the Presidential Medal of Freedom from Bill Clinton in 1995 and was the first Black historian to chair a history department at a traditionally white university, Brooklyn College.[11] But when I first met him, I didn't make the Greenwood connection. It wasn't until later that it dawned on me that he was the son of the great lawyer Buck Colbert (B. C.) Franklin.

When I was growing up in North Tulsa, all I knew about B. C. Franklin was that there was a park named after him. When I learned about Greenwood, he became one of my heroes, especially after I decided to become an attorney. After being held in one of the concentration camps post-Massacre, B. C. Franklin set up his makeshift law practice inside a Red Cross relief tent and began defending the rights of Greenwood's survivors, taking statements and writing complaints. That's where the famous photo was taken, the image I return to whenever I am in need of strength: Franklin and his law partner, Isaiah Herculaneus Spears, still dressed like lawyers, seated at either end of a wooden desk on a floor made of loose bricks, holding open law books. In those difficult days, it was Franklin who did the hard early work of establishing a legal foundation for reparatory justice.

John Hope Franklin was royalty to me, and when I found out he had graduated from Booker T., I was pumped and proud. He was always teaching and telling stories about his life, like how he overcame racism to become the first Black history professor at Duke University. He also reminded me just how pervasive racism was back in those days. For example, he talked about when he was a young professor in the 1960s, walking through the lobby of a fancy hotel, when a white guest came up to him and said, "Boy, the bag's in the car!" The man had assumed one of the country's great historical scholars was a bellhop.

I'm so grateful to have had the privilege to spend time with these living legends, and that I had the sense to shut up and listen to them. Being with Dad Clark, Wess Young, and Olivia Hooker was like being in history, especially for someone with a degree in the subject. I was in awe of them until it hit me after talking with them, helping them find hotel room keys, letting them taste my food at restaurants, and navigating other everyday interactions that they were not just historical figures but real people just like me.

The highlight of the trip came on May 11, 2005, when Dad Clark and Dr. Hooker walked into the halls of Congress to testify before the Congressional Black Caucus (CBC). Among the members of Congress present were Representative John Conyers (D-MI—who would later co-sponsor the John Hope Franklin Tulsa-Greenwood Race Riot Claims Accountability Act of 2007) and Uncle Don's friend Representative Charles Rangel (D-NY).[12] Seated at a long table in a room packed with spectators, Dad and Dr. Hooker shared their experiences of the Massacre and the destruction of Greenwood, and you could have heard a pin drop. Shortly afterward, I gave my testimony discussing the continued harm of the Massacre. This is part of what I said:

> Until I was in college, I had no idea that the Massacre had even happened. I knew I was living in a decaying, neglected community, but I had no idea how it had come to be that way. Tulsa's code of shame and silence, which prohibited any discussion of the Massacre and its aftermath, left me and other young Blacks to conclude that our poverty, poor health, and dying businesses were our fault. Only later did I learn that they were the effects of the Massacre—the destruction of wealth, seizure of property, the dispossession of generations—still stunting Black Tulsans' lives decades later. The Massacre is not an artifact of the past. It is still happening.[13]

On May 15, 2005, a few days after these national treasures shared their stories and pain with the members of the CBC—and almost eighty-four years to the day after the Massacre—the U.S. Supreme Court declined "without comment" to hear *Alexander v. State of Oklahoma.* Our case was dead.

Even worse, the decision came without comment from the court.

Later, I would learn that this was common, but at the time, I was furious. To me, it meant no one had the courage to say, "The law is right here, but what happened in Greenwood was wrong." I was especially disgusted that Justice Clarence Thomas hadn't said anything.

One of the worst things to happen to the cause of the Black justice movement and progress in breaking barriers was Clarence Thomas taking the great Thurgood Marshall's seat on the Supreme Court. In Justice Marshall, we had a man who said, "Where you see wrong or inequality or injustice, speak out, because this is your country. This is your democracy. Make it. Protect it. Pass it on."[14]

Think about all it took to get Justice Marshall on the bench in 1967: all the cases, all the times he feared for his life,[15] the civil rights work he did during the "Second Reconstruction movement," which is what most people call the civil rights movement of the 1950s and 1960s, when Black Americans made real progress. Now the one Black member of the Supreme Court was silent about the horror and injustice that had been inflicted on the greatest Black community in history.

In 2003, when I started working with the Reparations Coordinating Committee, I truly believed that each of the then-living survivors would get reparations. They had lived for seventy-five years in silence and then endured years of waiting for the Oklahoma State Commission to deliver their landmark report, the first official government acknowledgment that the Massacre was an act of domestic terrorism. We all believed that once the world knew what had really happened, justice would prevail.

We were wrong. We got all the way to the U.S. Supreme Court and then they shut us down without an opinion. They wouldn't even grant the survivors the dignity of a hearing, and the survivors knew that without the force of law, all the conciliatory gestures meant nothing.

Three years earlier, in 2002, the Oklahoma Legislative Black Caucus had presented the survivors with gold-plated medals bearing the state seal.[16] After the Supreme Court denial, Dad Clark looked down at that hunk of metal hanging around his neck and said, "We never got an even playing field. All we got was these dang old necklaces. I could have bought this myself." Now I really understood the bitterness in those words.

After the Supreme Court decision, Professor Ogletree stepped up to offer one of the greatest lessons he ever imparted to me, and it had nothing to do with the law. We were in D.C. preparing to speak at the Thirty-Fifth Annual Congressional Black Caucus Legislative Conference, and I asked him how he could keep going when even the highest court in the land had turned its back on us.

He didn't raise his voice. He didn't need to. Calmly, he said, "Damario, bad judgments don't end movements. Courts may turn us away, but justice isn't theirs to deny. Our job is to keep pressing until the law catches up with the truth." Little did I know how that simple statement would sustain me through my own crushing defeats.

Two years later, on April 24, 2007, I returned to Washington, D.C., with Professor Ogletree, Dr. Franklin, Dad Clark, attorney Albert Brophy, and Dr. Hooker to testify before the House Judiciary Committee alongside other scholars and national civil rights leaders about the need for justice and reparations. Earlier that year, Congressman Conyers had introduced the John Hope Franklin Tulsa-Greenwood Race Riot Claims Accountability Act for consideration by Congress.

The bill was modeled after the Civil Liberties Act of 1988, which granted reparations of $20,000 to each surviving Japanese American held in internment camps during World War II and $10,000 to their descendants. The Conyers bill would have removed the statute of limitations from our case, which would allow lawsuits to move forward. At the hearing, New York Democratic Congressman Jerry Nadler said, "It is painful to realize that what can only be described as ethnic cleansing took place in our nation and that it has been virtually wiped from the history books. Thanks to the work of the 1921 Tulsa Race Riot Commission, we have another chance to confront the past."[17]

Unfortunately, the words of California Republican Darrell Issa reflected the consensus of Congress. "The remedies that were available in 1921 or remedies which were passed specifically envisioning a specific event, from what I can tell, have not yet been linked," he said. "In other words, the Civil Rights Act was not intended, discussed or created in order to deal with injustices of 1921 retrospectively."[18] Once again, white America would hide behind a legal technicality to avoid facing its legacy of virulent racism and doing the morally right thing. The bill never received a House vote. Although it was reintroduced each year through 2014, it never made it out of committee.

Dad Clark passed in 2012 at 109 years old; Dr. Hooker passed in 2018 at the age of 103. Neither lived to see justice done.

Reparations and justice for my people were foremost on my mind as I began my law career in earnest. After starting as a part-time "street lawyer" (an attorney who gets most of their clients from people walking into their office with a problem), I began to gravitate toward deeply personal cases that reflected the plight of Black Oklahomans.

One of the first was representing descendants of the Creek Freedmen Ron Graham and Fred Johnson who—like my paternal grandmother, Johnnie Mae Austin; my father, Ahmad; and me—had been illegally stripped of their citizenship rights by racist members of the Muscogee (Creek) Nation. We won the case in the Muscogee (Creek) Nation District Court in 2006,[19] only to have the decision overturned by the Muscogee (Creek) Nation's Supreme Court the following year. I've been trying to get my Creek clients justice ever since. In 2025, I was still in court fighting the same citizenship battle for my Black Creek brothers and sisters (more on that later).

Another pivotal early case was representing Carletta Mack. Carletta was an intelligent, college-educated woman, a rising star in corporate America, and the wife of a naval officer. She was also a member of the most disrespected demographic in the world: Black women. In 2007, while she and her husband were stationed in Oklahoma at Tinker Air Force Base, she gave birth to their second child via C-section at

OU Medical Center. Three days later, she developed a raging fever and began vomiting violently. "That went on for about a day," she told me. "I kept telling the doctors and nurses something was very wrong, but it was like they didn't believe I was really in that much pain. As soon as my fever started to subside, they sent me home. Two weeks later, the left side of my stomach started to harden."

Carletta told me that three weeks after she was discharged from the hospital, she had gone to see her ob-gyn, Dr. Catherine Gazzaniga, who sent her for a transvaginal ultrasound. "Which made no sense, because the pain was in my stomach, and I could feel the lump there," Carletta said. "From that, they saw something, but then I had to wait another two weeks for an MRI." Ultimately, the tests revealed that Dr. Gazzaniga, who performed Carletta's C-section, had left a laparotomy sponge (a cloth the size of a kitchen towel) inside her stomach during the procedure.

Carletta's terrible experience is not uncommon in the United States. About one in five Black women (21 percent) say they have been treated unfairly by a healthcare provider or their staff because of their racial or ethnic background, and six out of ten Black women said that they had to be extremely careful about their appearance and be prepared to deal with insults from clinicians or staff in order to receive adequate care.[20]

In a Pew survey from 2022, a majority of Black women ages eighteen to forty-nine reported having at least one of the seven negative health experiences highlighted in the survey. They were also more likely to prefer a Black doctor or other healthcare provider, presuming they would have a better experience than with a provider of another race.[21] One woman who participated in a 2022 study on racial discrimination in medicine summed up the situation when she said, "African-American women we're so marginalized we are not listened to, we're not taken seriously."[22]

After countless hours and more than $100,000 in expenses over three years, Carletta's case finally made it to trial in 2010. Even though my Black clients and I were facing a powerful white doctor with her army of white attorneys, experts, and insurance adjusters, I was confident we would win. I destroyed Carletta's doctor on the stand. She admitted that she had left the results of the initial radiology report sitting on her desk for weeks, and that despite the report revealing that something from the surgery had been "retained" (a fancy word for "left") in Carletta's stomach, she had never read it despite signing off on it. On cross-examination, I got the defense's expert witness to agree that the doctor is ultimately the captain of the ship and responsible for what happens during surgery.

The jury deliberated for nearly six hours . . . and then ruled 9–3 in favor of the defendant. After the trial, an elderly white lady who had served on the jury came up to us with tears in her eyes. She told us that they all believed the white doctor was liable, but the nine jurors who voted against us didn't want to damage her reputation. I lost it. I shouted, "What about Carletta's pain and suffering? Isn't that just as important as this doctor's reputation?"

The verdict was devastating. I had lost this "slam dunk" case. I had lost the "slam dunk" Black Creek case on appeal. Professor Ogletree and our team had lost our Massacre reparations case. But more than that, I was beginning to doubt that I would ever be able to get justice for Black people in a hardened system that seemed hell-bent on preserving white supremacy. Even though Carletta told me she felt vindicated by how passionately I had represented her, I felt like I had let this family, and my people, down. A couple of days after the trial, I told Carletta how sorry I was and even said, "I don't know if I'm going to practice law anymore."

So began some dark, difficult times. On February 26, 2012, George Zimmerman shot and killed Trayvon Martin in Sanford, Florida. On April 6 (Good Friday), two white men—nineteen-year-old Jake England and thirty-two-year-old Alvin Watts—drove around North Tulsa in their white pickup and randomly shot five Black people. One of the shootings happened on the corner near where I grew up and my mama and my in-laws still live.

Dannaer Fields, forty-nine, Bobby Clark, fifty-four, and William Allen, thirty-one, died of their wounds; David Hall and Deon Tucker survived. Tulsa police found and arrested the two men, but with the country already on edge after the murder of Trayvon, the "Good Friday Shooting" had poured salt into Tulsa's racial wounds.

The Black community wanted England and Watts charged with a hate crime, but both local and federal investigative authorities downplayed the possibility. In fact, at the press conference announcing the arrest, then–Tulsa Police Chief Chuck Jordan said, "We're gonna let the evidence take us where we want to go. There are motivations other than race in these kinds of incidents, and we're gonna look at it."[23]

The community was incensed. To show support, Reverend Jesse Jackson came to Tulsa the following Friday to attend the funerals of the three men who had died. He spoke at the First Baptist Church on North Greenwood Avenue, one of the few entities that survived the Massacre. I wanted to show support for my community, but, due to work stress, I had developed a case of Bell's palsy, an inflammatory condition that causes paralysis of the nerves on one side of the face. My face was twisted and frozen and I could barely speak, so I just stayed home, out of sight. My doctor told me that about one-third of the people who develop Bell's palsy never regain full function of their facial muscles. I was terrified. My whole life was about speaking, and I had been silenced with an uncertain chance of recovery.

Finally, in early 2014, when I was thirty-eight years old, things began to turn around. I regained facial function and was able to speak normally again. Along with Dr. Hooker, I participated in a big story about the Massacre on Al Jazeera. I became the legislative liaison for the Oklahoma Policy Institute,[24] where I advocated for policies that would improve the lives of members of the most vulnerable and marginalized communities.

A few months later, I called my mentor Melvin Hall, who was a partner at the Oklahoma City office of Riggs, Abney, Neal, Turpen, Orbison and Lewis, where I had been a runner years before. I told him

I was interested in joining the firm, and he set up a meeting with the great David Riggs. During the meeting, David had my résumé in his hand and said, "You've done all of this in this short amount of time. How come I've never heard of you?" I didn't have an answer, but it didn't matter, because Riggs Abney brought me on as "of counsel" (a lawyer affiliated with a law firm but not a partner or an associate).

On my first day, I passed David in the hall, and he turned to me and said, "I have a shooting case I might need your help with." He asked me to sit in on a call with a wonderful woman named Zondra Magness. She was the mother of a twenty-one-year-old Black man, Monroe "Trey" Bird III, who had been shot in the back by a white security guard named Ricky Stone in the parking lot of an apartment complex in South Tulsa. The bullet had severed Trey's spinal cord and left him paralyzed from the neck down. Tulsa County District Attorney Steve Kunzweiler had used Oklahoma's "stand your ground" law as justification for not bringing criminal charges against Stone, despite the fact that forensics and blood tests showed that he had shot Trey in the back from a distance of forty yards as Trey drove away from him, and that he had been intoxicated and in possession of marijuana.[25]

A few years earlier, six-foot-eight Trey had been playing basketball at Okemah High School. Now he was facing the reality that he would never move again. We spent the first few months fighting with the family's health insurance company to get him the necessary medical treatment. Despite our efforts, the insurer declined to cover the specialty care Trey needed to adapt to life as a quadriplegic.[26]

When he was kicked out of the rehab facility, Trey had nowhere to go but his mother's home in the rural, all-Black town of Boley.[27] Lying in a hospital bed in the middle of his mama's living room, Trey told me he sometimes dreamt that he was back on the basketball court; then he would wake up and remember he would never walk again. He also told me he just wished he could at least scratch his face when it itched. Less than a month later, he died from a blot clot in his leg that caused a pulmonary thromboembolism—a common complication that could have been prevented if he had been in a proper care facility.[28]

We filed a wrongful death lawsuit against the security guard, the owner of the security company, the owner of the apartment complex, and the property manager. The suit was successfully settled (the biggest win in my career to that point) a few years later, in 2018, but a young man's life was still lost and a family torn apart. There seemed to be no end to Tulsa's willingness to protect some white people's impulse to commit violence against Black bodies under the guise of "feeling threatened."

However, due in part to my effective work on behalf of Trey and his family and on behalf of thirteen African American women suing a disgraced Oklahoma City police officer, Daniel Holtzclaw, for on-duty sexual assault, my profile as a civil rights attorney was rising.[29] I was building a national reputation. In September 2016, I took a case that would change my life forever.

I had been planning to drive down to Norman for my fraternity's (Omega Psi Phi) annual tailgate party before the OU–Ohio State football game. But it had been a long week and I was tired, so I decided to get some sleep and drive down in the morning. Before we went to bed, Mia and I saw on the news that there had been a police shooting about a mile from where we grew up. Praying it was no one we knew, I turned off my phone and went to sleep.

At around five o'clock in the morning, I woke Mia up and said, "I feel like somebody's calling my name." When I powered my phone on, one of the calls I had missed was from Dr. Tiffany Crutcher. Tiffany and I went to middle and high school together. She and Mia had gone to college together and were sorority sisters, but our families also had strong ties that went back more than eighty years. In fact, our mothers had been pregnant at the same time while our families went to the same North Tulsa church. Tiffany had been living in Montgomery, Alabama, and running a private mental health practice, among other successful ventures.

I called her on my way to the tailgate. When she answered, her voice was raw with grief. "The police shot Terence," she said. "They killed my brother. We need an attorney, Damario. How quickly can you get to the house?" I was right outside of Tulsa and told her, "I'll be there in thirty minutes." I hurried home to take off my game day gear and put on my suit and tie. On my way out, I shouted to Mia to call her friends in the local media to see what they could find out and who we could trust with the story. Then I drove to the Crutcher family home.

Terence, a father of four, had been killed when Tulsa police officer Betty Jo Shelby came upon his SUV. Three days later, the Tulsa Police Department released police helicopter footage showing four officers with weapons trained on Terence as he walked slowly toward his vehicle, arms in the air. The officers in the helicopter hovering overhead can be heard saying, "That looks like a bad dude" and "It's time for a Taser."[30]

Seconds later, Officer Tyler Turnbough fired his Taser. Shortly thereafter, Officer Shelby shot Terence, and he fell to the ground with a hole in his chest. Instead of offering first aid, all four police officers backed away and watched as Terence bled out. Violating department policy, they even shut off their body cameras and turned away eyewitnesses, telling them to leave the scene instead of taking statements.

In May 2017, Betty Jo Shelby became the first Tulsa police officer to be tried for killing a civilian in the line of duty. It was a weeklong trial with national media coverage. District Attorney Kunzweiler, who had refused to criminally prosecute security guard Ricky Stone, charged Shelby with first-degree manslaughter, bowing to the intense international scrutiny. The pressure intensified when I joined civil rights attorney Ben Crump, Reverend Al Sharpton, the Crutcher family, and hundreds of Black Tulsans on a protest march through Greenwood. A 120-voice gospel choir sang in Terence's honor while the crowd chanted, "Hands up! Don't shoot!"

Kunzweiler did the minimum at the trial, not even retaining one policing expert to counter the three who had testified on behalf of Shelby. After nine hours of deliberation, the jury returned a not guilty verdict, and the moment the judge spoke the words "You are free to go," Officer Shelby took off running like she was trying to qualify for the Olympics.

Two days later, the jury foreman released a letter to the court that was eventually made public. "Many on the Jury could never get comfortable with the concept of Betty Shelby being blameless for

Mr. Crutcher's death," the statement read, "but due to the lack of direct or even circumstantial evidence that she was acting outside of her training in the 30 feet prior to Mr. Crutcher reaching the window of that SUV, the Jury was forced by the rule of law to render a not guilty verdict."[31] Once again, the justice system had told Black people, "You don't matter."

To her credit, Tiffany used her grief to, as she likes to say, turn "pain into purpose." She left her medical career to start the Terence Crutcher Foundation, a nonprofit focusing on criminal justice and policing reform, strengthening communities, and policy advocacy here in Oklahoma. But in 2021, she summed up the feelings of most of Black Tulsa when she said, "Here in Tulsa, explicitly and specifically, there's not a really good relationship between law enforcement and the Black community. . . . There's no trust there."[32]

PART THREE

OWNERSHIP

There are two kinds of ownership: reclaiming our minds, bodies, and futures from the limitations of white supremacy and exploitative systems, and controlling our stories, businesses, land, and ideas while honoring Black history and culture as the source of our power. In the tradition of Greenwood co-founder O. W. Gurley, we own land, businesses, professional practices, investments, and our narratives with the potential to build long-term wealth, generational prosperity, and political influence.

As the true battle for justice began, the principle of ownership became critical. The threat of gentrification of North Tulsa became a reality. We—Greenwood, the survivors, the descendants, the diaspora, the social justice brotherhood and sisterhood—had to own our story and not allow anyone to tell it but us.

They told three of us young black boys, Douglas Jackson, Virgil Whiteside, and me, that we could help to defend our people. They told us that the mayor of the City of Tulsa had opened the Armory and given two machine guns to whites and that whites were using those machine guns to mow down our people. They told us we could be part of history, that we could help defend North Tulsa. And so we did! Our job was to stay behind the steps of Paradise Baptist Church and load and reload guns for the human chain of black defenders. And so we did. But the shotguns and rifles those black men had could not compete with those machine guns. But those brave men sure did try to save North Tulsa and me and my buddies sure did our part to help them!*

—Binkley Wright, Massacre survivor, as told to Eddie Faye Gates

Oklahoma's all-Black towns were a destination for migrants fleeing the South. African American leaders of sixteen counties in Oklahoma are shown in this photograph. Edd Roberts Collection, Oklahoma Historical Society, 961735.

CHAPTER 7

FINDING PHIL JACKSON

By 2018, Terence's murder wasn't the only thing riling up Tulsa's Black community. The Centennial of the Massacre was now just three years away, and the prevailing sentiment among the survivor and descendant community was that the city was planning to turn what should have been a solemn commemoration into a celebratory tourist attraction that would benefit only the city's white power brokers. They were raising $30 million to be used for memorials, ceremonies, and other high-visibility commemorative projects. *Governing* magazine[1] interviewed me for an article, and I let its readers know what the real deal was.

I said that the city owed reparations to the survivors and descendants, concrete measures that would enable them to rebuild the economic futures that the Massacre had stolen from them. But the rest of the article showed that Tulsa's real plans included cultural tourism and projects like the construction of a new BMX arena in Greenwood. To me and many others, those plans spelled one thing: *gentrification*.

No one from the government spoke about payments being directed to the people whose families had suffered the harm of the Massacre, its aftermath, and urban renewal. Instead, there was talk of healing, commemorations, educational programs, and memorials. I believe that such things are valuable for teaching people about the past and preserving memories. But unless they are married to resources that lead to tangible outcomes that improve the lives of those harmed, they are just half measures designed to assuage guilt, generate positive PR, and shut Black people up.

Then, on May 27, 2019, just days before the ninety-eighth anniversary of the Massacre, the gaslighting appeared to end. The leadership of the Tulsa Regional Chamber of Commerce held a press conference at the Greenwood Cultural Center (GCC) where president and CEO Mike Neal announced that the chamber was donating a copy of its meeting minutes from the weeks following the Massacre to the GCC. Neal also acknowledged that "the racism that enabled the massacre also shaped the economic disparities in our community."[2]

At first glance this appeared to be a big deal. After almost a century of denial, some of the most prominent perpetrators of the Massacre—the city and the chamber—had finally admitted that the violence had taken place. They also admitted that nearly a century later, the effects were still being felt by the survivors and their descendants. The minutes themselves were filled with the racial bias of the age and reflected the prevailing story that it had been the Black citizens of Greenwood, not the white terrorists, who had started the violence. Here is an excerpt:

> A minor arrest had been made and publicly announced, the defendant being a negro boy. Under bad advice and led by a group of negroes exhibiting a spirit of lawlessness, a group of probably fifty negroes left the negro section of the city, came through the business section and marched on the courthouse. There was no occasion for their coming. The member of their race was not in jeopardy at all, but under the inflammatory action of lawless negro leaders demands were made of the sheriff and insults hurled at the white citizens attracted by the negro mob. The shooting began and the riot was on. . . . Tulsa feels intensely humiliated and standing in the shadow of this great tragedy pledges its every effort to wiping out the stain at the earliest possible moment and punishing those guilty of bringing the disgrace and disaster to this city.[3]

Look closely at the language. The word *negro* appears six times, implying that the Black residents of Greenwood caused the violence. The only people called "citizens" were the whites who had gathered at the courthouse to lynch Dick Rowland; the outnumbered Black men were a "mob." And you'll pardon me if I take no comfort in the phrase "The member of their race was not in jeopardy at all." After more than a century of lynchings and massacres, it would have been lunacy for the leaders of Greenwood not to fear that their brother was in mortal danger.

But while the chamber labeled the donation as a gesture of reconciliation, to many of us it felt more like an attempt to sanitize their role in the Massacre, its aftermath, and ninety-eight years of continuing harm. The minutes exposed the clear intent of the chamber and city leaders to seize the valuable land owned by Greenwood's residents while blaming everything on the Black citizens they had just attacked. Worse, the minutes revealed that even in the immediate aftermath of the death and destruction, the people who had encouraged and supported it were already making efforts to "spin" events for the newspapers in Boston, New York, and Washington, D.C.

Tulsa's leaders may have hoped that the donation of the records would placate the people of Greenwood and the activists who continued to demand reparatory justice. It did not. In fact, it had the opposite effect. So, it was an interesting twist of fate that around this time, as I was searching for a way to somehow get a viable reparations case back into the courts, I reconnected with Eric Miller.

In early June 2019, I watched on C-SPAN as the House Judiciary Committee convened a hearing on H.R. 40, a bill that would establish a federal commission to study the impacts of the legacy of slavery on African Americans and recommend proposals to provide reparations.[4] Out of fifteen witnesses, the only one who talked about Greenwood and the need for reparations in Tulsa was Eric. Watching his testimony confirmed it was time to resume the fight for justice for Greenwood. I reached out to him on social media, and when I asked him to be my partner in the fight, he was ready.

Now we needed to figure out how to bring a new legal case that would have a chance of succeeding. Eric drafted a powerful new federal complaint, but I was concerned that if we filed a lawsuit similar to *Alexander v. State of Oklahoma*—a federal civil rights lawsuit—we would run into the same roadblock that had stopped Professor Ogletree and John Hope Franklin: the statute of limitations. Eric and I were determined to file a lawsuit anyway, even if it was doomed and the court fined us, as a form of protest. We wanted to send a message: *We will not be silent*. We agreed with a quote often attributed to the great writer Zora Neale Hurston: "If you are silent about your pain, they will kill you and say you enjoyed it."

It was Spencer Bryan, an old classmate, who stepped in with a different idea. We attended Carver and Booker T. at the same time, and more than two decades later, we were both civil rights attorneys often working together on cases. Spencer is one of the smartest attorneys I know, but he lived in Denver, so we were always on the phone discussing legal strategies. One of us would throw out an idea and the other would say, "No, that won't work." Then one day in late November 2019, we were sitting around our offices, talking on the phone and brainstorming ideas when Spencer brought up the recent judgment against Johnson & Johnson.

In August 2019, the Oklahoma attorney general's office had used a century-old Oklahoma statute to win a landmark ruling[5] awarding $572 million to victims of the opioid epidemic, arguing that J&J had created a "public nuisance" by aggressively marketing opiate-based drugs to physicians and misleading doctors and the public about the addictive nature of the drugs. But it wasn't the amount of the award that caught our eye. It was the successful use of the Oklahoma public nuisance law.

When you think of the word *nuisance*, you might think of something trivial like a dog that tips over everyone's garbage cans. But in Oklahoma law, a public nuisance is "one which affects at the same time an **entire community or neighborhood** [emphasis mine], or any considerable number of persons."[6] The state defines a public nuisance as "unlawfully doing an act, or omitting to perform a duty, which act or omission . . . annoys, injures or endangers the comfort, repose, health, or safety of others . . . or in any way renders other persons insecure in life, or in the use of property."[7]

Spencer said, "What if we used the public nuisance law?" It was like stadium lights coming on, or like seeing the sun rise from orbit and illuminate the entire Western Hemisphere. *Oh my God.* I said, "That could work. That could really work. I think that could work!" Now I was hyped. If we were right, our lawsuit was suddenly no longer theoretical. It was no longer a protest. Now we fit within a cause of action Oklahoma state law recognized.

The Massacre had affected an entire community both in the form of the immediate destruction of Greenwood and in the ongoing harm that the descendants of those residents continued to experience. The Massacre and the acts that led to it had endangered "the comfort, repose, health, [and] safety" of the people who lived in Greenwood in 1921. Through urban renewal, disinvestment, redlining, and excessive policing, the same entities responsible for the Massacre had also inflicted ongoing trauma on Black Tulsans in the form of high poverty rates, poor health, incarceration, and police violence. In other words, the nuisance created in 1921 had never abated and had never been remedied.

Most important, under Oklahoma's public nuisance law, statutes of limitations do not apply if the nuisance is ongoing! If we could successfully argue that the entities responsible for the Massacre had created an ongoing public nuisance, they would not be able to hide behind the statute of limitations or the fact that all the responsible individuals were deceased.

On December 2, I sent my weekly update email to my legal team, and it included this: "Per 50 O.S. 7 there does not appear to be a statute of limitations on a public nuisance case. . . . Remedies include abatement, civil damages, and indictments! . . . We can actually have a grand jury empaneled to indict those we believe are responsible for the public nuisance and/or open a true criminal investigation into the Massacre."

We had our strategy.

There is zero doubt that the Massacre, the racism that bred it, and the actions that followed it have harmed the Black people of Tulsa in vital, measurable ways. Before the Massacre, about 30 percent of Black Tulsans owned their own homes, while white homeownership was only slightly higher at 35 percent. But a team from the National Bureau of Economic Research found that Black homeownership in Tulsa declined 4.2 percent by 1930, and that by 2000, the percentage of Black Tulsans who owned a home had dropped by more than 25 percent.[8] By 2010, the homeownership gap between Black and white Tulsans had grown to nearly *32 percent.*[9]

Throughout American history, business ownership has been one of the most reliable ways to build wealth, and in 1921, Greenwood was home to more than 190 thriving businesses, from shops and theaters to cafés and grocery stores, nearly all of them Black-owned. Even after the Massacre, nothing could stop surviving Black entrepreneurs from rebuilding, and by the 1940s, the district was home to more than 240 mostly Black-owned and -operated businesses.[10]

But after urban renewal and decades of neglect and systematic exclusion from economic development, Black business ownership and career opportunities in Tulsa are nearly nonexistent. Data from the Brookings Institution shows that while Blacks make up about 15 percent of Tulsa's population, only about 1.25 percent of the region's nearly twenty thousand businesses are Black-owned, while Tulsans living in Black-majority neighborhoods have little or no access to jobs in so-called financial hub industries like finance, insurance, and real estate.[11]

Eric and I were confident we could show that the nuisance inflicted on the people of Greenwood continued unabated into the present day. There is a huge body of scholarship and research into the economic, social, and health consequences of the Massacre; we knew we could show that since 1921, Black Tulsans had grown worse off in literally every way we measure a population's quality of life. But could we convince a court in the face of a barrage of motions to dismiss and delay tactics from the defense? The truth was, we lacked the resources to mount such a huge, complex, expensive case. Without another source of funding, the city and other defendants could delay us into bankruptcy.

This all weighed on my mind as I left Mother Randle's house in January 2020. We had no money, no precedent for the case we wanted to bring, and no major law firm standing behind us. I went home that night and said to Mia, "I need more help."

She looked at me for a moment and then asked, "Who was Michael Jordan's coach?"

"Phil Jackson," I said. "What does that have to do with anything?"

She nodded. "You need a Phil Jackson."

As usual, my wife was right. I needed an army and someone to help me build it. Immediately, I thought of Bryan Stevenson. You might know Bryan through his *New York Times* bestselling book *Just Mercy,* which became a 2019 movie starring Michael B. Jordan and Jamie Foxx. But he's also a law professor, a racial justice warrior, and the founder of the Equal Justice Initiative, which offers representation to people who have been wrongly convicted or been the victims of poor legal counsel. Long before I met him, Bryan was a hero of mine. But I hesitated.

"I can't reach out to him," I said to Mia. "He's Bryan Stevenson."

"Well, you're Damario Solomon-Simmons," Mia said. How can you not love this woman?

In January 2020, I emailed Bryan, explaining that I was representing the last survivors of the Tulsa Race Massacre, and that I was in desperate need of resources and a guide. Finally, in early April I was able to get on Zoom with him. I told him I had a viable claim that I thought would win in court and that I needed his advice and counsel. I needed introductions to other attorneys and firms that might help me and resources for expenses. I said, "I need you to be my Phil Jackson. I cannot do this without you. I need you to walk with me."

Bryan said he would help me in any way he could, but the level of help I received was beyond what I could have imagined. Like my Uncle Don, Bryan opened doors. When he called or emailed someone and said, "I would like you to talk with Damario," I would get a call from that person the next day. When Bryan referred me to a senior partner at a large law firm, a board member at a foundation, or the director of a social justice nonprofit, I wasn't just some small-firm lawyer from Oklahoma. I was important. My case was important. Big-time, powerful people took my call, took me seriously, and usually gave me what I needed.

Now I was able to put together a winning team. There was me and my then-assistant Jill York; Eric Miller; Spencer Bryan and Steven Terrill, my former classmates; Adoja Aiyetoro, another brilliant lawyer and law professor who had been co-chair of the RCC with Professor Ogletree out of D.C.; a solo practice civil rights lawyer in Virigina named Maynard Henry; and two young Tulsa lawyers I was mentoring, Lashandra Peoples-Johnson and Cordal Cephas. None of us had the resources needed to sustain such an expensive legal fight. But with Bryan's help, we punched above our weight.

Now we had to determine who we would represent in our lawsuit. I can't just sue someone because I think their actions were unjust; I have to sue on behalf of someone who was harmed. We had already signed Vernon AME Church as a client. Vernon AME was one of about twenty Black churches in Greenwood before the Massacre, and its basement—where hundreds of Greenwood residents sought shelter as kerosene bombs rained down from planes and fires raged on the streets—is the only structure still in existence from 1921.

We had also signed jazz musician Hal Singer, who had been part of the original lawsuit, *Alexander v. State of Oklahoma,* that was dismissed. Hal was a toddler at the time of the Massacre and escaped after the white woman his mother worked for put him and his mother on a train bound for Kansas City, but their family home burned to the ground. He had been living in France since the 1960s and was dying of cancer, but he was up for the fight. Sadly, Hal would pass away just a couple of weeks before we filed our case with the Oklahoma district court.

Dad Clark, Olivia Hooker, and Wess Young had also passed, which left only one known living survivor: Mother Randle. She turned 105 years old during the time Eric and I were preparing our complaint, but she was just as committed as Hal Singer had been to seeing justice done. I was happy to make her my lead plaintiff, but I couldn't help wishing I had more survivors to include in the suit.

Then in May 2020, I saw an interview with a woman, Viola Fletcher, who lived in Bartlesville, Oklahoma, and was about to celebrate her 106th birthday. The story mentioned that she had grown up in Tulsa, and I realized that there was a good chance she was a Massacre survivor. The story said that her family had held a drive-by birthday celebration because of the pandemic, so I also had the name of her grandson. With some social media detective work, I was able to connect with her grandson Freddy, who took care of her.

I told him about my case, Mother Randle, and Bryan Stevenson, and Freddy agreed to set up a time for me to meet with his grandmother, who still lived on her own in the same one-bedroom apartment she'd called home for thirty years. A few days later, I made the forty-five-minute drive north to Bartlesville, and Jill and I met with the woman we came to know as "Mother Fletcher."

Being in the presence of survivors is like being in the presence of God. I knew many survivors growing up, but by then they had all passed away. Now here was history, alive and breathing and smiling and talking to me. Sitting with Mother Fletcher was awe-inspiring, and it didn't hurt that while she couldn't hear well, her mind was razor-sharp. She was also eloquent, regal, and beautiful, with a wonderful way of talking that made it sound like she was singing.

I told her all about the lawsuit and my long fight for justice for the survivors. She confirmed that, yes, she had lived in Greenwood when the Massacre had occurred in 1921, and that she remembered it clearly. I told her what I had told Mother Randle: I could not guarantee that we would be successful, but I believed we had a real case, and she would be an integral part of it. I told her that she deserved justice and that I wanted to get it for her and her family. And she was down. They all were. Just like that, I had two survivors.

Then things got even better. I spoke to another of Mother Fletcher's grandsons, Ike Howard, and he said, "You know she's got a brother who's alive, right?"

What?

Ike told me about Hughes Van Ellis, whom the family called Uncle Redd. He was ninety-nine years old and lived in Denver. I said, "Is he in good shape?"

Ike replied, "Well, he just came back from a cruise." I took that as a yes.

In a few weeks, I had gone from one survivor to three! But we kept things quiet. The city and the other defendants didn't even know that Mother Fletcher and Uncle Redd were part of the case until a month after we filed. They were our secret weapons: more people who had actually been in Greenwood on those terrible days, who (in the case of Mother Fletcher) could corroborate Mother Randle's testimony, who could speak to the years of harm that followed the Massacre, and whose mere presence carried an incredible moral force.

With three survivors on board, we were nearly ready to file a case we knew would shake Tulsa and America. Then things started to happen quickly.

My team and I were busy organizing descendants, litigating Massacre-related open records requests, and researching and drafting the petition for the lawsuit. I hired four new staff members to try to keep up with the work, but I still needed more. I was also paying for everything out of my own pocket, and I wasn't able to take on a lot of other legal work. I was working sixteen- or eighteen-hour days and not getting paid. Stress, anxiety, and purpose kept me in the office long past the point where I should have stopped. I was building a firm and juggling other big cases, but everything orbited around the Massacre fight. All I could think about was how old the survivors were and how desperately I wanted to get them some kind of justice before they passed. That conviction, more than anything else, made me believe that if I stopped working, even for a moment, we might lose our last, best chance at justice forever.

Adding to my stress, our public nuisance strategy was going to be *expensive*. My plan was to mobilize the descendant community, not as fundraisers but as an army of advocates, storytellers, and organizers who would keep Greenwood's cause alive in their own cities and neighborhoods while making it part of the national conversation. Because of this, raising money became about more than dollars. Every check written and every event held was also a chance to raise awareness—to declare that our case could be the spark for reparatory justice in Black communities everywhere. We designed this fight to live both inside and outside the courtroom, with descendants leading the charge.

But contacting and rallying all those descendants, fundraising, managing press coverage . . . it would all cost a small fortune even without the usual legal expenses like lawyer and staff salaries, research, and so on. We got some outside help, including terrific pro bono work from Human Rights Watch, but it was obvious early on that the cost of properly mounting this historic public nuisance lawsuit could rise into the millions of dollars. We desperately needed a vehicle to help us fundraise, organize, educate, and activate the descendant community.

That's how our 501(c)(3) nonprofit, Justice for Greenwood (JFG), was born. It became the core around which we could organize the descendants, Tulsa, and the national Black community behind our work. I knew we weren't just in a legal battle. We would be fighting a *narrative* battle, too. If we wanted to win, we had to control the *framing* of that battle. We needed to teach the history not just of Greenwood but of the way the nation's systems—healthcare, education, criminal justice, corrections—had harmed and betrayed the Black community. We needed people to understand the importance of Greenwood to the national battle for racial and economic justice. We needed to say, "Pay us the reparations you owe us, as if we are first-class citizens entitled to equal protection under the law. Make us whole and able to take care of ourselves. Give us back what you stole from us and let us decide what to do with it."

Bryan Stevenson understands the power of the narrative. When I talked to him about this, he told me that progressives had made a big mistake when they built their narrative around diversity, equity, and inclusion—the right-wing bugaboo known as DEI. "There's a lot I think we should have done differently," he said, explaining that we lost the narrative because instead of talking about DEI, we should have been calling the fight what it really is. "It's anti-bigotry," he said. "That's what we should be calling it. You've been denying Black people in your company opportunities because they're Black. You've been denying women opportunities because they're women. It's discrimination, it's bigotry, and it's bias against Black people and women, and you should stop it. We're going to call it the anti-discrimination policy. If we could do that, if we could go back ten years and frame it that way, there would be no DEI to attack."

I totally agree that the racial justice movement's emphasis (then and now) on DEI was a big strategic mistake. It wasn't just that, as with "Defund the Police," they gave the "bad faith Right" an easy target for ridicule and fearmongering. The so-called Left also fell into the trap of engaging with the state on the state's own turf, through channels that the state created and could control. Orisanmi Burton, an associate professor of anthropology at American University, made exactly this point in his online conversation with Charisse Burden-Stelly, an associate professor of African American studies at Wayne State University.[12]

"Part of what needs to be nurtured is a historical consciousness of the intent behind the reform and the history of how that reform was implemented," Professor Burton said. "The reform becomes the actual goal of the movement. The movement gets subsumed around defending this reform, which was instituted in the first place as a counter-revolutionary method. DEI is a precise example of this. People on the left are put in positions where they have to defend DEI, which is not even a radical or revolutionary demand at all."

We built Justice for Greenwood as a vehicle that would allow our movement to engage with the state, the media, and the public on our own terms and to push the narrative that would help us achieve our goals—one not of race but of harm for which recompense and fairness has been long denied. I drafted the nonprofit bylaws and the articles of the organization and filed them.

It usually takes four to twelve months for the IRS to respond to a 501(c)(3) application. Justice for Greenwood's 501(c)(3) status was approved in just six weeks, on May 31, 2020—ninety-nine years to the day after the Massacre. Again, it felt as though God was at work behind the scenes. Now we had an organization, a slogan, and a mission people could rally behind.

Unfortunately, I couldn't talk about our strategy or Justice for Greenwood, because I couldn't risk our opponents finding out about our plans before we filed. Outside of Mia and my small team, I carried the news mostly in silence. I would smile to myself in quiet moments, then lock back in on strategy as if nothing had changed. It was like holding a miracle in my hands but having to keep it hidden. The mix of joy and secrecy left me restless, waiting for the day when the world would finally see what we had built.

But my exultation over JFG's founding didn't last.

On May 25, 2020, I and millions of others watched in horror as a white Minneapolis police officer knelt on the neck of a handcuffed, helpless Black man for nine minutes. Because a seventeen-year-old girl named Darnella Frazier chose to stand her ground and film (an act of love and defiance), we all watched George Floyd panicking, crying, and saying again and again, "I can't breathe," while bystanders pleaded with Officer Derek Chauvin to take his weight off the man's neck. With his last breaths, George cried out for his mama. It was almost ninety-nine years to the day since Dick Rowland had been arrested.

The murder of George Floyd evoked all the fear and rage Black Americans feel when we confront the humiliating reality that law enforcement in the United States exists not to protect us but to protect white people *from* us. But what happened to George Floyd was even worse. There was no cop's word versus suspect's word here. George had been on his stomach on the street, handcuffed. He had not been a threat. This was murder, plain and simple.

Chauvin's act said, *I have power over you, and I will demonstrate it by taking your life.*

Millions of Americans took to the streets to protest and shout that Black Lives Matter. Four officers eventually went to prison, but little else changed. Like so many, I was furious, but I knew that all the protests in the world wouldn't make any difference without accountability. If we were to move forward as a nation, we needed more than protests, good intentions, or thoughts and prayers. We needed *reparations*.

Legislators, journalists, and well-meaning activists often fail to understand that reparations are not about helping or charity. Governmental investments and services to Black communities don't equal reparations or restorative justice. Neither does philanthropy. In fact, community service projects and charitable works often provide cover for acts of performative racial justice that allow well-off weekend do-gooders to feel good about "helping poor Blacks" while voting against critical state and federal programs our communities so desperately need. Reparations are about administering justice by settling a debt.

We were now less than one year from the Centennial of the Massacre, and we kept working on our lawsuit. I had never worked as hard on any single issue. It consumed me. I was working virtually seven days a week and losing weight. But my clients were centenarians, and I heard the clock ticking. I would do whatever was needed to bring them justice. A debt was owed. If I didn't collect it, who would?

Finally, on September 1, 2020, I was on my way to the courthouse to physically file the documents—until I noticed that there was a typo on the signature line! Big deal, right? For us it was. My team and I had worked endless hours to create the most complete account ever put in a court document of the harm inflicted by the Massacre. Descendants, activists, supporters, lawyers, and members of the local and national media were gathering at the Greenwood Cultural Center, waiting for a huge announcement. Copies of the lawsuit would go to the press and from there, into the history books. And I had a typo! Fortunately, I was able to get into my Gmail account using a computer in the courthouse's law library, open the document, and fix the typo. I printed a hard copy, then went downstairs and filed the lawsuit that would define my career.

With that crisis averted, my law clerk Jourdan Johnson whisked me to the GCC for an 11:00 A.M. press conference where we would announce that we had filed our public nuisance lawsuit, *Randle, et.al. v. City of Tulsa, et.al.*, in Tulsa County District Court. It was during the middle of the pandemic, so Covid protocols capped attendance. Reporters from all over the world stood, masked and distanced, cameras blinking red. The absence of a larger crowd and knowing we were live streaming to the world only heightened the tension.

"Good morning," I said, steadying my voice. "I am attorney Damario Solomon-Simmons, and along with my team, I am so excited to announce this lawsuit to finally get justice for Greenwood that we've been waiting on for over ninety-nine years." I paused, letting that number—ninety-nine years—settle. "This is a truly historic and emotional day. As I walked in this morning, I passed the pictures on these walls—survivors who fought for justice until their last breath. Too many of them died waiting."[13]

I lifted a page, my voice tightening. "Two weeks ago, we lost one more. Hal Singer, at one hundred years old, passed away before this case could be filed. My team had been in touch with Mr. Singer and his family, and they were excited about this litigation, hopeful it could finally bring the justice that had been denied for so long. Before his death, he wrote us a letter. Let me read just a piece: 'I have never had any faith in the justice system of the United States when it comes to Black people. . . . But we must fight for our rights and our dignity.' "

I folded the page and looked at the masked faces. "That is exactly what we are doing here today. Fighting for rights. Fighting for dignity. Fighting to repair what was stolen."

I introduced the rest of my legal team, all of whom had prepared presentations to deliver. They revisited the horror of the Massacre and laid out our public nuisance strategy in detail. Then a reporter called out the question I knew was coming: "Attorney Solomon-Simmons, why is this lawsuit different from the one that was filed back in the early 2000s? Why should people believe this time will be any different?"

I leaned into the mic. "Excellent question. That was a federal case, built on federal civil rights law. This is a state case, rooted in Oklahoma's public nuisance statute. And here's the critical difference: A nuisance does not expire. It does not run out of time. It exists until it is abated. The City of Tulsa itself has admitted the effects of the Massacre continue to this day. That means the harm is ongoing, and the law requires it to be repaired. This lawsuit isn't about symbolism or commemoration. It's about restoration, repair, and respect—finally giving back what was stolen."

That was quite a day. Months of secrecy and late nights were over. The fight for Greenwood's dignity was no longer hidden in draft briefs and conference calls. It was alive, on the record, before the world.

The announcement sent shock waves through the country and the Greenwood descendant diaspora. Overnight, calls and emails started pouring in from descendants of Massacre victims from all around the world wanting to be named in the lawsuit. We couldn't do that, because doing so would undermine the public nuisance claim, and the statute of limitations would cause the individual claims to be dismissed. But the flood of emails showed us that people were hungry for justice. I reassured them that their voices would be heard.

A few months later, something almost as important happened. Bryan Stevenson connected me with the international law firm Schulte Roth & Zabel (SRZ). Bill Zabel, one of the founding partners, is a legal legend who wrote the winning brief for the ACLU in *Loving v. Virginia,* the case that legalized interracial marriage.

Sara E. Solfanelli, the firm's special counsel for pro bono initiatives, invited me to attend SRZ's annual virtual town hall and talk about Greenwood and the case. I ended up presenting to about five hundred people—SRZ's largest town hall audience in years. Everybody was blown away by my presentation, but I didn't know that Paul Roth and Bill Zabel, two of the founding partners, were on the call. After everyone else left, Bill stayed on to talk.

He was shocked that he hadn't known about Greenwood or the Massacre. "D, how come I didn't know about this?" he said to me. "I can't believe this happened." I told him about how the city and county had suppressed the history of the Massacre and about my team's commitment to justice for the survivors and families. Finally, Bill said, "Whatever you need. If you need thirty lawyers, we're going to give you thirty lawyers. If you need sixty lawyers, we're going to give you sixty lawyers. Whatever you need, you let me know. We're going to help you."

In Bryan, I had my Phil Jackson. Now I had my army. I was ready to go to war.

There's a lot of prejudice here, a lot of prejudice in Tulsa, a lot of prejudiced people. Haven't thought about . . . now, somebody come from way back like I did and seen things as I saw, people know what I'm saying, but I feel like—I don't feel like we all that safe. I don't.*

—Lessie Benningfield "Mother" Randle

At Archer Street and North Greenwood Avenue, survivors stood amid the ashes of once-thriving Black businesses—the Williams Building, Gurley Hotel, Dixie Theatre, *Tulsa Star,* and Dreamland Theatre—symbols of prosperity reduced to rubble. Courtesy of the Oklahoma Historical Society.

CHAPTER 8

PRESSURE

The climax of that war started with my dramatic walk into Judge Caroline Wall's courtroom for our May 2022 hearing. I introduced you to this real-life courtroom drama way back in the preface, so let me refresh your memory. My team and I had filed our landmark public nuisance lawsuit, the defense had filed a motion to dismiss, and now we were before Judge Wall to argue that our lawsuit should continue to the discovery phase. If she ruled for us, we would stay alive to fight another day. If she ruled against us, our case would be crippled and maybe finished.

The gavel dropped and the room snapped to order. Judge Wall's voice carried across the packed chamber: no applause, no outbursts. The bailiff laid down the rules—six months in jail or a $500 fine for anyone who forgot this was a courtroom, not a rally. The pews creaked as people settled in. The weight of a century hung heavy in the air.

I rose from the counsel's table, smoothed my tie, and announced: "I have the great pleasure of representing Viola Floyd Fletcher, who is 107 years old. She'll be 108 in eight days. I have the great pleasure of representing Lessie Benningfield Randle along with my colleagues, my co-counsel, who is 107 years old. And I have the great pleasure of representing this young man who is . . . Mr. Hughes Van Ellis, who is 101 plus years old. And collectively, Your Honor, these three individuals, the last known living survivors of the Tulsa Race Massacre, have waited 300 years plus for an opportunity to have a day in court. They've waited

300 years plus to have an opportunity to prove that the Defendants caused a public nuisance that continues to this very day."

I reminded the court of the standard: "Oklahoma is a notice-pleading state. We are not required to prove causation, damages, or an abatement plan at this stage. We need only a short, plain statement of our claim. In over a hundred pages, we did more than was required. And at this stage, every allegation must be taken as true, construed in the light most favorable to us."

Then I looked directly at the judge: "We are not here to fix racism or 'societal ills,' as defendants try to suggest. Nowhere in our petition will you find that. What we ask is far more precise: that the nuisance created by the 1921 Massacre—arson, murder, looting, unlawful detention, disinvestment—finally be abated."[1]

I pivoted to the first prong of nuisance law: Was a crime committed? "What crimes were committed by the triggering act of the Massacre?" I said. "You had murder where they shot us to death—murder in violation of 21 O.S. 701.7. You had murder where they stabbed us to death—violation of 21 O.S. 701.7. You had murder where they clubbed us to death—violation of 21 O.S. 701.7. You had murder where they burned us to death, as this photo shows—a charred Negro killed in a Tulsa riot—in violation of 21 O.S. 701.7."[2]

Each time, I said *us*. Shot *us*. Stabbed *us*. Clubbed *us*. Burned *us*. I wanted the court to feel that these crimes still bled into the present. Then I turned to the second prong: What makes a nuisance? My voice boomed through the courtroom.

"Your Honor, what could be more offensive than destroying an entire neighborhood? . . . What could be more offensive than saying you want to run the Negro out of Tulsa? What could be more offensive than a grand jury recommending that Greenwood be policed by white officers so a 'proper relationship' could be maintained? That policy still permeates Tulsa policing to this very day."[3]

From the gallery, I heard a low "Amen."

The hearing stretched for more than three hours. My presenting team—Eric Miller and SRZ attorneys Michael Swartz and Randall Adams—and I laid out the irrefutable evidence. The Tulsa Police Department and Tulsa County Sheriff's Office had deputized and armed white Tulsans to murder, loot, and burn nearly forty city blocks. The state National Guard had joined angry white mob in killing and looting. In the aftermath, city and county officials conspired to prosecute Black leaders as instigators, despite knowing who the real criminals were. For the next one hundred years, these entities profited while Black Tulsans bore the harm of an unending public nuisance.

As we approached the three-hour mark, we clashed with the defense over the principle of *unjust enrichment*—that when one party benefits unfairly at another's expense, restitution is required. They argued it didn't apply. We answered line for line. Finally, Judge Wall called a recess, instructing both sides to confer about a particular passage in our petition. My team gathered in the jury room. The defense stayed behind. After a few intense but exciting minutes, I stood and told my team, "That's it. We're done. We don't need to say anything else. She's already made up her mind."

When we returned, I stood once more in front of the bench. "Your Honor, we've conferred. We rest on our briefs and prior arguments. Nothing further."

The courtroom was still with the kind of heavy silence that anticipates something important happening. I sat down, my hands folded on the table, outwardly composed, pulse pounding. Three hours of argument behind us, every slide and every word laid down like bricks in a wall I prayed would hold. The presence of the survivors in the room pressed on me like a firm hand on my back, steadying me: *Don't falter now*. I turned and caught a glimpse of them: Mother Fletcher, small but unbowed, her hands folded over a neat handbag; Mother Randle, her gaze fixed steady on the bench; Uncle Redd, his back straight as if he were still a young soldier. They had waited a lifetime for this moment.

Part of me felt certain we had done everything humanly possible; part of me braced for the gut punch of dismissal. The courtroom held its collective breath. I knew if what we had said that day wasn't enough, nothing ever would be.

Then the judge stunned us all. "Now, before I announce my ruling," she said, "I want to make sure that every item of safety and decorum and dignity for everyone present is observed. So, I'm going to ask counsel for Plaintiff: Would you like the Court to permit time for those of your Plaintiffs who might need assistance, do you want me to have everyone else wait for them to exit the courtroom or not?"[4]

What!?!

Eric and I looked at each other, shocked. I quickly answered, "No, Your Honor," and then I turned to Eric and whispered, "Did she say she's going to rule now?" We had all expected a ruling to take days or weeks. But she was going to give us her ruling *right now*. Our whole case, our whole community, hung in the balance. *Oh my God.* I felt a rush of fear. Had we done enough?

Then Judge Wall said, "It is just approximately before 5 P.M. and so once the Court does recess, I'm going to request that in accordance with the court procedures that are in place for everyone's safety and security, that those of you, unless you have a reason to be here present after 5 o'clock, you should quietly and calmly exit the building without lingering in the hallways. I think that's what the deputies would request."

My heart sank. She was calling for calm and dispersing the audience. She planned to rule against us; I was sure of it. Then with no fanfare, she spoke. Everything started moving in slow motion. I was so keyed up on adrenaline that I could see every detail, hear every sound. Behind me was a gallery full of Black people whose hopes for justice hung on the words the judge was about to say. The tension in the room was as thick as the smoke from the fires that had burned in Greenwood. No one made a sound.

"The Court finds, based upon all of the argument of counsel, which is in court and also filed of record, that based on all the premises the Motion to Dismiss is granted in part and denied in part. The Court will file a written order and mail it to all counsel of record."[5] *Bang!* The gavel hammered down and court was adjourned. Still, complete silence.

Granted and denied? If the motion to dismiss had been granted in part, it had also been denied in part, which meant . . . we had survived!

The realization shouted in my brain: *WE SURVIVED!* Our lawsuit could go on. We would live to fight another day!

All the tension blew away like clouds. I exploded out of my chair and jumped as high as I have ever jumped in my life, hugged Eric, and shouted, "We survived!" Then I turned to the crowd, a sea of what seemed like hundreds of Black faces, none of them exactly sure what to do. I threw my arms into the air and shouted, "Justice for Greenwood!"

Everyone leaped to their feet and started chanting, "Justice for Greenwood!"

"Justice for Greenwood!"

"Justice for Greenwood!"

People cried. People hugged. People jumped up and down.

It was pandemonium. It was unbelievable. It was a release. It was a relief. It was one of the greatest moments I've ever had as an attorney.[6]

Getting to that unforgettable scene required nearly two years of legal work, coalition building, interviews with the press, frustrating negotiations, and simply keeping ourselves moving forward, beginning less than a month after we filed our lawsuit in September 2020.

On October 2, 2020, we announced on Instagram that Mother Fletcher would be joining our lawsuit. Social media exploded. Twelve days later, we began deposing the survivors. On October 14, 2020, Lessie Benningfield Randle became the first survivor of the 1921 Tulsa Race Massacre to give a sworn deposition. When I asked Mother Randle how that made her feel, she smiled and answered, "Glad I am still here to do it!"

The litigation plan my team and I put together included getting the survivors under oath as soon as possible. Normally, you're not allowed to take depositions (sworn testimony taken outside of court, where a witness answers questions from lawyers and the exchange is recorded for use in the case) so early in a lawsuit, especially if there are pending motions to dismiss, as there were in this matter. But we did some aggressive lawyering and requested that the court allow us to take early discovery based on the argument that our clients were more than one hundred years old and could pass away at any time. The judge agreed, and we were able to set up this historic testimony.

For Mother Randle's deposition, we sat in the Survivors Room at the Greenwood Cultural Center on Greenwood Avenue. The room we were in looked out onto a tranquil pond, with pine trees shading a little sitting area. It was a deceptively beautiful view. That land was once owned by some of the most prosperous Black entrepreneurs in the country, but now it was owned by the city and state and occupied by Oklahoma State University. Inside the room, the walls were covered in stunningly heartbreaking black-and-white portraits of about two dozen survivors. Beneath each was a short bio about their lives.

They had all been part of Professor Ogletree's 2003 federal case, and they had all died brokenhearted that the justice they sought and so rightfully deserved had not come. Now here Mother Randle was, the first survivor ever to give her story under oath, sitting beneath their portraits. The symbolism gave me chills.

The pandemic was still raging, so to protect the health of this fragile lady, the deposition occurred over Zoom. There was a computer set up in the room, and the white male lawyers representing the City of Tulsa, the Oklahoma Military Department, the Board of County Commissioners, the Tulsa County Sheriff's Office, the Tulsa Development Authority, and the Tulsa Regional Chamber of Commerce each had their own little window where they could listen to the testimony.

Mother Randle was beautifully dressed, with her hair and nails done, and wearing her best "church" hat. I asked her to describe what she could remember from the night of the Massacre.

She said, "I saw the soldiers' pistols, of course, that's how they—I knew they was soldiers. And someone told us that they had called for the soldiers to come in and assist, so they called whoever the soldiers were at that time and the soldiers came in and stopped them. It was quite a mess. I never want to see anything like that anymore."

I asked her what else she had seen.

"Well, we saw a truck, a flatbed truck, and they had loaded, just threw dead bodies on the truck, had them stacked up on the truck," she said. "We saw that, like I said, I was very small, so I can't remember just—but I do remember that."

I asked her if she still remembered seeing the bodies.

"Yes, at times when I get to talking about it, like now, I do remember kind of," she said. "I wouldn't recognize them by, you know, name or anything, but I remember seeing dead bodies, which was not all."

I asked if she knew what had happened to the bodies.

"I hear—we heard that they took those bodies down and threw them in the river, but I don't know that to be true, but we heard that, that was a rumor that they threw those dead bodies in the river. So we don't really know because we didn't stop and stay around to see, you know. We was getting out of the way, so—but it wasn't pretty, I saw it wasn't pretty at all."[7]

Tulsa County's attorney raised an objection to one of my questions, but none of the attorneys present asked Mother Randle a single question.

Two days later, on October 16, my team and I went to Mother Fletcher's home in Bartlesville to take her sworn deposition. It was a surreal scene: me in my mask, the all-white team of defense attorneys on Zoom, in the cramped apartment of a woman who clearly lived in poverty but who sat regally in her chair in the corner of the room. I asked her what she remembered about the night of May 31, 1921.

"Well, I was asleep, as far as I've been told," she said. "We were all aroused up by getting up and getting dressed so we could leave, yes . . . All this, the whole family was there, the parents and all the children, we were all together, and we were blessed to all get together and get out of town. When we heard that we was supposed to leave, everybody gathered up and left."

I asked her what she heard.

"Noise, the noise of guns shooting and smell the smoke and see the fire flashing and people, a lot of people running and in a hurry to gather up and leave," she said.

I asked if she was afraid for her life.

"Well, yes," she said, "wondering why we had to be—deserve that time and to leave, you know, Mama, where are we—I guess the question was, where are we going and why, and so that's what we were told is that everybody should leave town . . . they were coming through town and killing all the black people, so that was our understanding."

I showed Mother Fletcher the opening scene of the television series *Watchmen*, which masterfully re-creates the horrors of the Massacre in its first episode. The defense objected, with one attorney objecting that the scene came from a "science fiction TV show" and was therefore subject to interpretation. But when I asked Mother Fletcher if what she had seen on the screen matched her experience from that night, she said it did.

Me: Mother Fletcher, did you see those type of images that we just watched on the screen?

Mother Fletcher: Yes, sir. Yes, sir.

Me: You saw black men being shot by white men?

Mother Fletcher: Being shot, yes.

Me: You saw white men burning up black businesses?

Mother Fletcher: A business and homes, yes. Yeah.

Me: Did you see black bodies in the street?

Mother Fletcher: Yes.

Me: Did you have to run with your family like the people on the show?

Mother Fletcher: I had to run, yes, my family.[8]

Again, not one of the defendants' attorneys asked a single question.

Now, with three survivors as part of the case, the attention from the public and the media became even more intense. We were less than a year out from the Centennial of the Massacre and nobody could get enough of the story of Mother Randle and Mother Fletcher battling Father Time and white supremacy in their quest for justice. It seemed like every major news outlet was calling daily: BBC, Al Jazeera, CBS, NBC, CNN. Every day after we filed our lawsuit, I got more than a hundred calls, emails, DMs, and texts. I did so many interviews, podcasts, and presentations that I started to feel like an AI chatbot repeating the same phrases over and over. But this was the work of controlling the public narrative.

Ironically, the pandemic helped us. People were stuck at home and had all the time in the world to share the story and get involved. Zoom gave me virtual access to some of the most prestigious speaking venues. I was averaging three major Zoom presentations a week, speaking to the likes of Harvard Law, the National Bar Association, and grassroots organizations. Every time I logged onto Zoom, I felt the power of the story breaking through. The pandemic had given me a megaphone to speak to the world. I was drained, but the cause was like a battery for my soul. Every morning, when I got up and plugged into it, it recharged me. It felt like the entire nation was truly listening to Greenwood.

The experience could also be nerve-racking. Some of my Zoom appearances were interrupted by hackers posting vulgar, racist, and pornographic material. A hacker broke into my presentation for the University of Wyoming Black Studies Center, screaming, "Nigger lives matter!" with corresponding visuals.[9]

Many in the racial justice community were ready to put all their passion and resources into the effort. We weren't far removed from George Floyd's murder, so white supremacy and racial reckoning were top of mind for millions of people. Now there was a real-life case for reparations to support. That had always been part of our strategy. The struggle for reparations is sometimes too theoretical and abstract, which gives white people the opportunity to placate their conscience by saying, "Oh, isn't it a shame what happened to those poor Black folks in Tulsa?" while doing nothing. Now I had a viable case with a valid claim and multiple flesh-and-blood survivors. Ignoring it was not an option.

Folks were fascinated with the survivors. They were the living embodiments of the Black struggle. As October moved along and H.R. 40 gained traction in Congress, people all over the country saw how critical Tulsa was to the reparations fight. Not only was there no dispute that the Massacre had taken place, but we also had a mountain of evidence: living survivors, video, hundreds of photographs, insurance claims, and more. If we were going to win, it was going to be here, now. Support poured in.

We needed a forum where we could interact with and organize descendants and keep them informed and involved, so in October 2020 we started doing monthly virtual town halls, and by January 2021 we had gotten really good at them. We did a virtual town hall for seventy-five to one hundred people every month through 2021, and we kept our people informed and motivated.

But the most satisfying reaction to the lawsuit came from the City of Tulsa, the chamber, and the other defendants. They were *stunned*. They hadn't even known that Mother Fletcher or Uncle Redd existed! After the chamber released the 1921 minutes in 2019 and said, "We're sorry and we must make amends," they had figured Black America would accept their gaslighting because nobody could possibly file a lawsuit that wouldn't be laughed out of court. The statute of limitations had their backs. They could do their little mea culpa song and dance and we would just go away.

Instead, borrowing from Kendrick Lamar, we "popped out and showed 'em." We said, "No reconciliation without reparations!"[10] That became my mantra. I also made it clear to anyone who would listen that some of the money being raised toward the Centennial should go to the survivors and descendants, saying, "Greenwood is not a tourist site . . . it is a crime scene!"

The city, county, and state had no idea what had hit them. In their disbelief and panic, they embarked on a campaign to belittle our cause for reparations while deliberately smearing me and my reputation. Meanwhile, we started building our case.

While our main targets were the state, county, and local governments and the chamber, they all operated through their quasi-public Tulsa Race Massacre Centennial Commission (TRMCC). Back in the early 2010s, the city and Tulsa elites had realized a few unsettling things.

First, Tulsa was beginning to attract unwanted attention due to its history of police corruption and violence against Blacks. For example, in 2010 six Tulsa Police Department officers were indicted on corruption charges after a federal grand jury investigation.[11]

Second, with the hundred-year anniversary of the Massacre only a few years away, an even brighter spotlight would be directed at Tulsa's long history of white supremacy and racial oppression. After decades of ignoring the survivors' calls for justice, the city needed to erase the true story of Greenwood's destruction and make it look like all was forgiven without doing anything to make victims whole or offend the racists who wanted to pretend the Massacre had never happened. In 2015, the TRMCC formed and recruited prominent Black Tulsans to be their public face and voice.

(To be clear, throughout the rest of the book, when I talk about battling "the commission" or the TRMCC, I'm really fighting the City of Tulsa, State of Oklahoma, and the chamber.)

After its formation, the TRMCC announced a $30 million fundraising campaign to renovate and expand the beloved Greenwood Cultural Center in time for the Centennial. Since its opening, the GCC had become a magnet for locals and visitors who wanted to learn more about not just the Massacre but Greenwood, Black Wall Street, the history of Black Tulsa's innovation and economic development, and towering figures like A. J. Smitherman and Dr. Olivia Hooker. As a son of Greenwood, once I learned the truth about Black Wall Street and the Massacre, serving on the GCC board was a dream of mine, one that was realized in 2010. However, that same year Republicans took control of state government for the first time in history and immediately cut our funding. So, throughout my four-year term, we had to eliminate much-needed programs, terminate loyal and productive employees, and sell off assets just to keep the lights on.

Since then, the building, at a historic site on Greenwood Avenue, has continued to deteriorate. Because of this, there were a lot of people in the Black community, me included, who were initially on board with the TRMCC's plan. But after a while many began to question the commission's motives. For one thing, they had shown no interest in involving survivors or descendants. In 2015, as the TRMCC was forming, a prominent descendant who had been working for years to help bring the Massacre to light sent an email to the commission, asking to play a role. In part, the TRMCC wrote back:

> The current commission is a working committee for planning. It is not an open committee to the public. All members are elected, or public officials, or have ties to private funding to make this 5-year initiative happen. Survivors and their families, and interested individuals will be able to join a committee and or be recognized once the current commission finalizes all funding mechanisms and National designations required for long-term tourism and historical benefit.[12]

This raised suspicions that the city and the TRMCC intended to exclude survivors and descendants from any involvement in the process of creating a commemorative facility or determining Greenwood's future. Our fear was that the true purpose of the TRMCC was not restorative justice but creating the cosmetic appearance of cooperation, healing, and racial harmony to serve the interests of wealthy white folks. Like a city hosting the Olympics, Tulsa would put on its best face, only instead of sweeping up all the litter, the city would hide its history of racial violence and embrace of the KKK behind speeches and ribbon cuttings.

In 2016, G. T. Bynum, a former city councilman, won the mayor's race by talking about how he was haunted by the Black-white inequities of Tulsa. After his election, he created the Office of Resilience and Equity, which was charged with closing the equity gaps in Tulsa's economy, schools, transit, and more. (By some measures, those gaps did narrow.)[13]

However, Bynum also enforced the status quo when it came to Greenwood, stating that he thought paying reparations would divide the city.[14] The city would acknowledge the Massacre, memorialize it, apologize for it, and leverage it commercially, but under no circumstances would they spend a dime to make whole the families who had lost everything, including the bodies of many of their murdered loved ones.

On April 16, 2020, the TRMCC announced in a letter to Mayor Bynum that it was withdrawing from negotiations with the Greenwood Cultural Center to build its museum, Greenwood Rising, on the GCC's location. "We made a gallant effort to forge a collaboration among the Centennial Commission, the Greenwood Cultural Center, and the John Hope Franklin Center for Reconciliation," the letter read. "Despite great strides, the parties have been unable to reach agreement on a fundamental aspect of the construction of Greenwood Rising: its location."[15]

On April 28, the TRMCC proudly announced that it had secured a new location for what would be called the Greenwood Rising Black Wall Street History Center. The state-of-the-art museum and interactive history center would be built at the corner of Greenwood Avenue and Archer Street—the historic heart of Black Wall Street.[16] The property Greenwood Rising would be built on was owned by white developers. Not a square foot was owned by the Black descendants of Massacre victims or survivors.

Having kicked the hornet's nest, now we did everything to ramp up the pressure on the city and the TRMCC to come to the negotiating table. By publicly calling out the $30 million being raised without a cent being earmarked for survivors and descendants, I had given the community a rallying cry. We dominated the narrative among the people of North Tulsa and the nation. While the city was doing damage control, the country was talking about justice and reparations for the survivors and descendants. We continued to get positive coverage, and amid the increased public awareness, the calls for reparations only got louder.

On November 6, 2020, Dr. Tiffany Crutcher led a ceremony where she and I and members of the Tulsa Community Remembrance Coalition and the Equal Justice Initiative collected six jars of soil from parts of Greenwood where Black people had been murdered during the Massacre, including soil from the land where the home of a forty-two-year-old man named Reuben Everett (a direct ancestor of award-winning singer and actress Janelle Monáe), who was shot defending his home, had stood. The soil collection was part of a project Bryan Stevenson was leading, where people all around the nation were collecting soil from sites where Black people had been lynched.

Collecting that sacred soil was one of the most moving things I've ever done, and it stood in welcome contrast to the chaos of the previous couple of months. Court filings, press conferences, Zoom calls—it was all loud and fast. But that morning was quiet, reverent.

There was one jar. One vessel for all of us. We lined up, each person stepping forward, scooping a handful of dirt, and pouring it in. We kept our distance because pandemic rules still defined our personal space. Yet even through the masks, you could feel the intimacy: eyes locked, shoulders slumped, tears wiped away. I felt the urge to hug everyone, to share the weight and the love, but instead pressed my hand to my chest and nodded.

Layer by layer the jar filled, until it was more than soil. It was memory made tangible—grief and honor and witness sealed together.

It was in this atmosphere that I was approached by a member of the TRMCC Steering Committee who was also a senior program officer at the George Kaiser Family Foundation (GKFF), the most powerful force in Tulsa and the state's largest philanthropic organization. Run by one of the leading oil and business families in the nation, the GKFF has assets totaling around $5 billion.[17] The GKFF was also a key power behind the commission, and I had a good working relationship with them through my longtime association with the executive director.

I was told the TRMCC was interested in working with Mother Randle (who at that time was still the only survivor named in our written complaint), and we discussed ideas that I wanted to bring to the TRMCC for their consideration. After the somber soil collection ceremony, this was great news. We set up a Zoom call for November 13 between my team and TRMCC leadership.

I was excited that within two months of filing our lawsuit we were going to have a meeting to discuss possible collaboration with TRMCC decision-makers I'd had good relationships with for many years. I sent an email with these goals for the meeting:

- Learn how the commission proposed to incorporate Mother Randle into its work
- Understand the commission's position on restitution for the living survivors and known descendants of Massacre victims
- Determine whether the commission would support allocating a portion of the $30 million raised for the Greenwood Rising Center to restitution for living survivors and known descendants of Massacre victims
- Determine whether the commission would support dedicating a percentage of ongoing revenue collected by the Greenwood Rising Center to pay outstanding insurance and city/county claims that were unjustly denied
- Determine whether the commission would support a true criminal investigation into the deaths of those recently found in unmarked graves at Oaklawn Cemetery
- Determine whether the commission is, or would be, willing to compensate individuals for the intellectual property (family narratives, photos, videos, etc.) it had requested

In response, I got an email stating that TRMCC leadership would not attend. Further, the email made clear that anyone from the TRMCC who did attend would not be there in their official capacity. Instead, we would just be "friends catching up."

I was disappointed, but I chose to take the meeting anyway with those who logged in, and thought we had a frank, productive conversation. I was told that the attendees would brief the rest of the TRMCC on my requests for action on reparations, and that my team and I would receive a formal response from the commission about next steps. But as 2021 rolled in and my team and I kept working, I heard nothing from the TRMCC. On January 4, 2021, I sent them an email asking about their response. More silence.

Two days later, I and millions of other Americans watched in horror as Donald Trump incited a mob of thousands of his supporters (most of whom he pardoned days into his second term) to storm the U.S. Capitol. Before the day was over, about 140 law enforcement officers would be injured,[18] members of Congress would be hiding for their lives, the halls of the Capitol would be desecrated with human feces, and the certification of Joe Biden as the next president would be disrupted.

But to many of us watching in shock from Tulsa and around the country, the footage of that day was eerily familiar. We saw a mob of mostly white men, filled with rage, committing acts of violence and vandalism in an attempt to forcibly maintain their privilege and assert their white supremacy. It was a sobering echo of what Black communities like Greenwood across the United States had endured too many times, and a reminder of what we were fighting for.

The insurrection was also a stark reminder of the racial disparities that still haunt this country. As gut-wrenching as January 6 was, it pales in comparison to what happened to Greenwood on May 31–June 1, 1921. On January 6, rioters broke windows and barriers, terrorized the members of the House and Senate, and threatened to hang Vice President Mike Pence. One person was shot by a Capitol Police officer; there were no fires. In Greenwood, thousands of white terrorists stormed the streets with firearms, shooting and killing innocents at will and burning the entire district of more than ten thousand people to the ground. Yet while more than fifteen hundred people were charged with crimes for their roles in the January 6 riot, not one was prosecuted for their role in the Massacre.

The restraint of law enforcement officers on January 6 was also telling. Apart from the woman killed as she climbed through a broken window, officers and Secret Service agents did not fire on the enraged white mob. But what if the people attacking the Capitol had been

Black? There is no doubt in my mind that officers would have opened fire, and the steps of the Capitol would have been strewn with dead and wounded Black bodies bathed in a river of blood.

Most important, the mayhem of January 6 was part of the legacy of this country's systematic denial of accountability for white violence. President Trump's despicable pardon of everyone accused of insurrection-related crimes drove this home in 2025, but even in 2021 it was clear that we as a country were reaping what we had sown. I said as much in an insurrection response video I released:

> This is what happens when you allow lynchings to happen without accountability, without arrests, without convictions. This is what happens when you allow whole communities like mine—Greenwood, Black Wall Street—to be burnt down to the ground by a mob just like the mob we saw yesterday at the Capitol. A mob of violent, criminal, terroristic, thug white people who were able to create terror, break into buildings, steal property, fight officers, injure people, and then be walked out as if they were leaving a football game. . . .
>
> . . . It's the same here in Tulsa. Just talking about the Massacre is not going to prevent it from happening again. The people that committed the Massacre, they went on with their lives, just like the Confederates. They became leaders, elected officials, city fathers and mothers, because there was no accountability. They didn't face any arrests, they didn't face any trials, they didn't pay any compensation or restitution, they didn't repair what was broken.
>
> They just went on with their lives saying, "Black lives don't matter."[19]

Life revolved around our case. Mentally, I was on overdrive, revising briefs, taking calls from the press, and leading strategy sessions at all hours. Even when I tried to rest, my brain couldn't shut off. The only things that kept me going were my anchors: daily meditation, constant prayer, and most important, Mia. She worried about me day and night, convinced that I was running too hot and the stress would harm my health.

I would come out of my office after another sixteen-hour day and she would ask me to slow down, maybe delegate some of the things I was doing. I would shake my head and say, "I can't. It's all too important." I could tell she was frustrated, but as she has from the beginning, she stood by me. She hugged me and kissed me and told me how proud she was. I went to sleep, got up the next morning, and went to battle again.

If I hadn't had Mia and those daily practices, I would not have made it through. Meditation and prayer gave me rhythm, a way to quiet the noise so I could bring everything I had to the fight. Mia reminded me who I was and that I was equal to the task.

Emotionally, I was riding high because my plan was working. The story was spreading, and the survivors were finally being heard. But at the same time, I heard the clock ticking. I knew time was running out for my three survivors, and the weight of that reality pressed on me every day. Pride and pressure braided together, each one fueling the other.

On January 20, 2021, I sent an email to the TRMCC, making it clear that because our clients were more than one hundred years old, time was of the essence. I asked them how they proposed to work with and compensate Mother Randle but mostly about the issue of paying a portion of the millions the TRMCC was raising for the Centennial to the survivors and the descendants as part of a comprehensive reparations package.

At the time, the TRMCC was at war with itself. One of its members was Oklahoma Republican Senator James Lankford, who was taking heavy fire from Tulsa's Black community for being an election denier and trying to stop the certification of the 2020 presidential election. He poured gasoline on the fire with an open letter in which he stated that he hadn't realized that his actions could be seen as casting doubt on the legitimacy of Black votes. The calls for Lankford to be kicked off the commission grew louder.

However, on January 25, the TRMCC infuriated many of Tulsa's (and the country's) Black citizens by allowing Lankford to keep his seat on the commission.[20] They also sent me a letter on January 28 explaining that "this Commission established a mission significantly different from the Oklahoma Commission to study the Tulsa Race Riot of 1921, appointed by the state legislature in 1997 and sunset in 2001. The final report from that commission recommended five (5) separate reparations to the survivors, descendants and to the community of Greenwood. That report answers many of the questions you raise." I also obtained a copy of their January meeting minutes that quoted a member of TRMCC's leadership saying she and "other members of the Commission received an email from Damario Solomon-Simmons, who is legally representing survivors of the race massacre. . . . There are no plans to raise additional funds [on behalf of survivors]."

On February 2, 2021, we filed our amended petition with the district court, introducing Mother Fletcher and Uncle Redd as co-plaintiffs. This raised the pressure on the defendants even more. With the new filing, they also learned that we had a big New York law firm, SRZ, on our team, were monitoring every move they made, and had the ability to respond to it immediately. But what they did next still managed to take us by surprise with its tone deafness and dishonesty.

The TRMCC took out a full-page ad in a special Black History section of *USA Today* with the headline "TULSA TRIUMPHS" over a montage of Black Wall Street murals and renderings of the still-under-construction Greenwood Rising museum. The ad copy began, "Tulsa, Okla. is leading America's journey to racial healing."[21] Pure propaganda. The idea was to promote Tulsa as leading the nation in racial equity and justice. The spend on the ad had probably been around $200,000, money that should have gone to the survivors.

At our March 2021 Zoom town hall, dozens of descendants and supporters from around the country hammered the city for its duplicity and contempt. Brooklyn Williams, whose grandfather was

A. J. Smitherman, publisher of *The Tulsa Star,* which was destroyed in the Massacre, talked about the effect of that lost wealth on her family. "It wasn't just his newspaper business and the home, but he also had a printing plant," she said. "Those things were valued pretty high. If this event never took place, for sure our family would have been living pretty high on the hog right now."[22]

On March 23, the commission participated in a statewide TV show where in response to a question about the survivors' claim for reparations they said they were dedicating part of their work to Mother Randle. To our team this created the false impression that she was a beneficiary of their fundraising campaign, so we sent a cease-and-desist letter to the TRMCC demanding that they stop using the names of survivors to drum up support for their work.

We also sent out a press release that included a statement from Mother Randle: "My family and I were shocked to hear that the Commission is 'dedicating' much of their work to me since they have refused to meet with me, did not allow me an opportunity to participate in the Commission's planning, and declined to enter discussions on how I, a living survivor of the Massacre, feels about their activities around the Centennial. . . . My family and I still invite the Commission to meet to discuss how the Commission could tangibly support me and the other two known survivors who have waited 100 years for justice."[23]

With less than two months to go until the Centennial, the city, the TRMCC, and my team were no closer to resolving anything. But we kept up the pressure.

Although safe in my maid's quarters, I could see that red blaze in the sky over our beloved Greenwood. When I did get down to Greenwood after the riot, I was so hurt by what I saw. To wake up and see nothing but ashes and buildings burnt to the ground—I couldn't keep the tears from falling.*

—LaVerne Cooksey Davis, Massacre survivor, Licensed Practical Nurse, and dedicated member of Mount Zion Baptist Church, as told to Eddie Faye Gates

Fifty women, men, and children stand in front of a church, possibly Vernon Chapel AME Church in Tulsa. Collection of the Smithsonian National Museum of African American History and Culture, Gift of Princetta R. Newman.

CHAPTER 9

THE POWER OF MORAL AUTHORITY

In May 2021, with the Centennial just weeks away, I took Mother Fletcher and Uncle Redd to Washington, D.C., where they shared their stories before a nationally televised House Judiciary subcommittee meeting about the trauma of the Massacre.

Getting there wasn't easy. The trip was expensive. I couldn't just jump on a plane with the survivors. I had to take their caretakers and members of my team. The total cost would be more than $15,000. Journalist Tiffany Cross, then-host of MSNBC's *The Cross Connection,* who did a sit-down interview with the survivors a week before the trip and became part of our national support team, convinced one of her friends to donate half of our travel costs. Then my good friend Angela Rye connected us with Rashad Robinson and Color of Change, and they were kind enough to cover the balance.

(Angela is another person who deserves some recognition here. I met Angela when I was a national board member and reparations director for the National Black Law Students Association. She was an officer for the western region of the NBLSA and went on to become executive director and general counsel to the Congressional Black Caucus [CBC]. After that, she became an outspoken, sharp political strategist and commentator on CNN. She's an articulate, smart, powerful Black businesswoman who ain't taking BS from anyone, and she's stepped up again and again to help me with the work.)

One crisis had been averted, but another was warming up in the bullpen. On the day we were set to fly to Washington, violent storms delayed our flight for several hours. That's just an inconvenience when you're my age, but it's another matter when your star witness is 107 years old. Uncle Redd was flying from his home in Denver and he got out fine, but we sat around the Tulsa airport with Mother Fletcher, trying to get another flight. Finally, we found one, but it only had three open seats. We had a party of seven.

Mother Fletcher, her grandson Ike, and I got on that flight and flew to Charlotte while Mia and the rest of my team waited for a different flight. When we finally got to D.C., it was about midnight.

Our luggage had gone on the other flight, which meant Mother Fletcher had no change of clothes, but she was supposed to testify before Congress at 10:00 A.M.! Mia and the rest of the team got in at about 3:00 A.M., and my amazing wife was at a nearby Target that morning before they opened. She shopped for Mother Fletcher, went to the hotel, and helped this 107-year-old woman whom she had never met get dressed.

With that crisis resolved, we headed for Capitol Hill and ran into yet another one. After January 6, the U.S. Capitol was on lockdown. When our bus arrived, security told us that no vehicles were allowed close to the Capitol, so we would have to park about a mile away and walk. Fortunately, my good friend Congresswoman Sheila Jackson Lee heard about what was happening and let the guards have it. "Oh, hell no," she said. "These are one-hundred-year-old people." She called the Capitol Police, and they let us bring our Sprinter van onto the Capitol grounds.

Security led us into the building, but the white female police officer on duty said, "I can't let you in. This is a restricted location. You're going to have to go this other route." Representative Lee was having none of it. She came to the security checkpoint and snapped, "Do you see these people? Get your sergeant down here, now." The supervisor came down, and they figured it out. We barely got to the floor of the House in time, but then the survivors stepped up to the microphone and the world stopped for a while.

It was the first time Mother Fletcher had set foot in Washington,

D.C. The Capitol was grand and intimidating, but she sat at the witness table as if she had been preparing for this moment her entire life. I was right beside her, putting on her headphones, turning the pages we had written together, and leaning in to adjust the microphone so her words carried. Her voice was calm and steady, almost defiant: "I am here seeking justice. . . . I still see Black men being shot, Black bodies lying in the street. I still smell smoke and see fire. . . . I hear the screams. . . . Our country may forget this history, but I cannot."

She went on for several minutes more. When she finished, silence gripped the room. Suddenly, it erupted into a standing ovation. My chest tightened, but I kept my head up, fighting back my emotions.

Then it was Uncle Redd's turn. I crossed the aisle to sit beside his wheelchair; cameras surrounded us. His voice carried the cadence of a soldier:

> I am 100 years old. I am a survivor of the Tulsa Race Massacre. Because of the massacre, my family was driven out of our home. We were left with nothing. We were made refugees in our own country. My childhood was hard, and we didn't have much. We worried what little we had would be stolen from us, just like it was stolen in Tulsa. You may have been taught that when something is stolen from you, you can go to the courts to be made whole; you can go to the courts to get justice. This wasn't the case for us. The courts in Oklahoma wouldn't hear us. The Federal courts said we were too late . . .
>
> When I returned home from the war, I didn't find any of this freedom I was fighting for overseas. Unlike White servicemen, I wasn't entitled to GI bill benefits because of the color of my skin. I came home to segregation, a separate and unequal America. Still, I believed in America . . .

Then his voice cracked.

> We are not asking for a handout. All we are asking for is for a chance to be treated like a first-class citizen who truly is a ben-

> eficiary of the promise that this is a land where there is a "liberty and justice for all." . . . I want to say I appreciate being here, and I hope we all will work together. We are one. We are one.[1]

That broke me. Tears spilled behind my mask, hidden as I bowed my head. I put my arms around him, holding him close while flashes popped and applause thundered. In that embrace, I felt the century of pain and the weight of carrying it forward.

Finally, Mother Randle, who had been too frail to make the trip, appeared onscreen to make the final plea. "America is still full of examples where people in positions of power, many just like you, have told us to wait," she said. "Others have told us it is too late. It seems like justice in America is always so slow or not possible for Black people. We are made to feel crazy just for asking for things to be made right. There are always so many excuses for why justice is so slow or never happens at all. I am here today, 106 years old, looking at you all in the eye. We have waited 100 years, no, we have waited too long, and I am tired. We are tired. Lastly, I am asking you today to give us some peace. Please give me, my family, and my community some justice."[2]

Until that point, no one had really heard the survivors speak. No one had seen the depositions, and they hadn't been in a lot of national interviews yet. Before their appearance in D.C., it had been easy for skeptics to say, "This Black lawyer probably got these hundred-year-old people who don't even know what the hell is going on." Now, here were these century-old folks traveling twelve hundred miles from Tulsa to talk clearly and passionately about their experiences. Instantly, we were above-the-fold national news. It changed everything.

As the applause died down and the cameras kept flashing, pride surged through me—pride that I had placed my clients and my community in front of the entire world, and they had delivered their truth with unshakable power. Even Ohio Republican Congressman Jim Jordan, a hardcore MAGA disciple, and Louisiana Republican Congressman Mike Johnson, who's now Speaker of the House, were courteous and respectful. As I gathered my notes for my own testimony, exhilaration became certainty: *There is no way we lose this time.*

Oklahoma representative Regina Goodwin spoke, and then Tennessee Democratic Congressman Steve Cohen, chairman of the subcommittee, said, "Our next witness is Damario Solomon-Simmons. . . . We welcome you, and you are recognized for five minutes." It felt like someone had fired a starting gun. I leaned into the mic, and as I spoke, I saw every pen taking notes go still, and every photographer stop clicking their shutter.

"I am here today because the city of Tulsa has failed us. They bombed us. They burnt us. They killed us. They looted from us. They destroyed not just our property, not just our livelihood and our lives, but our legacy, our generational wealth, the idea of Greenwood, a freedom mind state, landownership, and wealth concentration. They took that from us, and then, they put in a system of policy violence that continues to this very day. So much so that, right now, as I speak, the same perpetrators of the massacre—the city, county, chamber, and State—are utilizing the massacre to pad their own pockets."[3]

As if the committee were my jury, I laid out the evidence, step by step. I explained that even Tulsa's current mayor admitted the disparities. In North Tulsa, life expectancy was eleven years lower than on the white side of town. Poverty rates were twice as high. Homeownership lagged far behind, schools were underfunded—a direct result of the 1921 Tulsa Race Massacre.

I told them these weren't just statistics. They were proof that the Massacre had never ended, that one hundred years later, Greenwood was still burning. I wanted every representative in that chamber to understand that without repair, harm multiplies. Without reparations, a wound festers.

After the survivors finished testifying, Representative Hank Johnson (D-GA) rose from his seat and came down off the dais. He walked straight over to me and the survivors. "Mother Fletcher," he said, leaning in so we could all hear, "You have been denied justice for far too long. I'm moving forward with introducing my bill." The survivors' visit led to the introduction of federal legislation: H.R. 3466, the Tulsa-Greenwood Massacre Claims Accountability Act of 2021, sponsored by Representative Johnson. A few days later, in a press release, he explained that the bill would "provide victims of the massacre—survivors and their descendants—access to the courts that they've been thus far denied due to statute of limitations restrictions."[4] But in that moment, what mattered was the conviction in his voice and the fact that he said it standing eye to eye with us, not from behind a microphone.

I relished spending so much time in D.C. with the survivors, and while I had great relationships with all three of them, one of the best parts of that time was that Uncle Redd and I began to strike up a real friendship. When we flew back and forth to D.C., or when he traveled to Tulsa from his home in Denver, we spent a lot of time together, just talking and laughing. He loved to eat and would tell me stories about seeing combat in World War II or how he worked six and a half days a week for forty years to support his family. Imagine the perfect papa—kind, wise, full of tales, and with a twinkle in his eye—that was Uncle Redd. Every time I saw him, he would grab my hand and say, "My man, my man, this is my man right here."

While we were in D.C., we all went for dinner on the patio at the InterContinental Hotel on the Wharf, a beautiful, upscale entertainment and dining district built on the Potomac River—me, Mia, Eric Miller, Tiffany Crutcher, Tiffany Cross, Mother Fletcher and Ike, and Uncle Redd and his daughters, Malee and Muriel. It was a beautiful day, the food was wonderful, and the place was packed. Yes, Uncle Redd enjoyed all of that. But he was more interested in a certain former talk show host from *The View*. "Boy, I sure would love to meet that Sherri Shepherd," he said. "I would show her my dance moves." We roared with laughter.

Another thing I loved about spending so much time with Mother Fletcher and Uncle Redd was seeing how they still acted like a big sister and little brother. Mother Fletcher, always stately and proper, would remind her brother what camera to look at during a TV appearance or a photo shoot. If we were out at a restaurant, she would say to the server, "Can you please make sure we both get our food at the same time?" It was beautiful to see two people who had lived so long still have that brother-sister bond.

But the high point of the D.C. trip was our meeting with Kamala Harris, then vice president of the United States. Angela Rye had connected me to the vice president's people, and I sent them an email saying the survivors would love to meet her if she was available. I got an email back saying that the vice president would love to meet them but also asking if I was related to Ken Simmons out of Oakland. I replied, "Yes, I am. Ken Simmons was my great-uncle."[5] Harris's people told me she would like to meet the survivors, but she also wanted to meet me.

What? I felt a rush of gratitude for my Uncle Don. I remembered him telling me I should change my name to Simmons because the name would open doors for me worldwide. Reading the email that Kamala Harris wanted to meet me, I could hear Uncle Don laughing and crowing, "I told you so! Now go do our name proud!"

There were some fireworks at the rest of the hearing, like when I shut down one of the two Black conservatives the Republicans had trotted out to argue *against* justice for the survivors. But my mind kept drifting: *What if I miss her? What if the meeting starts without me?*

When the gavel finally came down, I pushed past the crush of cameras and reporters calling my name. No quotes, no interviews. I hustled out of the Capitol, heart pounding, racing toward Blair House, the vice presidential residence.

I arrived, took a Covid test, and waited. Then one of the VP's staff came out and said, "Which one of y'all is Damario?" I raised my hand. Everyone started to get up, and the staffer said, "No, just Damario." The staffer and what appeared to be a Secret Service agent walked me into an ornate meeting room decorated with grand carpets and luxurious draperies. The meeting was winding down. The survivors sat around a long, gleaming conference table, their names displayed on placards in front of them, cameras placed discreetly around the room. Vice President Harris sat at the head of the table, listening intently as

Uncle Redd raised his finger to emphasize a point. A few feet away, Mother Fletcher clasped her hands, her mask slipping as she leaned toward Harris to say something.

Harris wasn't distant or formal, like a typical politician. She leaned in, smiled, and nodded when the survivors spoke. She touched their hands, laughed at their jokes, and spoke their names as if they were family. She *listened.* I could feel history being honored, not just observed.

As I slipped quietly into the room, Harris caught sight of me. Conversation stopped, and with that wide, confident smile, she pointed across the room and said loud enough for everyone to hear, "That is my cousin right there!"

Wait, what? Pause for backstory: One of the attorneys I worked with at Riggs Abney was Drew Edmondson, who was Oklahoma's attorney general for sixteen years. His family knew the Simmons family well, and when Drew was running for governor, he went to the National Association of Attorneys General conference and met Kamala Harris, who was then the California AG.

Later, he called me and said, "Damario, I met your cousin, Kamala Harris, who is running for U.S. Senate. She knew all about the Simmonses, the Creeks, everything." I didn't see how Kamala could be my cousin. Her mama was Indian, and her daddy's Jamaican. But after she and Biden won in 2020, my cousin Ken Simmons II posted a photo on Facebook of him and Kamala with a caption that said, "Congratulations to my cousin becoming the first African American vice president!"

I called Ken, and he explained to me that she was not my cousin by blood, but Uncle Ken had introduced her parents, had walked her mother down the aisle, and had basically been her godfather. He explained that we weren't related by blood, but we were related by family, good people, and love.

Heads turned toward me, and the vice president of the United States told the whole room about the Simmons family of Oakland, and about Christine Simmons (Uncle Ken's wife) being the reason she went to Howard and pledged Alpha Kappa Alpha. Standing there, hearing the vice president of the United States call me her cousin in front of my clients and her staff, I felt ten feet tall.

My clients had testified before Congress. New legislation had been introduced. I met with the vice president of the United States, who acknowledged me as family and promised to do all she could to help us in our cause. The trip had gone from being a comedy of errors to an unqualified triumph. A trio of gentle, fragile centenarians had stared down the United States Congress and the Tulsa Race Massacre Centennial Commission, and the rich and powerful people had blinked. The power of the survivors' moral authority had won.

Back in Tulsa, the temperature was rising. We were now less than two weeks from the Centennial. The city fathers had a week of events planned, including a candlelight vigil at Greenwood Avenue and Archer Street; the dedication of the Greenwood Rising Black Wall Street History Center; multiple symposia and panels, including the Tulsa Race Massacre Roundtable; and finally, a prime-time celebration called "Remember and Rise," which would be televised nationally by CBS and feature the Black Democratic political leader and voting rights activist Stacey Abrams and a performance by John Legend.

To the city, the chamber of commerce, and the white elites, all that meant tens of thousands of tourists spending money in the region and days of positive media attention. To me, it meant the chance to finally get justice. After the survivors' testimony aired on national television, the pressure on Tulsa officials skyrocketed. For years, they had managed to dodge, delay, or dilute calls for reparations. But now the entire world had seen Mother Fletcher, Mother Randle, and Uncle Redd pleading for justice before Congress. I was lobbying the national media, senior members of the Congressional Black Caucus, leaders of national civil rights organizations, and high-ranking Black corporate leaders to run stories, stand with us, and make calls to Tulsa decision-makers.

Now the BBC, Al Jazeera, CBS, CNN, NBC, *The New York Times*,

The Washington Post, and more ran stories nearly every day asking the same question: "What is being done with the $30 million raised in the name of the Massacre? Is any of the money going to survivors or descendants?"

I could feel the pressure building in my inbox and phone, too. Every day, I got an avalanche of emails, texts, DMs, and calls from journalists, lawyers, community groups, and everyday people asking what Tulsa was planning to do. The pressure was measurable in airtime, column inches, celebrity endorsements, and the city's growing fear of reputational damage on a global stage. They knew they could no longer hide behind silence. It was time to meet and hammer out the details of an agreement.

In more than twenty years as a litigator, one of the things I've learned is that the more the pressure builds, the more likely the other side is to make a deal. That's why so many cases settle right before going to trial. When a trial is in the distant future, the plaintiff and defense teams can go back and forth. But get within a few days of a trial and suddenly everybody's interested in settling. The Centennial celebration would be my courtroom, and the press and a national television audience would be my jury. I was certain that pressure would bring everyone to the table. By late May, the power brokers on the commission—foundation heads, business leaders, and elected officials—were ready to have another meeting. Thank God!

I sent them our demands in writing. First, the survivors would get $1 million each to ensure their comfort for the rest of their lives. Second, for the survivors to participate in the Centennial events, $10 million of the $30 million the TRMCC had raised for Greenwood Rising had to go to descendants, as well as one-third of the ongoing revenue generated by Greenwood Rising. Third, the commission had to make a public statement of support for our litigation against the perpetrators of the Massacre. Finally, the commission and the city would help to raise $50 million in seed money to start a reparations fund to repair long-term harm.

On May 24, 2021, the pivotal Zoom meeting took place. There was a lot of talk about what would be appropriate to give the survivors, and the commission members and their allies insisted that it would be difficult to come up with more than $100,000 per survivor in seven days.

Bill Zabel, whose clients include billionaires, was on the call but had said little for about an hour. But when the talk turned to dollar amounts, he had heard enough. "That's de minimis, the amount of money they're talking about," he said. (In legal terms, the Latin phrase *de minimis* refers to something so insignificant that it's not worth consideration.) "Three hundred thousand dollars is what you raise in an afternoon for inner-city kids for an after-school program. We are talking survivors of the worst race massacre in American history here!"

The TRMCC also balked at the $50 million in seed money, and in the end they said they couldn't meet our demands. I informed them that the survivors and descendants we represented would not participate in any Centennial activities. As we ended the call, I was disappointed that the survivors' moral authority, which had compelled Congress to act, was not powerful enough to get a deal done with the TRMCC. However, it was powerful enough to assert our will in other ways.

On May 27, I got a message from the news director for our local CBS affiliate asking, "Did you blow up the Centennial?" At that moment, my phone and inbox exploded with calls and emails from national reporters and producers asking me to comment on my role in canceling "Remember and Rise."

I googled the news and saw that John Legend and Stacey Abrams had announced they would not participate in "Remember and Rise" since the survivors were not going to be there. John even issued a long statement supporting Justice for Greenwood and asking his fans to donate to us. Around the same time, President Biden announced that he was coming to Tulsa for the Centennial but that he wouldn't be attending any of the commission's official events. Instead, he would come to the Greenwood Cultural Center and meet with the survivors. On May 28, the commission publicly announced that the event had been canceled due to "unexpected circumstances with entertainers and speakers."[6]

This was a *major* black eye for the city. They had booked high-profile events featuring national business leaders, elected officials, and civil rights leaders, but now these folks were calling to tell me that they stood with me, the survivors, and Justice for Greenwood. Many of them followed John Legend and Stacey Abrams and withdrew from city-endorsed events, choosing instead to participate in events put on by Justice for Greenwood and our partners. After five years of meticulous planning, over about forty-eight dramatic hours the city's Centennial fell apart because of their refusal to support reparations. This was *huge,* a real-life David vs. Goliath story. It was an example of the ThinkGreenwood principles—Community Love, Freedom Mind State, Ownership, Wealth Circulation, and Willful Resilience—in action.

We had gone toe-to-toe with the moneyed interests of Tulsa and stood on principle enough to get John and Stacey to do the same. We did it by sticking to three basic principles that any movement can use to make progress. First, know your story. Not just what's happening, but who it affects and why. Find the moral center of the issue that touches people's hearts. Second, build an army of allies, from national broadcast journalists to influential TikTokers, who will share your story and shape public opinion in your favor. Third, get your army to tell your story and keep telling it to anyone who will listen. That's how you build pressure.

A group of committed people stood together in unity and love to defend what they knew to be right. Our best weapons were the righteousness of our cause and the dignity and perseverance of the three survivors and the power of their recollections, together with the fact that most folks know right from wrong. Three centenarians went up against the corporate might and wealth of Tulsa's elite and the power of the state, and the city's narrative went down by a TKO. However, my goal was to win reparations for my clients and community, not to "blow up" events, so the work was far from over.

Predictably, the city and the TRMCC didn't go down without trying to take me with them. A smear campaign began against me and the survivors. On May 28, a TRMCC spokesman (who hadn't even been part of the negotiations) held a press conference in the parking lot of the Greenwood Cultural Center and told several bald-faced lies, including that the city's Centennial event had been called off because I had allegedly contacted the commission at the eleventh hour and upped our financial demands.[7]

On that same day, I escorted Mother Fletcher and her grandson to a dedication ceremony at the Gilcrease Museum in North Tulsa. Tiffany Crutcher had been working to preserve the legacy and memories of our survivors for future generations. Through the foundation she had launched in her brother Terence's name and memory, she had partnered with the museum and a tech company to record the survivors' oral histories and create an installation that used AI to compile life-size, interactive conversational videos.

After pulling into the museum parking lot, I helped Mother Fletcher out of the car and into her wheelchair. We were coming up the hill when out of the corner of my eye I saw a reporter from the *Tulsa World* standing in front of the entrance. He started walking toward us. He had been blowing up my phone and questioning the veracity of the survivors' stories.

When I saw him coming, I leaned down toward Mother Fletcher's wheelchair and said, "That's the *Tulsa World* reporter who's trying to discredit you as a survivor. We're just gonna ignore him and walk on past." But the next thing I knew, the reporter and I were nose to nose while he demanded to know why I hadn't responded to his requests for a comment. "Damario, you're a fraud, a con artist," he sneered. "That's why you don't want to talk to me, because you can't prove these people are really survivors." I could feel my blood pressure rising, and I foolishly took the bait and forgot where and who I was for a moment.

The reporter and I began screaming at each other. Needing to defuse the situation, I started to walk away . . . and then this white man grabbed my chest like I was his little boy. For a second, I only saw red. In that moment, my fury at all who had smirked and lied to us while denying us justice gathered in my fists. That ready-to-fight OU linebacker was still in me, and for a second that linebacker was ready to knock this man on his ass.

Then, in a moment of clarity, I saw that other people walking up to the museum had noticed us. I came back to myself and realized that we were making a scene in front of my 107-year-old client. The day wasn't about me; it was about the survivors and descendants. So, I took a deep breath, walked away, and went into the museum.

The city and its allies in the media had begun to show their true colors, dragging my name through the mud and trying to turn the community against me because their keynote speaker and headline performer didn't want to be associated with an event that did not center on reparations or honor the last living witnesses to the Massacre. Together, the white press and the TRMCC thought they could shame me, a civil rights attorney, because I stood up for my clients . . . because I did the thing I was born to do.

The city's words about reparations and respecting the survivors were empty, but that's a common problem when it comes to racial justice. People talk about how they love Martin Luther King, Jr., John Lewis, and Frederick Douglass. But talk is cheap. When everything is on the line, most folks don't want to back up their talk with action. They would rather post on social media and pretend their words alone can change anything. But change requires sacrifice. You do what John Lewis did and get in good trouble. You do what MLK did with the Montgomery bus boycott. You take risks. You show up. You have to be willing to pay a price. In his address on West India emancipation, Frederick Douglass said it best:

> If there is no struggle, there is no progress. Those who profess to favor freedom and yet depreciate agitation, are men who want crops without plowing up the ground, they want rain

> without thunder and lightning. They want the ocean without the awful roar of its many waters.
>
> This struggle may be a moral one, or it may be a physical one, and it may be both moral and physical, but it must be a struggle. Power concedes nothing without a demand. It never did and it never will.[8]

My team and I put everything on the line to go against the Tulsa power structure. We were uncompromising. It was our job to provoke and disrupt. We were on the right side of the issue. Moral authority was with us. Moral authority had moved Congress. Moral authority had collapsed the plans of a city backed by billions of dollars. We were out for justice, and whatever it took to get it within the law, we were willing to do.

I always tried dialogue first. I met with people, sent letters, and shared the unforgettable stories of the living Massacre survivors. And at every step I heard, "We'll get back to you." Then, nothing. The powers that be of Tulsa misunderstood my motivation, the nature of my work, the relationships I had built, and the political and human capital that I had accumulated. They assumed I was just another lawyer, but they were mistaken. During all my years as part of the community, from learning how to talk to my neighbors who walked into Gibbs candy store (where I worked in my youth) to helping people as a street lawyer, I've been connecting with power players and regular folks. They know me. They trust me. I'm not just *for* them. I'm one of them.

That's still true today. I work out at the same north side Hutcherson YMCA where I attended Daddy Brown's "wild game" holiday dinners as a boy. It's seven minutes from my house, and I've been going there my entire life. It's the "Black Y," where I work out with people from the community. The other day, I was lifting weights with my headphones on, and this brother came up to me and tapped me on the shoulder. When I took off my headphones, he said, "Man, I just want to say thank you for the hard work. You're helping so many people. I appreciate you."

That feels incredible, and it's because the people I'm representing are my people. I love that when I leave my house to visit the gym, see my insurance agent, or go to my pharmacist, I'm seeing people who I know and who know me. I take pride in my community, even though we don't have as much as we need on the north side of town. I love that I can be on TV one day doing an interview for the BBC and the next morning I'm at the Y working out next to my favorite mailman, Eric.

So, when it came time to choose sides—to choose who they would support—most of the community chose me, my team, our clients, and our cause.

Not every response to my work was supportive, however. I was the public face of the fight for reparations and the cancellation of "Remember and Rise," and while the majority of what I heard was positive, there were threats, including some that were vile and racist. If you think it's dangerous being a Black man in the United States, try being an outspoken Black lawyer getting in the face of the white power structure. I was sky-high because our narrative was getting international attention, and I wasn't even thinking about my own safety, but you know who *was*? Mia.

Thanks to all the post-D.C. coverage, I had a long string of public events, and a few days before they started, Mia sat me down at home with a look I've come to know very well. "We need security," she said. "You need somebody with you wherever you go." I started to protest, but she knew exactly what to say to quiet me down. "You're just so focused on the work, as you should be, but you need somebody equally as focused on protecting you as you are on getting justice." What could I possibly say to that? Plus (and this is another recurring pattern in my life) Mia was right. I said, "Who are we gonna get that I can trust?"

She already knew. "Call Tyrone." No. For real.

Tyrone Lynn is a retired Tulsa Police Department homicide detective and crisis negotiator known as a tough cop and a stand-up guy. His sons are like my nephews, and Mia and I are close to him and his wife, Rhonda. Back in 2011, he made national news when a disturbed man climbed the three-hundred-foot Clear Channel radio tower in Tulsa and refused to come down for six days. Tyrone had already retired, but he was such a brilliant negotiator that the city asked him to try to talk the guy into coming down . . . which he did.[9]

By the time Mia suggested that I call him, Tyrone had moved to Houston, but I called him and said, "Man, I need security. Can you come up here tomorrow, stay through the week, and go to these events with me?"

Without hesitation, he replied, "Absolutely." Aside from being a great friend, Tyrone is also a pro, so he knew that my increased visibility and outspokenness made me a potential target. He got on a plane, spent the week with me, and since then he's been my director of security and one of my most trusted advisers.

Today, I don't go to a lot of public events, particularly when it's been advertised that I'm going to be speaking, unless he's there with me. These days, if I'm going somewhere, my mama will ask, "Is Tyrone going with you?" If I tell her that he is, she always says, "Well, please tell Tyrone I appreciate him."

The days counting down to the Centennial were a whirlwind as the survivor and descendant community held its own commemoration luncheon that was authentic, heartfelt, and focused on reparatory justice. At that event, to a roof-shaking ovation and cheers, Justice for Greenwood presented Mother Randle, Mother Fletcher, and Uncle Redd with checks for $100,000 each. There were hundreds of people in attendance, including A-list civil rights leaders and dignitaries from across the country and around the world, including Representative Sheila Jackson Lee, attorney Ben Crump, and Rashad Robinson, president of Color of Change.

Meanwhile, Dr. Tiffany Crutcher organized a series of cultural events for the Black Wall Street Legacy Festival that weekend, including a procession through Greenwood that featured the survivors riding in a horse-drawn carriage and waving to the crowd. Despite the unusually cold weather, there were thousands of people in the streets. All the major news stations had reporters on the ground, many broadcasting live from Greenwood. At that moment, the eyes of the world were on Tulsa.

NBC had been requesting an interview with a group of descendants and activists, and we helped bring it together. On May 29, Tiffany Cross came down to Tulsa and met with Laurel Stradford (great-granddaughter of hotelier J. B. Stradford), Dr. Tiffany Crutcher, Chief Egunwale Amusan, and Nehemiah Frank (founder and editor in chief of *The Black Wall Street Times*). Sitting in a loose circle in a Greenwood parking lot to observe social distancing, these veterans of the fight for reparations shared their views on Tulsa's refusal to act, on the conspiracy of silence, and on the pain of seeing year after year go by without justice.

Chief captured the frustration of the reparations community. "People ask me, like, 'Chief, what does it mean to have this one-hundred-year Centennial?' It means 365 more days of oppression and the failure to remedy through justice. That's all it means. Nothing different. It's another year that you failed, that the city failed, that society failed, and that those of us who are descendants, we still stand on this sacred ground with that charred baton that has been left in our hands. That's all it means."[10]

But May 31 was the big day. I woke up energized but also with a heavy spirit. It was a century to the day since Greenwood was destroyed, and despite the setbacks with the Centennial Commission, I still believed reparations were possible. I never saw the Centennial as a celebration, but as a platform. It was a chance to demand justice, to elevate the voices of our survivors and descendants so that they could never again be ignored or erased. For a century, Tulsa had said no to the rightful call for justice, but on that day, the wall of refusal seemed to be crumbling.

That morning, Greenwood community leaders braved the rain to hold a soil collection ceremony, organized by Dr. Crutcher, on Standpipe Hill, where one hundred years earlier the men of Greenwood had made their last stand. The soil was placed in engraved urns.[11] The Oklahoma National Guard (one of the defendants in our case) also issued a public apology, stating for the first time that they did not do their job to protect the people of Greenwood.[12]

Later that day, CBS aired an interview conducted by Gayle King, the CBS morning personality, and that was where Uncle Redd again showed off his great sense of humor and love for the ladies. He told Gayle all about living in a tent and bathing and doing laundry in the river for years because his family had lost everything. Then, at the end of the interview, he asked Gayle how old she was, and when she told him he said, "You're too old for me," even though he had more than thirty years on her. I about fell out of my chair laughing!

During the Centennial, I got to spend more time with the survivors, and it reminded me why I, and everyone else, loved them so much. Mother Fletcher was always very dignified, and sometimes she didn't care for Uncle Redd's candor. We were taking a break during the Gayle King interview when I heard Mother Fletcher say to him, "Why are you telling them that about washing the laundry in the river? It's embarrassing!" Always the big sister, looking out for the family name and keeping her baby brother in line.

To end the day on a high note, we hosted a live town hall for hundreds of descendants of the Massacre, local and national leaders, and scores of media members at the Greenwood Cultural Center. Angela Rye presided over a packed house including survivors and members of the CBC leadership, like the legendary Representative Barbara Lee (now mayor of Oakland) and Delaware Representative Lisa Blunt Rochester (now a United States senator), and national civil rights leaders like Nicole Austin-Hillery of Human Rights Watch (now of the Congressional Black Caucus Foundation).

We were observing pandemic protocol, so the chairs were spaced wider than usual, but the room still pulsed with anticipation. When Mother Fletcher and Uncle Redd entered, chatter stopped and everyone rose instinctively—some clapped, some cried, some pressed a hand to their heart.

The gathering opened with a prayer that set the frame: "This is not a celebration . . . this is a crime scene." Angela Rye charged the room: "You were called here not to celebrate, not to grieve, but to do the work." Then she pulled Dr. Tiffany Crutcher and me to the front. "Give them their flowers," she said. The applause thundered.

When I spoke, I kept it plain. I laid out the purpose of Justice for Greenwood—reparations for survivors and descendants, accountability for those who'd profited, resources to rebuild. I reminded them that the case we had filed wasn't about one plaintiff but an entire community. "We are the Greenwood diaspora," I said, and the crowd roared it back.

Congresswoman Brenda Lawrence called the Massacre genocide. "It is a debt that America owes," she said, "and we're going to make sure they pay it." Barbara Lee insisted on truth and reconciliation. Lisa Blunt Rochester recalled a boy who feared Tulsa's history would be banned from his classroom. Sheila Jackson Lee, fierce as ever, declared, "Reparations time is now." Michael Swartz and Sara Solfanelli of SRZ described pouring millions of dollars' worth of legal work into the case. Descendants like Jaya Rapp (a direct descendant of Massacre survivors Lee Neal, Simeon Lee Neal, and Susan Brown Neal) and Raven Williams (a direct descendant of A. J. Smitherman) stood to name their ancestors and demand that family stories not be exploited but honored.

Then the survivors spoke. Uncle Redd raised his hand and said, "To the president of the United States, I'm pleading for justice and reparations. I have waited one hundred years for this. We are one." Mother Fletcher leaned forward and softly added, "My brother spoke for both of us."

I closed with a reminder of what bound us together. "Greenwood was a love story," I said. "Dick Rowland was just a shoeshine boy, but the community loved him as much as A. J. Smitherman, J. B. Stradford, or Dr. A. C. Jackson. That's who we were. That's who we must be again."[13]

The answer roared back, louder with each repetition: "We are Greenwood!" In that moment, the diaspora didn't feel scattered. It felt like family.

But the most heartwarming part came after the presentations. Descendants started mingling and meeting one another, and I heard strangers chat for a few minutes about their ancestors, and then exclaim, "Oh my Lord, your grandfather and my grandmother were neighbors in Greenwood!" or "My great-grandfather was your great-grandfather's family doctor!" It brought the long-dead residents of Greenwood back to life, and it was beautiful.

President Biden was scheduled to meet with the survivors at the GCC the following day, so the Secret Service shut us down early to sweep the building. I headed to the Hotel Indigo in downtown Tulsa to meet my legal team from SRZ. We knew this was a critical time. The cancellation of the Centennial celebration and the breakdown of negotiations meant the pressure on the city to reach a settlement had eased. We hoped Biden's visit, the press coverage around it, and the words of Reverend Jesse Jackson (who was in Tulsa to speak at the dedication of a prayer wall at Vernon AME Church) would restore our leverage and momentum.

The hotel lobby was overflowing with people from across the world, and the energy was high. Then a big, unmistakable voice drew my attention. I stood up and headed toward the bank of elevators, calling out, "I know that ain't nobody but Barbara Arnwine in my city!" Immediately, I saw the renowned civil rights attorney. The former longtime president of the prestigious Lawyers' Committee for Civil Rights Under Law, Barbara is a petite Black woman but a giant in our field of civil rights.

"Damario?" Barbara said, turning around, a smile spreading across her face. We hugged and I asked her if she was staying at the hotel. "No, I'm going up to visit Reverend Jackson," she said. "You better come up with me. You know he'd love to see you."

I didn't realize that Reverend Jackson had been staying at the Indigo, or I would have already been in his room paying my respects and soaking up his wisdom. I didn't intend to pass up the opportunity now.

I told my team I'd be back in a few minutes and then stepped onto the elevator with Barbara. On the way up to his room, I thought back to the first time I'd met him. In 2013, I was invited to Chicago to appear on his radio show and participate in a Saturday morning community forum. Reverend Jackson had converted a former synagogue on East Fiftieth Street into a command center, broadcast studio, and community gathering place, and it was here that he taped his radio show and offered free food and services to the people in his community.

When I arrived, people were milling around, with no security and nobody checking IDs. Anyone in the neighborhood could just walk in off the street and get something to eat if they were hungry, something to drink if they were thirsty, or information about healthcare or other social services.

It was beautiful. I saw this global icon easily and happily fellowshipping with anybody who came into his building—not simply making promises in televised speeches but *acting* on those promises. Reverend Jackson gave the people in that neighborhood hope. They knew this world-famous leader was not just *for* them. He wasn't just a celebrity. He was one of them. He's one of my role models for servant leadership.

Barbara and I stepped off the elevator, and she knocked on the hotel room door. When it opened, I saw Reverend Jackson seated on a chair across the room, with his son (and current Illinois congressman) Jonathan standing beside him. Not only did we share a passion for civil rights and pride in our people, but we were also both proud members of the great Black fraternity Omega Psi Phi, and I walked over to greet him with our fraternity's handshake. Then I stopped dead. Sitting on the couch opposite Reverend Jackson, next to Barbara, was the same TRMCC spokesman who a few days earlier had slandered me at his press conference. Tension filled the room.

I took a seat next to Reverend Jackson and started to speak with him about the Centennial and about what he might say to the Tulsa City Council in a couple of days. He spoke about how the movement needed to be careful. "We don't want to get played by all the pomp and circumstance surrounding the Centennial," he said. "We need to keep our focus on the fight for true economic justice for the community, not on performative gestures that have no substantial impact on Black lives, wealth, or health."

As usual, Reverend Jackson had stated the issue succinctly and forcefully. But after he finished, I pointed at the TRMCC spokesman and said, "That ain't what *he* believes." I was pissed, so I called the man out not just for lying on me to the national media, but for giving cover to the white power structure looking to exploit the Massacre. He responded by accusing me of disrespecting Reverend Jackson. I replied, "I'm not disrespecting my frat brother. I just want him to know who he has in the room with him."

"Okay, okay," Reverend Jackson broke in. "Damario, I understand your frustration, but let's stay focused on the real powers that be."

We had a chance to do just that the next day when President Biden came to Tulsa and dealt the city leaders a major blow by bypassing their TRMCC-sanctioned events to meet with the survivors and give a speech at the GCC. He spoke about measures aimed at narrowing the racial wealth gap and called on Congress to pass the George Floyd Justice in Policing Act.

"For much too long, the history of what took place here was told in silence, cloaked in darkness," he said to the large crowd. "But just because history is silent, it doesn't mean that it did not take place. And while darkness can hide much, it erases nothing. It erases nothing. Some injustices are so heinous, so horrific, so grievous, they can't be buried, no matter how hard people try."[14]

Nice words, but I couldn't help noticing that not only did the president not announce any reparatory measures, he didn't even say the word *reparations*. Instead, Uncle Redd, not President Biden, authored the most memorable part of that event. Roland Martin, host of #RolandMartinUnfiltered, a hugely popular daily digital show focused on the Black community, was on-site to do a live broadcast, and from out of nowhere Roland and Uncle Redd just started singing "We Shall

Overcome." I looked over and saw them, singing and swaying, and slowly, all the conversations in the room came to a stop. After a moment of awed quiet, the gathered civil rights leaders and politicians all joined in to sing the old spiritual.

Uncle Redd had a fine sense of timing and was a natural showman. In 2021, when he was one hundred, he and Mother Fletcher flew to Ghana to receive honorary Ghanian citizenship. During an event celebrating the diaspora, Uncle Redd asked for the microphone. Someone held the mic in front of him, and he stuck one finger in the air, looked at the people gathered around him, and said, "We are one. Come on. We are one." The rest of the people in the room started chanting, "We are one! We are one!" He had great instincts and seemed to know just what people needed to hear.

That evening, I sat on a panel called "The Color of Wealth: The Destruction of Greenwood & Tulsa's Legacy of Loss"[15] with the CEO of the anti-poverty Robin Hood Foundation (and current Maryland governor) Wes Moore, economist Darrick Hamilton, Joi Chaney of the National Urban League, and SiriusXM Urban View 126 radio host Karen Hunter. We discussed the racial wealth gap in Tulsa and the need for reparatory justice. Unsurprisingly, the disparities between Black and white Tulsans were stark.

Black people in Tulsa were far less likely to own their homes, and even if they did, their homes were worth much less than those owned by whites. Blacks were less likely to own their own businesses, owned less than 10 percent of the assets that white Tulsans owned, and had an average net worth of about $8,000 per household compared to about $145,000 for white households. In other words, Black people in Tulsa weren't just poorer than white people. Compared to the wealth owned by whites, theirs was microscopic.

As Ofronama Biu, now chief economist and senior research director at the Maven Collaborative, said on the call, "Wealth is the most important measure of economic security and well-being. Wealth allows families to better cope with unexpected shocks such as sickness, unemployment, and even the negative consequences of the pandemic. Given the iterative and intergenerational nature of wealth accumulation, without redress the Tulsa Race Massacre that occurred over one hundred years ago is inseparable from the great differences that exist today."[16]

If that's not a description of ongoing harm, I don't know what is.

On June 2, the Tulsa City Council held a tense, emotional three-hour public meeting. The council had been talking about passing a nonbinding resolution that would "acknowledge, apologize, and commit to making tangible amends for the racially motivated acts of violence perpetrated against Black Tulsans in Greenwood in 1921." I was vehemently against this resolution and lobbied my city councilwoman privately to convince her to vote against it.

Why? Because at this moment in time we still had an opportunity to extract tangible concessions from the city. Public opinion and media coverage were still giving us considerable leverage over Tulsa and its supporters. Joe Biden had just become the first president to publicly acknowledge the Massacre. The national media were still giving the survivors their close-up.

The documentary *Dreamland: The Burning of Black Wall Street,* executive-produced by NBA superstar LeBron James, had just been released. Another NBA star, Russell Westbrook, released his own documentary, *Tulsa Burning: The 1921 Race Massacre,* on the History channel. The entire country was talking about Greenwood and saying, "Tulsa, what are you going to do about this?" There was overwhelming pressure on the city to take meaningful action on reparations.

As far as I was concerned, the resolution was the same kind of empty "we'll get right on that" rhetoric we had been hearing for decades. If the council codified that language as Tulsa's official position on the Massacre, they would be giving the city an escape hatch. The city would feel justified in saying, "What more do you want? You got an apology and a commitment to do . . . something." Our bubble of pressure would deflate like a balloon.

That's what Reverend Jackson told them when he got up to speak to the hushed audience. He said that reparations are about economics, and that while everything Tulsa had been trying to do—museums, ceremonies, vigils, pathways—were not bad ideas, reparatory justice must begin with *economic* justice. "We have not seen justice yet. And until we see justice, we are the land of the oppressors and the home of the cowards," he said."[17]

Some people think Black people are being greedy when we talk about monetary reparations. But we live in a capitalist economy where, unfortunately, cash is king. To build a better life, you need capital. Reparations make people whole by giving them the money they need to rebuild the lives they should have had if they had not suffered the harm. They can have more control over where to live. They can start businesses and purchase income-producing assets. They can send their children to college. They can afford better healthcare. Most important, reparations are the *only* way to reduce the tremendous racial wealth gap.

When you try to make Black people feel bad about asking for money, you're saying that you don't believe we deserve the same equal rights under the law as everybody else. It's easy to go to an MLK Day speech or go to an MLK Day parade with an MLK T-shirt on, but it's a lot harder to support the work reflected in Dr. King's quote, "We must recognize that we can't solve our problem now until there is a radical redistribution of economic and political power."[18] When it comes down to actually giving Black people what we are owed, what do you say?

A nonbinding resolution doesn't pay outstanding claims. It doesn't compensate survivors for their losses. It doesn't pay restitution for the people who were murdered. It doesn't give Massacre victims like Mother Randle the money they need to move out of a crumbling house in a neglected neighborhood.

In the end, the resolution passed unanimously, providing the city with some positive press coverage. It acted as the pressure relief valve the powers that be needed. Negotiations ceased. We filed our response to the defendants' six motions to dismiss, but I feared that we had missed our best opportunity to get reparations by settling with the city while the world watched. The country's attention would soon turn elsewhere, and Tulsa would have no incentive to meet with us or pay reparations.

We were going to court.

PART FOUR

WEALTH CIRCULATION

Individual business ownership is one aspect of building resilient, vital Black communities, but business alone has never created—and will never create—enough wealth and power to remedy centuries of harm. The people of Greenwood understood this truth deeply. They practiced the genius of concentration—of mind, money, and mission. They built schools, financed businesses, and created institutions where education and enterprise worked hand in hand. They knew education was not merely opportunity—it was the infrastructure of economic growth. They pooled resources, circulated dollars, and turned knowledge into wealth.

Their triumph was no accident; it was the deliberate concentration of intellect, discipline, and purpose within a community determined to prosper together. When we educate strategically and build wealth collectively, we move from survival to sovereignty.

On reaching the house I saw my piano and all of my elegant furniture piled in the street. My safe had been broken open, all of the money stolen, also my silverware, cut glass, all of the family clothing, and everything of value had been removed, even my family Bible. My electric light fixtures were broken, all the window lights and glass in the doors were broken, the dishes that were not stolen were broken, the floors were covered (literally speaking) with glass, even the phone was torn from the wall. . . . My car was stolen and most of my large rugs were taken. I lost seventeen houses that paid me an average of over $425.00 per month.*

—Robert Tyler Bridgewater, M.D., Massacre survivor,
physician, and founding member of Vernon AME Church,
as told to Mary Parrish

A postcard shows the smoke cloud over the area where the conflagration reportedly started. The scene is from the perspective of the roof of the Hotel Tulsa. The original is in the Department of Special Collections, McFarlin Library, the University of Tulsa.

CHAPTER 10

KEEPING IT IN THE COURT

On September 28, 2021, I arrived at the Tulsa County Courthouse for our first hearing, where the court would consider the defendants' dismissal motions. As I walked into the building, my mind wandered to Professor Ogletree and the lawsuit he had led for a different group of survivors, and how his regal, proud gravitas in the courtroom had inspired me. By this time, he had been diagnosed with early-stage Alzheimer's disease, but I knew he would smile if he could see how far we had come.

Beside me walked my co-counselors: Eric Miller, Kymberli Heckenkemper, Michael Swartz, Angela Garcia, Sara Solfanelli, Randall Adams, McKenzie Haynes, Lashandra Peoples-Johnson, Cordal Cephas, and Steven Terrill. Before we even entered the courtroom, I could hear the buzz of voices that could only come from a big crowd, the kind I had never heard in a courtroom before. When we walked in, I saw where the noise was coming from: dozens of supporters, all of them masked and many wearing purple Justice for Greenwood shirts, nearly all of them talking excitedly at once. Several news outlets had sent reporters or camera crews to cover the hearing, and they had packed the room to overflow capacity.

I guess I have to take the blame for that. After tensions surrounding the Centennial and the unfinished business of reparations, our community was ready to rally behind something, so a few weeks before the court date we had launched a "Don't Dismiss Us" campaign.

The night before, on September 27, we'd held an emotional prayer rally at the Greenwood Cultural Center that hundreds had attended. Now it looked like they had all turned up at the courthouse . . . and brought friends!

As moving as the show of support was, it was a problem for the fire marshal, so we were forced to move the hearing to the spacious Carlos Chappelle Ceremonial Courtroom on the sixth floor.[1]

As everyone got settled in the new venue, I looked over and saw the large bronze plaque attached to the wall, detailing the life and career of Judge Chappelle, a direct descendant of Massacre survivors and the first Black presiding judge in Tulsa County. His presence reassured me. Then, because the courtroom was so full and the spectators so passionate, Judge Wall admonished those in attendance about courtroom conduct:

> I understand this is a very sensitive matter to many people and people may get emotional from time to time. It is not appropriate in the courtroom proceeding to express any kind of outburst of any kind. And I would caution you, if you feel that you're getting—if anyone feels that they're about to have an emotional outburst or say something, you need to excuse yourself to the hallway and remain quiet. If you cannot remain quiet, you must leave the floor. I will give everyone this warning. Any violation of the court orders is punishable—can be punishable by a finding of contempt which can be punishable by six months in jail and/or a $500 fine.[2]

In all my years in court, I had never seen or even heard about a judge saying something like this before a motion to dismiss hearing. She was telling a room full of Black people that if they made a sound they could be held in contempt. But I didn't allow that to distract me. I sat quietly at the counsel table and rechecked everything from my notes to my PowerPoint slides, ensuring that I was thoroughly prepared. It's a kind of calming ritual that helps me quiet my emotions and focus on the task at hand.

John Tucker, the lead attorney for the Tulsa Chamber of Commerce, led things off for the defense. John, a senior partner at one of Tulsa's largest and oldest firms, has been practicing law for ten years longer than I've been alive. Wearing a bow tie and sounding every bit the Southern lawyer that he was, John started his argument off by saying, in part: "I would be remiss if I didn't observe, as the Court has already, that there's a substantial public interest in this hearing . . . evidenced by the large number of folks . . . that are attending here today and why we moved to this larger courtroom. I would suspect that they are here because they are concerned, as many people in Tulsa are, about some of the issues that underlie the concerns of Plaintiffs expressed in this lawsuit which have to do with the racial and economic disparities and discrimination that exist in Tulsa, and with the geographic disparities that exist in Tulsa."[3] His job was to minimize the importance of our case, and "issues" was one way to do that.

A few minutes later, pointing toward the big north-facing window, Tucker said, "I think the Plaintiffs' eloquent argument in a sense sums up the frustration he feels and many people in the audience feel about what happened in 1921, and the fact that as we look to the north [toward Greenwood] we see that that's not a prosperous community."[4]

I hid my surprise at this admission. We had come to the courthouse exhaustively prepared. This would be the first time Black victims of the Massacre had a hearing in the Tulsa County District Court. This was history. So, to hear the defense freely admitting that there was a problem that needed to be rectified was startling.

There was a reason for this. The defendants were confident that all they had to do was show up in court and make a pro forma argument for dismissal and the system would do what it had done since 1921: find in their favor and against Black people.

When my turn came, I rose and introduced myself and my clients. I reminded the court (as I would in May 2022) that Oklahoma is a notice-pleading state, so every allegation at this stage must be taken as true. If we were allowed to proceed to discovery, we would then have to prove the validity of our claims.

The arguments stretched for six hours—the longest motion to

dismiss hearing of my career. Point after point, the defense attorneys insisted the harms were too old, too private, too far beyond the reach of nuisance law. I countered that a nuisance exists until it is abated. The defendants had admitted the harm continued to the present day, so the duty to repair remained under Oklahoma law.

At the conclusion of arguments, Judge Wall announced she would issue a written order within ten days. Then she stepped off the bench, walked toward our table, and gently took me aside. "I just wanted to let you know that I'm in a prayer group with some of the defendants," she told me quietly, "but that doesn't impact me."

Stunned, I gently nodded, but as the judge disappeared through the door that led to her chambers, my stomach churned. Nevertheless, I decided against asking her to recuse herself. I still believed Judge Wall gave us our best chance of being treated fairly by the Tulsa County court system. I had argued high-profile, racially based cases before her, including my Trey Bird case, and she had been fair and applied the law properly. Also, we had made it further than anyone before us. For the first time ever in Tulsa County District Court, survivors of the Massacre had been heard on the record.

So, we waited. Ten days, no decision.

Thirty days, no decision.

Meanwhile, I was working on other strategies. Since 2020, part of my plan was to enlist the U.S. Department of Justice (DOJ) in the fight, and while we waited for Judge Wall's findings, I decided to put that part of the plan into motion. Back in August, I had sent a letter to the DOJ requesting that the department open the first federal investigation into the Massacre. There were several good reasons to get the DOJ involved. First, with H.R. 40 going to the full House of Representatives, a federal investigation might give the bill the final push it needed to pass a floor vote. Second, the extra pressure of government scrutiny might encourage our defendants to settle. Third, a federal investigation with federal resources might turn up evidence that had not yet come to light. Finally, the perpetrators of the Massacre, especially the corporate and governmental actors, could finally be held criminally accountable.

In October, the move paid off. My team and I met over Zoom with attorneys from the DOJ, led by Kristen Clarke, assistant attorney general for the Civil Rights Division, and Barbara Kay Bosserman, deputy chief of the Cold Case Unit. We laid out the facts: the Massacre as a means to steal Black wealth, the connection of the city's modern-day white power structure to the perpetrators, the importance of a federal investigation to the overall pursuit of justice. Then DOJ personnel started asking questions. One of the most interesting lines of discussion concerned the possible existence of documents in the hands of Tulsa's powerful families or entities that might shed further light on the Massacre. This got my blood pumping! If the DOJ had the power to subpoena documents and witnesses, we might have a whole new look into the causes and conspiracies behind the Massacre.

This case fell under the purview of the Civil Rights Cold Case Records Collection Act of 2018,[5] a bill introduced by the great John Lewis and passed in 2008 that authorized the federal government to reopen and investigate unsolved racially motivated murders that occurred between 1920 and 1980. It was reauthorized in 2016.

As the meeting came to an end, I was fired up. The potential involvement of the DOJ gave our case a whole new dimension. I would spend the next few years working to get the DOJ on board.

Over the next two months, there wasn't much legal work to do on the public nuisance case, so my team and I did everything else. We sued the City of Tulsa for violating the Oklahoma Open Records Act by denying us access to public records related to the Massacre. We filed suit to reopen the estate of Dr. A. C. Jackson, the brilliant surgeon murdered during the Massacre, so his family could finally protect his name, image, and likeness. We dealt with endless press requests. I was pursuing other cases, including my Black Creek citizenship case. While we waited, believe me, we were busy.

I was in my office working on a case involving a client who had been killed in jail when I got an email from my best friend, attorney

Jeff Trevillion, who serves on the board of Justice for Greenwood and is a partner at a big law firm in Oklahoma City. One of the other partners sent an email to the whole firm, and Jeff forwarded it to me with a one-word message:

"Damn."

The email read: "$465 million opioid judgment against J&J reversed. Supreme Court says public nuisance law does not support judgment."[6] Damn is right. This was the case that had given us the idea to apply the public nuisance law to the Massacre, and after I heard about the decision, I felt like I had been punched in the stomach. I couldn't believe it. Then I read paragraph 39 of the order, which said in part:

> The Court has allowed public nuisance claims to address discrete, localized problems, not policy problems. Erasing the traditional limits on nuisance liability leaves Oklahoma's nuisance statute impermissibly vague. The district court's expansion of public nuisance law allows courts to manage public policy matters that should be dealt with by the legislative and executive branches. . . . Further, the district court stepping into the shoes of the Legislature by creating and funding government programs designed to address social and health issues goes too far.[7]

The Oklahoma Supreme Court had written this decision specifically to stop our case. I was sure of it then and I'm still sure of it today.

On the surface, the court had found that the lower court had overreached its application of the public nuisance statute and that the law could not be applied to the manufacturing, marketing, or selling of products. The ruling specifically stated that "public policy matters" should be addressed by executive or legislative action.

No problem! We would just go to the state legislature or Congress or the mayor's office and they would take care of everything, right? Except the survivors and their descendants had done that over and over again and been told, "Not this time." The state had created the Oklahoma Commission to Study the Tulsa Race Riot of 1921 but then refused to act on its reparations recommendations. Mayor Bynum had even said that paying reparations would "divide the city"[8]—as if the city could be any more divided based on the quality of life of its white and Black residents. Oklahoma's executive and legislative branches have thumbed their noses at justice and repair for Black survivors and descendants for more than a century, and now we were supposed to rely on them?

That was the bad news. The worse news was that this language created a clear road map for Judge Wall to dismiss our case. I immediately sent the message to my team and called an emergency Zoom meeting. Within fifteen minutes, everyone was on the call. After some lively discussion, we decided that the J&J decision could actually make our argument even stronger, provided we responded with sound legal theory and took control of the narrative.

The ruling said a public nuisance claim arises when a defendant "(1) commit[s] crimes constituting a nuisance, or (2) caus[es] physical injury to property or participat[es] in an offensive activity that rendered the property uninhabitable."[9] No problem. With the Massacre and the years of harm that followed it, we were literally talking about the largest crime in state history. These crimes caused physical injury to people and rendered property uninhabitable. The defendants were still committing crimes that caused physical injury or rendered property uninhabitable.

We weren't talking about commerce, like selling pills. We were talking about ongoing actions inflicting grievous harm on a community of people and then denying them the means to overcome that harm. Public nuisance law clearly applied.

Next, the court's opinion stated, "The Court has allowed public nuisance claims to address discrete, localized problems, not policy problems." Again, not an issue in our case because we were seeking to repair the damage that occurred in the discrete, localized Greenwood community. That is *specifically* the role of the judicial branch of government.

To us, all of this made our case stronger, so we settled in to take control of the story. We immediately filed a notice of supplemental authority (used to inform the court about newly relevant cases, statutes, or regulations) and took the position that what the supreme court did was good for us. Justice for Greenwood launched a media offensive to counter the idea that our case was dead in the water. Calls went out to local Tulsa TV and radio stations and newspapers. We emailed national reporters and sent texts to producers I'd built relationships with over the years. "We need to get in front of this today," I told the team. "We're not going to let the defendants claim victory before the judge even rules."

Within hours of the first calls and messages going out, we'd booked interviews. Local anchors wanted me in studio. National outlets asked for Zoom calls. I made the rounds, repeating the same message to cut through the noise: "This decision narrows nuisance law in a way that we did not expect but believe helps us. The Court said public nuisance requires a crime. The Massacre was crime upon crime—murder, arson, looting, kidnapping. Our claim is exactly what the public nuisance statute was meant to cover."

By the time we got to the 2021 holidays, we had turned the story around.

All this activity is a clear example of Willful Resilience, one of the ThinkGreenwood principles. I constantly reminded myself and the team that setbacks were not endings; they were part of movement lawyering. I leaned on Mia, my spiritual practices, and the hope and fight of the survivors and descendants. Seeing Mother Fletcher continue to come to court, Mother Randle keep doing interviews, and Uncle Redd sitting tall in his wheelchair and talking about the trips he was planning to take lifted me up. If they could keep going, what business did we have giving up? The court had dealt us a potentially fatal blow, but instead of falling into depression or raging against the injustice, we acted. We brainstormed and found a path forward. We kept hope and our narrative alive.

Another dimension of Willful Resilience is managing the pressure and stress that a long fight can heap on people's shoulders. Throughout the long battle, some people on my team came close to burnout, and I didn't even see it. I'm not proud of it, but at the time I didn't care about the human cost of the fight. I just cared about getting the job done. I am specifically talking about the nonlawyers on my team. Lawyers understand what it means to work more than twelve hours a day; that's just part of being a lawyer. But my nonlegal staff were not used to this pace of work, and I didn't fully appreciate that. I just said, "This is what we do. This is not a nine-to-five job. This is a movement. We grind."

But my wife saw it. Without my knowledge, Mia became my team's confidante, the back-channel way of communicating concerns to me. They would call Mia and say, "Damario's insisting that we work another weekend." She would listen, wait two or three days, and then talk to me. She didn't say, "I talked to so-and-so and she's feeling overworked," because I would've quoted from Jeremiah 12:5 and said, "If you have raced with men on foot and they have worn you out, how can you compete with horses?"[10] In other words, if they were falling short at this stage, how would they keep up when the road really got rough?

Instead, she came to me and said, "Not everybody is like you. Maybe ease up on them and give them a chance to show you what they can do." My team was like a steam engine. I kept shoveling coal in, but there was Mia on the other end, quietly letting the steam out so the whole thing didn't blow up. Nothing ever blew up; we kept it together and kept up the fight. That was only possible because of Mia.

Still, the legal punching and counterpunching was frustrating. The legal process can drag on for months or years because everything triggers a new round of briefs, challenges, and arguments. So, I kept talking with Bryan Stevenson, trying to stay patient and keep my spirits up.

Bryan and I talked about how keeping the case in the courts was, in itself, a win. "The longer this goes on, Damario, there is the victory," he said. "The victory comes in the case being alive." Of course, he was right. I wanted to get a resolution as soon as possible while we had *living* survivors. But if we couldn't get the resolution we hoped for, "keep the case in the courts" became our mantra. The longer the case stayed alive, the more people talked about it, the more the media covered it, and the more the idea of reparations would become harder to dismiss or ignore.

That lesson applies to nearly every major civil rights fight. The Montgomery bus boycott lasted for 381 days, but its persistence forced the nation to confront Jim Crow. The Freedom Riders in 1961 endured beatings, arrests, and burned buses, but their refusal to stop traveling through the South forced federal action on desegregation. The principle holds today, too. In Palm Springs, California, Black and Mexican American families displaced in the 1960s kept their issue alive for decades before reparations finally moved forward. The family of Henrietta Lacks, whose cells were stolen and commercialized without consent, fought for recognition and repair for seventy years before finally reaching a settlement in 2023.

Keeping the fight alive doesn't just sustain pressure; it creates opportunity. It allows time to attract new allies, partners, and resources, to build coalitions that didn't exist at the start. It inspires the next generation of leaders who witness the struggle and choose to join it. Survival is not passive. It sets you up to win. That's why it's critical to keep fighting despite the odds, obstacles, and opposition. As long as you keep your issue alive, there is the possibility of justice.

Already, we had accomplished a great deal. When we filed in 2020, most people thought bringing a viable reparations case was a pipe dream. We proved them wrong. The media had made us national news. We'd had a visit from the president and made headway in Congress. Now, as we entered 2022, we were still alive in court. Tulsa, the Massacre, and reparations were part of the conversation from coast to coast. People who had never heard of Greenwood were asking questions. "Keeping it in the courts" was winning.

All the while, the legal jabbing and crossing continued.

We filed our supplemental brief on January 31, 2022.

The defense refiled for dismissal in February.

We responded and then waited on Judge Wall.

Away from the courtroom, patience was wearing thin. In February, we had a second Zoom call with the DOJ. This time, the participants included Uncle Redd, Ike Howard (Mother Fletcher's grandson), La-Donna Penny (Mother Randle's granddaughter), Chief Amusan, and Dr. Crutcher.

These people, who had been deeply wounded by the Massacre and decades of the city's malice, shared their confusion and disappointment that the DOJ still hadn't taken any action and seemed unsure if it *would* take action. There was talk of promises from President Biden and mutilated bodies found in mass graves. Overall, there was the fear that once again, a government entity would promise action but do nothing. Then Barbara Bosserman said, "I don't know if we can open the case, but if you work with the City of Tulsa, maybe you can get a grant."

After a beat of stunned silence I exploded with anger. How *dare* this stranger in her D.C. office insinuate that a check from the DOJ would satisfy us! My voice shot up so high it almost cracked. My hands flew into the air as if I were trying to swat the insult away. My words came fast and sharp, like gunshots. "We're not in this for money from the DOJ!" I shouted, leaning toward the camera. "We're in this to get the Justice Department to hold the perpetrators accountable!" (Later, Tiffany Crutcher told me I had "clicked off the safety.")

No one said a word. My outburst had been unprofessional, but I had no intention of walking it back. I was sick of our side having to be patient, take the high road, and exhaust ourselves to gain an inch of ground in the courts. I was sick of people thinking we were in this just for money when what we wanted was full justice.

Finally, Uncle Redd said simply, "He right."

Talk about the power of moral authority. With two words, Uncle Redd made it okay. Still, I was right to be furious at the suggestion. We were asking the DOJ to do exactly the kind of work it was created to do after the Civil War: investigating and prosecuting racial violence against Black people when states and local governments refused.[11] I was tired of seeing politicians (especially Democrats) lining up to say the right words about civil rights and racial justice but then refusing to use their power to effect real change. President Biden, who had sat with the survivors and promised to do everything to ensure that they got justice, had not directed his DOJ to act. That gap between rhetoric and action wasn't just frustrating—it was costing survivors their last chance at justice.

It's like Lizzo asks in "Truth Hurts": "Why men great 'til they gotta be great?" I honestly wish I had an answer.

Despite the DOJ's reluctance, we still felt good about the narrative, our network of supporters, and our legal prospects, so it's ironic that the next few weeks of 2022 were some of the most personally painful I've ever experienced. In March, I got a call from one of the most important people in my life, my cousin Stanley Keith Ransom. After Mia, Stan was my person. Born and raised in Kansas City, an AT&T worker and union steward, he was always a constant, wonderful presence in my life—and because he was seventeen years older, he became a mentor and surrogate father, too. We talked constantly about everything: family, football, fishing, and life in general.

I was sitting in my home office, surrounded by some of my books and athletic trophies, when Stan called and said, "I need to talk to you. I need to tell you something." I knew that tone, so I got nervous. He told me he had been diagnosed with cancer, but he immediately downplayed it. "Damario, don't get all choked up right now," he said. "We're still going through the tests. I'll let you know more, but right now, there's nothing to worry about."

That was the first blow. The second came a few days later when Mia had to get an MRI. She had been battling debilitating fibroids and endometriosis for years, and they were getting worse. Lately, she had been basically bedridden for two weeks out of every month because of bleeding. We drove to the Tulsa suburb of Broken Arrow, where the imaging center was, but I couldn't go in with her because of Covid restrictions. My wife was in there alone, in terrible pain, and I had to sit in the car, helpless. That's when I got a call from Stan's youngest daughter. When I saw her number come up, I thought it might have been some good news, but it wasn't. She said, "Dad didn't want to tell you, but he has stage four pancreatic cancer."

I'm no doctor, but I know enough to know that's a death sentence. When we hung up, I broke down in the car—just laid my head on the steering wheel and wept like a baby. When Mia was finally able to come back to the car, I told her and she cried, too. (Later, we found out that Mia's medical issues meant another surgery and that she would never be able to carry a child to term. That was the second blow.)

Two days later, I flew to Des Moines, Iowa, for a hearing in an important case related to racial discrimination experienced by thirteen ex–University of Iowa football players.[12] I cried during the entire flight. I cried that whole night at my hotel. I got up the next morning, killed at the court hearing, went to the airport, and cried all the way back home to Tulsa. Then I drove to Kansas City to see Stan. That was the first of six trips I made to KC over the next eight months.

The final blow of this awful time came a few days after I got back from Kansas City. My maternal family held monthly Zoom calls to keep in touch, just like a lot of families did during the pandemic, when seeing relatives face-to-face was risky. On the Zoom call that March, Stan told everybody about his cancer, and everybody reacted like you'd imagine, with shock, concern, tears, and offers of help.

When we were about to sign off, my Aunt Edna Cherry said, "Everybody, we'll see you next month!" Stan, sort of making a joke, said, "Well, hopefully. I don't know if I'll be here or not." But Aunt Edna wasn't having any of that. She said, "Oh, I'll see you. You'll be here." A few days later, on March 25, she died suddenly. We had her memorial on April 8.

As we drew closer to our all-important May 2 hearing, all this loss had left me exhausted and brokenhearted. But the movement and the people involved in it saved me. My phone buzzed constantly with calls of support. Students emailed to say they'd just learned about Greenwood and to ask how they could get involved. National civil rights leaders checked in. Donations came in with notes that said, "Keep going" or "We believe in you." My inbox was full of requests for interviews, panels, and podcasts.

What stands out the most, though, were the words of encouragement and appreciation from descendants. Timothy Mayo, a descendant from California whose ancestor U. D. Emerson had been a victim of the Massacre, appeared in an online video. In it, he said, "Damario is the epitome of what we call success. There should be funding so that Damario doesn't have to always start from zero again, and he can create young lawyers in his legacy."[13]

Along with the love of Mia, my family, and my team, the endless expressions of support kept me going through my grief, and I made it to May 1, the night before our hearing, when we held another prayer rally to get the community pumped before the big day.

I walked into the historic Mount Zion Baptist Church, rebuilt from the ashes of 1921, carrying the weight of history. Justice for Greenwood's "Pack the Court" campaign had worked: The sanctuary was jammed, purple shirts filled the pews, and the air was vibrating with anticipation. Eric Miller and Sara Solfanelli had flown in to stand with me. Before I spoke, my friend Terry Bradford leaned close and told me, "You're not walking alone. Look at what you've already built." I carried those words with me as I turned to the crowd.

I lifted my hand and let my voice ring out: "Tomorrow, we walk into court together. This is not just about three survivors. This is about a community that has carried pain for a hundred years, and tomorrow, we demand to be heard!" The church erupted in clapping and shouting, hands raised high. It felt like a revival, but the altar call was for justice. Behind me, banners spelled out our demands. In front of us, survivors and descendants nodded, elders wiped away tears, and young people were wide-eyed. I knew the briefs and filings had become more than words on paper—they had become flesh and spirit in the people.

When I finally walked out into the cool night air, I felt steady and hopeful for the first time in two months. Whatever the next day brought, we would walk into that courtroom as a proud army, our heads held high.

Back in chapter 8, I shared what went down in Judge Wall's courtroom that day, including the climactic moment when she denied part of the defense's motion to dismiss and we realized our case would go on, and the joyful chants of "Justice for Greenwood!" But why were we celebrating?

We hadn't won the case. We hadn't settled. We'd gotten nothing more than temporary reprieve, a partial denial of the defense's motions to dismiss our lawsuit. Was that cause for a cacophony of shouts, chants, and hugs? Was that technical decision by the judge really a reason to dance, cheer, and hope?

It was. Because prior to that moment, *every single time* anyone had come before a court with a legal action related to the Massacre, the court had crushed it. Cases were thrown out. Dismissed. Disregarded. Disrespected. We didn't just want our case to continue to the discovery phase, where we might see new evidence and learn new facts. We needed the state to acknowledge, finally, that the lives and pain of Black Tulsans mattered and that our cries for justice were worth being heard. On that day, we finally got that acknowledgment. Damned right it was worth celebrating.

After things calmed down, I walked out into the hallway outside the courtroom, my hands in the air like a boxer who's just won a decision, with Dr. Crutcher on one side of me and Representative Jackson Lee on the other. The hallway outside was chaos: flashing cameras, arms raised, shouts of victory reverberating off marble walls. Even amid the reporters and microphones, I could hear the chant continue: "Justice for Greenwood! Justice for Greenwood!"

Strangers hugged like family. Elders pressed my hand and whispered, "Keep going." I couldn't stop smiling. None of us could. I told reporters through a trembling smile, "We did it—and I cannot stop smiling about it. Over one hundred years of unjust defeats and denials, and finally our community will get a chance to use the judicial system to examine and document the horrors of the Tulsa Race Massacre." Even as I said it, I had to swallow hard to keep from breaking down.

"When you work on something for 20-plus years, you have defeat after defeat . . . you have client after client die," I continued. "To know I have three living survivors that are here with me right now to feel this partial victory, it means everything. It shows a precedent and model of how you can organize a community, how you can organize your colleagues and partners throughout the nation. This victory we've received is because of so many people working together from across this nation and building coalitions."[14]

Sitting in his wheelchair in front of the cameras and microphones, Uncle Redd said, "I've never seen nothing like this happen. That means it's going to change things. It's going to make people think . . . It's going to change, it's going to be better for everybody."[15]

Regina Goodwin, the state representative (now state senator) who represents the district that includes Greenwood, told *The Black Wall Street Times,* "Right now, we got life. And we're excited. All the hard work and creativity that Attorney Solomon-Simmons has brought to date is working. So we gotta keep pushing, pressing and praying." Later that day, a rainbow appeared over Greenwood. I took it as a sign that God was on our side, and a new day was breaking.[16]

But when reporters asked me what the next step was, I told them I didn't know. Judge Wall had granted part of the motion to dismiss and denied part of it. We wouldn't know which parts until she issued her formal written ruling.

Representative Jackson Lee spoke next and electrified the crowd when she said, "I am not a descendant of these souls who are buried in the soil in Greenwood, many unidentified to this day. But I take that to Washington. Sitting here, listening to the eloquence of the arguments, methodically block by block—I want the nation to hear this decision."[17] In the middle of everything, Bryan Stevenson called to tell me I had done a great job, and that keeping the case in the courts was a huge victory for the national racial justice movement.

Producers from CNN, MSNBC, CBS (and every network in America, I think) had been calling nonstop, asking if I could go live. Behind the scenes, Mia had been working overtime, coordinating with producers and holding down a conference room at the hotel across the street, while Gerry Johnson of Human Rights Watch was blasting the story through his network to get it to the international press.

I had to get to the hotel, where Mia was waiting, to do critical interviews, but as soon as I stepped away from the courthouse I was caught in a wave of congratulations. People pressed in close, masks slipping, hands outstretched. Some wanted to hug, others slapped my back, some raised their palms for high fives. It was pure love, but it nearly cost me the chance to make my biggest press hit of the night.

I hustled through the crowd, dashed into the hotel, slipped into a chair just in time, and the camera light blinked on. Joy Reid's face came into focus on the screen. On Joy's show, *The ReidOut,* I told the nation that after more than one hundred years, the survivors would finally get their day in court. Joy asked, "What does this mean?" and I answered, "It means everything. It means that Mother Randle, Mother Fletcher, Uncle Redd . . . will finally have an opportunity to have their day in court here in Tulsa, Oklahoma."

When the segment wrapped, I barely had time to exhale before CNN pulled me into another segment. This time, I wasn't alone. Sitting shoulder to shoulder with me was Uncle Redd, his frame thin but his presence unshakable. CNN's Omar Jimenez asked what this moment meant to him, and Uncle Redd leaned into the mic and said, "I'm prepared to live to 130 if necessary to see justice done."

It didn't stop there. The Associated Press and Reuters blasted the story onto the wires, and suddenly Greenwood was on front pages across the world. *The Guardian* ran a feature. The BBC put it on international radio. Our case, our survivors, and our fight for reparations were front-page news and the topic of conversation in London, Lagos, and Los Angeles.

That evening, we celebrated at a dinner at the upscale Polo Grill in Utica Square, an area of South Tulsa where people like me wouldn't have been welcomed when I was born, unless we were cooking or cleaning for white guests. When Mia and I entered the room, the guests—supporters and people from the community—stood up and cheered. As I looked out at the faces of the people who had believed in me and fought alongside me, I allowed myself to feel the joy of this victory, just for a moment.

That night, after the celebration wound down and talk of the day's victory had faded into a hum of "Good nights" and "I'll call you tomorrows," Mia and I drove home. We took the IDL highway, and as we approached our home, the twinkling lights of downtown to the south stood in stark contrast to the darkness looming over the area north of the highway. Stopping at a red light, I turned to Mia. She had been fighting a stomachache brought on by stress. We had been talking about Judge Wall's decision and if it would change anything.

"I wonder what it will mean," I said.

Mia just looked at me. I could tell she was trying to choose the right words. Finally, she said quietly, "It means we have a chance."

After the elation of the ruling faded, we were back to the waiting game. Remember, while Judge Wall had partially denied the dismissal motion, she had partially granted it. But which part? We ached to find out. Still, the survivors were happy to have the spotlight and tell their stories. My team was busy with fundraising and keeping the descendant community active. I continued to do interviews and appear on panels.

Then something almost as wonderful as the judge's ruling happened that also confirmed the power of the "keep the case alive" strategy. Ed Mitzen, the founder of Business for Good, a New York–based nonprofit, read about our case in *The Washington Post,* and it touched him so much that he reached out to the *Post* reporter, who put him in touch with Representative Goodwin. When I got the news, I was shocked but delighted: Mitzen and his wife were generously donating $1 million—$333,333 for each of the three survivors—to help pay for their care and comfort.

On May 18, in a ceremony at the Greenwood Cultural Center, with the survivors seated in their wheelchairs in front of family members and a line of Business for Good representatives, Mitzen presented them with an oversize check. At the ceremony, Mitzen said, "They had their homes destroyed, insurance claims denied. Whether it was 101 years ago or six months ago, it doesn't change the fact that they were clearly wronged. We felt badly that they had to work so hard to try to get what we felt was an obvious thing that was owed to them." But when her turn came, Representative Goodwin also made it clear that this gift, while generous, was not justice. "What you see here today is generosity," she said. "What you see here today is pure love. What you see here today is a man and a group of folks who care enough to give up their means so we don't confuse the two issues. The 101-year fight is ongoing."[18]

But that wasn't the only large donation received because we kept the case alive and in the news. Time for more backstory: Before the Centennial, I ran into a guy who had worked at the building Mia and I lived in thirteen years earlier. We had become friends, and now he was the manager of this great Tulsa restaurant. When I walked in for lunch one day, he saw me and his face lit up. He said, "Man, I really love what you're doing. I'm so glad to reconnect with you. I've got somebody I want to introduce you to. I think he would love your work. Give me your email and your phone number."

I did, and then I forgot about it. A few days later, I was driving home when I got a call from the gentleman who had been given my information. He said, "Damario, we've heard all about you, and we love what you're doing. We would like to make a donation." I thanked him for his generosity, but I assumed it was just a routine gift, so I texted him the donation link and as far as I was concerned, that was that.

Pam, my CFO, called me few minutes later as I was pulling into my driveway. "Damario," she said, "he wants to donate five hundred thousand dollars."

I almost crashed my car into the garage door.

At the time, Justice for Greenwood had very little money. That $500,000 enabled us to hire people and start new programs, and it was out of that money that I was able to give $100,000 to each of the survivors right before the Centennial in 2021. That gesture really touched this man, but I was just practicing what I had been preaching to the TRMMC and the city: If you raise money because of the Massacre, some of it should go to survivors and descendants.

Anyway, this generous gentleman and I stayed in touch. After the big hearing in May 2022, he and his wife offered me something I could hardly believe: a personal gift of $4.5 million because he believed so strongly in what I was doing. He said, "Damario, I want you to be able to continue the work and not have to worry about anything." I won't lie; money was tempting. I knew that if I had been paid for my time and hard work, the legal bill would easily surpass $4.5 million. That kind of money could have changed my life and Mia's overnight. But after praying about it, I directed that the gift be made to Justice for Greenwood.

It's not that I didn't want the money; I did. I'm not sharing this to make myself look virtuous. But this struggle has never been about me. It's about my people, my family, and my city. Greenwood deserves an organization strong enough to fight without fear, compromise, or dependence on the whims of others. That gift, born out of the power of keeping the story alive, has helped us do that.

And still Judge Wall's official written ruling had not come in. Finally, late in the afternoon of August 3, my phone buzzed with a new message from Judge Wall's bailiff: The order had arrived. I opened the attachment, my eyes scanning the first few lines before I shot it off to the team with a quick note: "Order's in. Review ASAP—let's huddle in ten." Within minutes, replies stacked up: "On it." "Wow." "Let's talk."

By 5:30 P.M., *The Brady Brunch* squares were filled on Zoom. The ruling was complicated and frustrating. On one hand, for the first time in 101 years, an Oklahoma court had not dismissed a Massacre-related lawsuit after the initial motion to dismiss. That was monumental.

But the order also cut deep. Judge Wall had dismissed all descendant plaintiffs for lack of "standing," reasoning that they hadn't shown a legally protected injury that could be redressed in court. She dismissed Historic Vernon AME Church, ruling that because the current church wasn't incorporated until 2019, it lacked standing. She had also dismissed claims that the Massacre's ongoing effects—from urban renewal to discriminatory policing—constituted a continuing nuisance, citing the Oklahoma Supreme Court's Johnson & Johnson opioid decision.

However, she left a door open. The survivors' claims tied directly to the destruction of Greenwood in 1921 could move forward. We had until September 2 to amend our petition as instructed.

The mood on Zoom was mixed. Should we appeal to bring the descendants and Vernon AME back in? How would we reshape our abatement plan? In the moment, what mattered was that we had survived another attempt to end the case. The path was narrower than we wanted, but it was still open. After a century of silence and denial, that was historic.

Having to redraft our petition was frustrating, but we had to follow the judge's order. After getting a short extension, on September 13, 2022, we filed our second amended petition, and we were back to the slow chess moves of litigation. Six days later, the defense asked for more time and didn't file their new motions to dismiss until October 17. Because there were so many motions to answer, we asked for more time, too.

In November, Judge Wall granted our request.

We filed our responses.

The defense filed their replies.

Just like that, we were back in the holiday season again and we still hadn't started discovery. The process was maddening, but morale never dipped. We all knew delay was the defendants' main strategy, but instead of wearing us down, it steeled our resolve. I reminded my colleagues, "Just like Greenwood, we don't just endure odds, obstacles, and opposition—we turn them into fuel." I leaned on the holidays as a time to do something Mia had been begging me to do: step back, breathe, and spend some much-needed time with her and my family. Hosting our loved ones for Thanksgiving and Christmas grounded me. Between the food, laughter, games, and just being together, those moments became a source of strength I carried with me into the new year.

By February, we were tired of waiting. We filed a motion to move forward with discovery, which would allow us to take more depositions (including Uncle Redd's), send subpoenas, file requests to produce information, and more. But Judge Wall denied our motion, and we heard nothing else from the court until May 5, when she set the hearing on the defendants' third motion to dismiss for May 10—Mother Fletcher's 109th birthday.

A week or so before the big hearing, figuring I would need some rest, I took Mia to Las Vegas for her birthday to see Usher in concert. I was looking forward to a great show and some relaxation by the pool . . . until I got an email from the Department of Justice asking for a meeting with the survivors. I knew cutting our Vegas trip short wasn't going to win me Husband of the Year, but what choice did I have?

After coordinating travel with the survivors and their caregivers, I flew to the capital with Eric Miller, Tyrone Lynn, Mother Fletcher, and Uncle Redd to meet with Barbara Bosserman and Walter Henry, a Black retired FBI special agent and ex-football player from Mississippi, to talk about what a possible investigation might look like.

With Judge Wall's order that the direct survivors' case was still alive, I knew it was important to keep them out front in this fight. Since my first appearance on her show, Joy Reid had become a friend and ally, so I asked Mother Fletcher and Uncle Redd if they would be willing to appear on her show while in D.C. Of course, they said yes, and after meeting with the DOJ, the three of us appeared in studio on *The ReidOut*.

I sat stage right, next to Joy. Mother Fletcher and Uncle Redd, seated in their wheelchairs, sat on the other side of the set, but they commanded everyone's attention. As I watched them answer Joy's questions, I noted that, amazingly, all their experience with the press had taught them how to take command of an interview. They knew just what to say and how to say it with dignity, humility, and perfect timing. It was impressive to watch.

Dapper in a bolo tie and a black blazer, Uncle Redd talked about the aftermath of the Massacre, when families that had lost everything tried to survive. "I had to go from town to town looking for work," he said. "We'd go from one town to the other, sharecropping to make a living." Talking about his long life, he said, "I'm still here. I'm here to fight."

Asked what justice would look like, Mother Fletcher said, "Everything is beautiful and rebuilt and restored. It's just time now that we have justice on all of that, where we can live that type of life over again." When Joy asked about the subject of reparations, this woman, who was more than twice my age, was sharp and ready. "The people that's entitled to it, I think they should get something back," she stated, looking Joy in the eye. "It may not be what they had, but it could be something better. There's always room for improvement."[19]

That interview put a charge into our narrative, and when we returned to Tulsa a few days before the hearing, we kept the momentum going. We set up another press conference with the survivors on the morning of the hearing. As I looked at Mother Fletcher sitting in her chair beside the podium, I said, "This is 2023. One hundred and two years ago, this woman was running for her life. This woman just turned 109 years old and she's in here fighting for justice. She's been waiting for 102 years."

Then we were back in Judge Wall's courtroom for the hearing on the latest motion to dismiss. I started off by informing the court that it was Mother Fletcher's 109th birthday. Everybody clapped, even the defendants and the judge, and we all wished her a happy birthday. I let that die down, and then I declared, "It is a shame that on her one hundred and ninth birthday, she's in this courtroom fighting for the justice that she's been seeking for 102 years!"

The hearing lasted a couple of hours, and it was mostly a rehash of the same ground we had covered back in May 2022. When both sides finished, Judge Wall said, "I'm going to decide this quickly." And that was that.

June passed. No word.

The July Fourth holiday came and went. Nothing.

For a few days, instead of working nonstop on cases or answering every text message from the members of the media, I spent more quality time with Mia, which lifted my spirits. On July 7, we decided to drive downtown to have dinner at a little Central American restaurant we like. I needed the distraction. As usual, I tried to drop Mia off at the front of the place like a gentleman and park the car. She did what she's done for thirty years: She refused to get out and said, "No, I'm walking with you."

With that marital ritual finished, I found a parking space and turned the car off. Mia got out, and I was about to get out when I saw a text from the same *Tulsa World* reporter who had grabbed and berated me back in 2021. It read: "Do you care to comment on the dismissal of your case?"

I felt the hairs on my arm stand up and my heart pound. I did not respond to him; instead, while trying to keep my hands from shaking, I hurriedly went to the online docket. I couldn't believe what I was seeing. Judge Wall had dismissed our lawsuit with prejudice, which meant the case was permanently closed and we were barred from ever bringing the same claim against the defendants again! Even worse, she had dismissed our case in a one-paragraph ruling with no explanation:[20]

> The Court determines Plaintiffs' Second Amended Petition fails to state a justiciable public nuisance claim under Oklahoma law. Plaintiffs' Second Amended Petition fails to allege a legally cognizable abatement remedy. Plaintiffs' Second Amended Petition fails to cure the defect in pleading which the court found to exist and liberally granted leave to amend pursuant to 12 O.S. 2012 § G.[21]

Just like that, three years of litigation, four contentious hearings, thousands of pages of documents, survivor depositions—all of it cast aside like trash. The news took everything out of me. I just sat in the car and stared at nothing. Time had stopped. Finally, Mia turned back toward me and saw the look on my face. She got back in the car and said, "What happened?"

I barely got the words out. "She dismissed us."

I sat in that car ten more minutes. Mia finally said, "Let's just go home." All the way home, I couldn't say a word. We pulled up to the house, I opened the garage, and Mia got out, but I stayed put. She looked at me. "Babe, I'm so sorry."

"I'll be okay. I just need a moment."

I sat in the driveway for another half hour.

Then I gasped. *The survivors*! I couldn't let them learn about this on the news! I had to pull myself together. I hurriedly texted and arranged a call with the survivors and their caregivers.

On the call, I started to tell them what had happened. Suddenly, I had the same feeling I'd had when the jury ignored Carletta Mack's pain to protect a white doctor's career. It was the same feeling I'd had when the Tulsa DA allowed Monroe Bird's intoxicated murderer to go free, when my Creek case was dismissed, and when Terence Crutcher's killer walked. I felt betrayed. Worse, I felt like I had failed these brave survivors. Somehow, I got the news out and was starting to choke up when Uncle Redd said matter-of-factly, "But can we appeal?"

Wait, what?

Suddenly, I felt like Superman, nearly dead after being poisoned with kryptonite, . . . but then somebody took the kryptonite away. A thousand volts of energy rushed into me. *Of course* we could appeal! I said, "Yes, absolutely, we will appeal!" I would "keep the case alive" at any cost, because who knew what could happen? We would file an appeal with the Oklahoma Supreme Court.

Now that we didn't have to worry about offending Judge Wall, we let her have it. My co-counsel Sara Solfanelli gave a blistering statement to *The Washington Post:*

"Inexplicably, nearly one year after defendants filed another round of duplicative motions to dismiss the lawsuit and more than 2.5 years after the case was filed, Judge Wall threw the entire case out," she said. "Black Americans, especially Black Tulsans, carry the weight of intergenerational racial trauma day in and day out—a weight they cannot relinquish or cavalierly dismiss. . . . The dismissal of this case is just one more example of how America's, including Tulsa's, legacy is disproportionately and unjustly borne by the Black community."[22]

I had an even more important task: getting back in front of the people who had supported this fight from day one to let them know we weren't dead yet. We called another press conference, this one at

Vernon AME Church. At the podium, I blasted the lack of substance in the order and how it had been issued without any notice. I also set a defiant tone. "We will continue to fight until our last breaths," I said. "Despite Tulsa and America's attempt to silence, change and gaslight the facts and truths of our collective racial history and trauma, we as survivors and all of those that believe in racial justice, we will not sit quietly or passively to allow mistruths or misjustices to persist. We will continue to fight. . . . We will not rest until there is justice for Greenwood."[23]

We faced one major challenge, though: *I'm not an appellate attorney.* No one on my team had any experience appealing a decision to the Oklahoma Supreme Court. Attorneys who specialize in appeals have a different set of skills from trial attorneys. They focus on reviewing and correcting possible legal errors in a case, not on presenting evidence or arguing in front of a jury or judge. They're experts in legal research, writing, and appellate advocacy. Everything was riding on this appeal, which meant that we needed a top-shelf appellate attorney.

Referrals led me to Jana Knott, a former staff attorney to Judge Noma Gurich of the Oklahoma Supreme Court. But I needed more than a great appellate lawyer. I needed a true believer in our cause, not just our case. I told Jana, "This is a passion. This is not just another case. I can't have somebody just because they're good with the law. We want an appellate attorney who is comfortable with this and all that comes with it."

Jana said, "I'm in. Let's go." Just like that, she was part of the team. She walked us through the technical appeal process, and we started working to prepare for an argument before the Oklahoma Supreme Court. In football terms, we were down to the fourth quarter. The next stage of moves and countermoves would decide the fate of our case and define my twenty-plus years in the fight to obtain justice for Greenwood.

I took my little girl by the hand and fled out of the west door on Greenwood. I did not take time to get a hat for myself or baby, but started out north on Greenwood, running amidst showers of bullets from the machine gun located in the granary and from men who were quickly surrounding our district. Seeing that they were fighting at a disadvantage our men had taken shelter in the buildings and in other places out of sight of the enemy. When Florence Mary and I ran into the street it was vacant for a block or more. Someone called to me to "Get out of the street with that child or you both will be killed!" I felt that it was suicide to remain in the building, for it would surely be destroyed and death in the street was preferred, for we expected to be shot down at any moment.*

—Mary Jones Parrish, Massacre survivor and journalist

Remains of the Midway Hotel. The original photograph by Francis Schmidt is in the Department of Special Collections, McFarlin Library, the University of Tulsa.

CHAPTER 11

TWENTY-FIVE MINUTES

When you file an appeal with the Oklahoma Supreme Court, they can choose to decide it themselves or kick it down to the Oklahoma Court of Civil Appeals. If you get sent to the court of civil appeals, you've got to go through the civil appeals process, get a decision from that court, and then appeal to the supreme court again. This can take a year. We really didn't want to do that.

On August 4, 2023, we filed our petition of error (a request for the court to reconsider the lower court's decision), our motion for oral argument (a request to argue our case before the court), and our motion to retain (a request that our appeal be heard by the supreme court and not kicked down to the court of civil appeals).

Three days later, we got an email from the clerk of the Oklahoma Supreme Court that had us all high-fiving each other. The state supreme court was retaining our case! Our goal was for the court to reverse Judge Wall's dismissal and allow us to proceed to discovery. This would be our last chance to stay alive. The defendants filed their opposition to our appeal and request for oral arguments on August 21, 2023.

We'd hoped that the court would rule on the case immediately, which it had the option to do. The case was on an accelerated appeal, where the court typically issues decisions without requiring additional briefing. Instead, it took nearly a month for the court to set a briefing schedule, which meant we wouldn't get a decision on our petitions until after the holidays. Disappointing, but we were "keeping it in the courts," so anything could happen.

Over the next few weeks, my team and I worked diligently to get our "brief in chief" (the document explaining to the court why we believe the decision should be overturned) completed early. I went back to punishing workdays where I'd only see Mia as we were both heading to bed. The days bled into one another as we charged ahead, constantly on our computers, on Zoom calls, or on the phone with one another. Everything was at stake now, so everything had to be perfect: *t*'s crossed, *i*'s dotted . . . and no typos.

Then the brief was done, and I headed down to Dallas with Tyrone for some well-deserved relaxation and to enjoy the greatest college football rivalry in the nation: the annual OU–University of Texas game, scheduled for October 7. I'd had three years of near-constant work, loss, and high-stakes legal poker. I needed a break from trying to fix the world to chill with my boys.

I watched the game with about thirty of my Omega Psi Phi brothers at a restaurant, and for a few hours it felt like the real world didn't exist. I was living and dying with every play. When our quarterback led a final drive and we scored with seconds left, the place erupted. We were all yelling, hugging, and jumping up and down, screaming "OU!" The next day, I took Mia to the State Fair of Texas. We ate, rode the rides, and laughed all day long. It was a perfect, relaxing weekend full of food, friends, fun, and football.

During those few days, I was finally able to decompress and let the work go. As you've probably figured out, I'm a workaholic. But the pressure of the case wasn't just affecting the defendants; it was affecting me, too. This leisure time was the tonic I needed. I felt relaxed, positive, and carefree. The work was still waiting for me, but I was able to set it aside for a short while and take care of myself and my wife.

And things just got better. Over the summer, I had paid for a trip with a fishing guide but hadn't been able to go. Now I cashed in my credit and booked a guided fishing trip for Monday, October 9. Tyrone and I made the two-hour drive east of Dallas to Lake Fork Reservoir.

We met the guide, Dee of Crappie Head Fishing, boarded the boat, and went fishing. The weather was perfect: sunny but not too hot, with a little of that fall crispness in the air. Dee was a cool brother, and we had a lot in common. All through that day we talked, laughed, and caught a bunch of fish.

I even turned my phone off. No buzzing, no breaking news alerts, no stream of texts or emails. Just water, wind, and laughter. I could feel my shoulders loosen, my chest lighten, and my jaw unclench. The only sound was the gentle slap of the water against the boat; the only tension was the tug of the line when a fish bit. I wasn't strategizing or preparing. I was straight chilling in a way I hadn't allowed myself to do in a very long time. It reminded me of the fishing trips I took with Daddy Brown. Fishing was for me what it had been for him: a welcome chance to catch a breath.

At the end of the day, on the way back to shore, I turned my phone on. I had a bunch of messages and missed calls, of course, but a couple of them stopped me cold. They were from Ike, Mother Fletcher's grandson.

I said to Tyrone, "Please call and see what he needs?" I was determined to spend at least one day away from everything having to do with work. After a couple of minutes, Tyrone handed me the phone. As soon as I asked Ike what was going on, he broke down.

Uncle Redd had died of cancer at the age of 102.

Over the past two years, Uncle Redd and I had become especially close. He wasn't just a client to me; he was a role model. After a hard one hundred years, he was finally having the time of his life being at the center of the national conversation. He had really wanted to live to see justice done, but he also knew there was a chance he wouldn't. I felt a lump in my throat as I thought about my friend who I wouldn't see again.

I just sat there in the boat with my head in my hands thinking about Uncle Redd—his smile, his jokes, his stories. I thought about the time he and I had made plans to set up a visit to the University of Colorado campus so he could meet Buffaloes head coach and NFL

Hall of Famer Deion Sanders. Uncle Redd was a big Colorado fan, and meeting "Prime Time" was on his bucket list. But he got sick before it could happen.

But what really hurt—hurts to this day, honestly—was that he never got to give his sworn deposition. He had been an infant during the Massacre, so he couldn't have told us about what happened on those two days. But he could've talked about growing up in the aftermath. He did just that once, when we were doing interviews in Bartlesville, where Mother Fletcher lived when I met her.

A few days later, Mia and I flew to Denver for the funeral. After the service, there was a dinner, and despite nearly breaking down a couple of times, I was able to speak about my friend. "I want to thank Uncle Redd's family, especially his daughters, Muriel Watson and Malee Craft, for allowing me the privilege of representing your father," I said. "Uncle Redd was more than a client to me; he was special, a man whose courage, humor, and faith carried us through some of the hardest moments of this fight for justice. I'll never forget the stories we shared and the dignity with which he carried the weight of history. Standing beside him in court and in Congress, I saw not just a survivor but living hope. Though he is no longer here in body, I know he is watching and helping from the other side, and I promise we will continue the fight for Justice for Greenwood until the work is done."

Then this woman I didn't know got up. She told the gathering that she'd met Uncle Redd several years back. She'd been severely injured in a car accident and was in so much pain and facing such a hard rehabilitation that she wanted to give up and die. But Uncle Redd befriended her, and she credited him with saving her life. "I didn't want to do the physical therapy," she told the mourners. "I didn't want to learn how to walk again. And it was Mr. Ellis who would call me, pray with me, encourage me, and tell me it was going to be okay. He told me that God is not through with me."

A few weeks later, there was a community-wide memorial service in Tulsa where everyone dressed in white because Uncle Redd was all about joy and happiness. I didn't want to go initially, not only because

I was focused on the November 6 deadline for filing our final brief to the state supreme court but because my grief had turned to anger. The defense's "delay of game" gambit had paid off, at least in part: One of the survivors had died. I was furious that their strategy had cost a great man the chance to see justice done. I finally showed up to pay my respects, but I wasn't in that headspace. The best way for me to honor my friend and client was to win the case.

We filed our final supreme court brief by the deadline, the calendar pages kept turning, and just like that, it was the holidays. Still no word from the court on our motions. Fortunately, I was busy: hosting my family for Thanksgiving and Christmas, working on other cases, and hiring some new faces at JFG.

In February, I set work and grief aside to go to the 2024 Super Bowl in Las Vegas, courtesy of the NFL's Racial Equity & Social Justice Council and Dr. Crutcher, who sat on the council. The Kansas City Chiefs beat the San Francisco 49ers, 25–22 in a thrilling overtime. But as off the hook as the game was, NFL Commissioner Roger Goodell's party at Caesars Palace was even better. I shook hands with some serious A-listers: California Governor Gavin Newsom; former NFL star, Super Bowl champ, and media personality Ryan Clark; and the first African American female U.S. attorney general, Loretta Lynch.

Then, a couple of weeks after the game, what we had been waiting for finally happened. I was sitting in my office, watching a deposition in another case on Zoom. During a break, I glanced at my inbox and saw a forwarded email from Randall Adams, a lawyer on my team: "I think the Supreme Court granted us oral argument in Randle??? Am I reading this right?"

For a second, I stared at the screen, making sure my eyes weren't playing tricks on me. Then I read the email, letting the words sink in: "Tuesday, April 2, at 1:30 pm." Game on! The supreme court had granted our motion for a hearing! Rather than everything being decided based on legal briefs, we would be able to get up in front of the justices and make our case! I let out a loud "YES SIR!," which brought Mia to my office door asking, "What happened now?"

I told her and she said, "That's amazing . . . when?" When I told her the date was April 2, in about six weeks, her eyebrows went up. "That's not far away. Will you be ready?"

"Of course." After months of grinding motions, here it was—the highest court in Oklahoma had decided that our case deserved to be heard. Relief, pride, and urgency all surged together.

Ironically, we had canceled our standing Tuesday 4:00 P.M. team meeting because we had nothing pressing to discuss. Not anymore! I fired off a message to the team that read: "WOW! Well, looks like we have something to meet about today at 4:00 P.M. after all!!"

On the call, everyone was practically vibrating with excitement. For the first time ever, a legal team representing survivors of the Massacre would be able to stand before the Oklahoma Supreme Court and plead our case. After everybody calmed down, I said, "Okay, how should we split up the oral arguments among different members of the team?" That's when Jana Knott, our appellate expert, spoke up: "Damario, we'll only have a total of thirty minutes for oral arguments."

Thirty minutes? To summarize four years of litigation, legal research, and a crime that had been taking place for more than a century? Our first hearing in front of Judge Wall had taken *six hours,* and my team had been at the podium for more than half that time. How would we possibly cover everything in half an hour?

I was mentally adjusting and talking about how we could split up the responsibilities when Jana said, "I don't recommend that. It's cumbersome, it's disjointed, and it's just not as effective to have many different people talking. One person needs to do it. Damario, it has to be you."

Excuse me?

Like I said, I'm not an appellate attorney. Not only had I never argued before the state supreme court, I had never even set foot in their courtroom. But I kept my cool and tried to project confidence and leadership. I told everybody on the call, "Whatever I need to do for the cause, I'm down." But for real, I was scared to death to have my first appellate argument be before the Oklahoma Supreme Court in a case of this magnitude. We had six weeks to turn me into a credible appellate lawyer. It was time for boot camp. Cue the training montage music from *Rocky*.

My SolomonSimmonsLaw staff and the team at SRZ printed out every court case we had cited in our brief and the other side had cited as well. That was hundreds of cases, and I had to know them all. I ended up with notebooks full of cases and another set of notebooks full of two-page summaries of the cases and the "holding" for each—what the case stood for, the law that came out of the case, who cited the case, where they cited it, and what claim they cited the case to support. During my argument, I had to have that information at my fingertips and know it by heart.

That meant I had to read the entire record of our lawsuit, all the way back to 2020: all the briefs we had written since our first filing, all the briefs written by all the defendants, and all the court transcripts. Basically, I needed to know everything that had occurred in the case by heart. I spent day after day in my office poring over years of legal briefs and research from both sides until my eyes burned and my head was splitting.[1]

Yeah, no problem.

I also had to learn how to present as an appellate attorney. That meant multiple rounds of "moot court" sessions—basically, practice arguments. Now, I hadn't done a moot since I was part of a competition back in 2001 when I was a 1L—a first-year law student. So, I really didn't know what to expect. We'd have three moots in person, and three on Zoom. The first was to take place at the Oklahoma City University School of Law on March 18.

When you do a moot, you get lawyers to serve as mock judges. They listen to your argument, pepper you with questions, and then give you feedback. We secured the president of the Oklahoma Bar

Association and Carla Pratt, an OU law professor who served as an expert for me in my Black Creek case. My best friend, Jeff Trevillion, arranged for two young lawyers at his firm to participate. Through this "crash course," I would learn the presentation skills of an appellate attorney—and not "crash" (I hoped).

As a trial attorney, I'm walking around the courtroom, putting on a show, belting out my presentation, and commanding everyone's attention. I rely heavily on evidence, exhibits, and visual storytelling, making complex facts easy to understand and emotionally engaging.[2] I interact with witnesses, cross-examine opposing experts, and argue to convince juries or judges to rule in my client's favor. My work involves creating a clear narrative, simplifying complicated legal concepts, stripping away jargon, and connecting with people's hearts and minds.

Think about the late Johnnie Cochran at the O. J. Simpson trial saying, "If it doesn't fit, you must acquit" while holding up a pair of gloves. He said that thirty years ago, and we still talk about it. That's a trial attorney.

That's not what an appellate attorney does. I would be standing at a podium. There would be no jury. Instead of facing one judge, I would be facing nine justices.[3] No walking around. No witnesses. No props or PowerPoints. My job was to use legal arguments to show how Judge Wall had misapplied the law in dismissing our case. I wouldn't be appealing to emotion but making arguments grounded in relevant case law, statutes, and expert analysis.

Also, the justices could pepper me with questions as soon as I got to the podium and said the traditional opening of any appellate argument: "May it please the court." They could be hostile, argumentative, or downright disrespectful. If I was not able to recall the relevant arguments, facts, and case law in real time, I could be humiliated.

I knew only one way to get myself ready: I went back to grinding sixteen to eighteen hours a day. Then, on March 4, two weeks into the intensive preparation, I wasn't feeling well, but I didn't want to listen to my body. It was like I had a cartoon devil on one shoulder saying, *You can't be sick. You got to be working,* with a cartoon angel on the other shoulder saying, *You need to relax or you'll burn yourself out.* All day long I fought with myself, knowing I should relax but afraid to do so.

Finally, on March 5, I was fatigued, had a slight cough, and had a hard time catching my breath. I told Mia, "Don't worry, it's just my allergies." However, when I was unable to get out of bed for most of the day, she made me go to Ascension St. John Owasso Hospital in Owasso,[4] a wealthy suburb about twenty minutes north of Tulsa, because we knew I could get right into the emergency room.

I told the ER staff, "I'm not feeling well and I'm having shortness of breath." They immediately brought in a wheelchair. *Whoa.* They told me that based on my symptoms, they needed to check my heart. I replied, "No, it's my allergies, not my heart, and I am not getting into no dang wheelchair." But then Mia said, "Damario, get in the wheelchair," in a tone I knew all too well. I sat down. A nurse took me to get an EKG.

After a while, a doctor came in and said solemnly, "We're going to hold you. We think you had a heart event, and we need to do some more tests." A heart event? What does that even mean? I asked the doctor. "Basically, it means a small heart attack." *Seriously?* Now I needed to do a CT scan with contrast to check the calcium buildup in my coronary arteries. The ER doc told me I also needed to talk to a cardiologist.

The cardiologist explained what was happening. Apparently, I'd had an abnormal heart rhythm. They were being extremely cautious, which explained the additional tests. Also, my heart rate was extremely high, and they had to get it down before they could do the CT scan. Eventually, they gave me IV medication to get my heart rate down.

They finally got my resting heart rate down, injected the contrasting dye, did the CT scan, and I was fine. A cardiac calcium score ranges from 0 to 400, and mine was 0.1. "Your heart is healthy," said the doctor after reviewing the results. But then what was going on? Next, the doc asked, "What do you do for a living? Are you under a lot of stress right now?"

I laughed before I could stop myself. I told the doctor, "Well, I'm an attorney, and I am about to go before the state supreme court to argue this issue that's 103 years old, and the hopes of my clients and community are riding on my back. So, yes, I'm under some stress."

I had been putting myself under unrelenting pressure since 2019, and that was without taking into account the impact of running my own law firm, Covid, George Floyd, January 6, the deaths of my Aunt Edna, Stan, and Uncle Redd, and everything else that had been going on. I had been working constantly, not getting enough rest, and putting everything on my shoulders. I was exhausted. Eventually the stress took me to the breaking point.

This was my body's warning shot. I was literally putting my health and life on the line for Greenwood and reparations for the survivors.

My heart scare changed how I prepared for the supreme court, right? Well . . . no. I didn't even tell the team about it. I took a couple of days to rest and then got back to work.

A few days later, we held our first full moot court session at Oklahoma City Law School. I was trash. I gave a passionate trial lawyer's performance, blew past my time limit, had no command of the case law, and struggled with tough questions. It was humbling. After that first moot, my insecurity about making the argument skyrocketed. *I don't know if I'm going to be ready. I don't know if this was the right move.* I had a long way to go and less than four weeks to get there.

Of course, there was no going back, so I resolved that I would be prepared, whatever it took. After a March 21 strategy session with Bryan Stevenson, things started to click. Bryan, who is believed to have made and won the most oral arguments in front of the U.S. Supreme Court of any African American attorney,[5] told me how bad he was on his first couple of arguments and shared the techniques he used to be successful.

Most important, he said I had to prepare and practice with the fire and fervor of the mighty Greenwood ancestors whose shoulders I stood upon. They had been waiting, he reminded me, all these years for their story to be told. He also reminded me that no one knew more, cared more, or believed more in the case than me, and that I should stand at that podium from a position of strength and confidence, knowing that I was born for this.

As we did more moots, I could feel myself getting better. I was more confident going through the questions. I knew the case material from muscle memory. I understood the road map I had to follow. As Jana and Sara had suggested, I started to look at my argument as a drive down a highway. The justices would ask questions, trying to steer me off the highway on different tangents. My job was to answer their questions concisely and get back on the highway as fast as possible.

One slight curveball: I wouldn't really have thirty minutes. I had to state our case, then the defense got their turn. Then I needed time for rebuttal. So really, I would have about twenty-five minutes to cover the totality of Greenwood, the Massacre, and the aftermath. So I condensed and condensed some more. We did another live moot, and another, and then one where we invited outside lawyers, including a couple of respected professors at the USC Gould School of Law. My reviews? Two thumbs up.

Our last live moot was at the University of Tulsa College of Law on Friday, March 29. Jana came over from Oklahoma City, and a few seasoned appellate lawyers from Crowe & Dunlevy's Tulsa office participated in person. The rest of the team participated via Zoom. Everyone came after me with tough questions, but when we were finished, everyone said, "You're good. You're ready."

I was. I felt ready. I got my game face on and went into final prep mode.

We were four days out, so I treated that time like I was back at OU prepping for a Saturday football game. I moved into the Colcord Hotel in Oklahoma City on April 1. Most of the legal team came to town to support me. We had one final "walk-through" moot that afternoon. I was feeling confident. The rest of the evening was about resting, relaxing, hydrating, and getting my mind right.

I was ready. The hearing would be held at 1:30 P.M. the next day, giving me ample time to rest.

April 2, 2024. I awoke at 6:00 A.M. When I inventoried my attire for the hearing, I realized that I had accidentally forgotten my traditional purple pocket square. No problem—Mia to the rescue! She ran to Nordstrom Rack to buy me a replacement. When she returned, I was in the zone, with my music blasting like the hotel room was a football locker room. Out came her phone. She started shooting behind-the-scenes video of my prep ritual for our archives, social media, and maybe someday a powerful documentary. Who knows?

I didn't think about the video. I dressed myself for court and got my mind right. I roamed around the room—head bobbing and singing along with "Clear Eyes, Full Heart, Can't Lose" by T. Powell and listening to remixed motivational speeches featuring two of my favorite speakers, Les Brown and Eric Thomas. I managed to put on my lucky Omega Psi Phi cuff links but fumbled my attempt to tie a Windsor knot in my signature purple tie (after all these years, you'd think I would have that down!). Once again, Mia stepped in to save the day.

Then she put her reporter hat on. "How do you feel?" she asked me. I said, "I feel great. I feel honored and privileged to be in this situation. I'm ready to go, and the main thing is I'm trying to make sure I stay calm and conversational, because I'm talking to nine people and nine people only." When I unwrapped my new pocket square, I found a surprise note from my beautiful wife that said, "You are the one, sir. You were chosen and created for such a time as this. I'm very proud of you. There is nothing you can't do with God and with me."

That was just what I needed. I had my ancestors with me, my wife with me, my team with me, and God with me. I had everything I needed to be successful.

Later, I prayed to God and talked as I always do to the ancestors and elders who have left this world but who inspired me while they were in it: Mama Brown, Daddy Brown, Professor Ogletree, Uncle Redd, Otis Clark, B. C. Franklin, and more. "God, thank you for this opportunity. Let me be your vessel and give me the strength and words. Ancestors, I stand on your mighty and powerful shoulders. God, speak through me. Ancestors, be with me." Then I recited a poem that I wrote for times like this called "I Can't Lose":

I can't lose
I am more prepared than they
could ever be

I can't lose
I am more passionate about the issue
and all will see

I can't lose
I was made to defeat
injustice and depravity

I can't lose
I am on the right side and just side
of the law, the moment,
and the history

I can't lose
I am simply better than they
will ever be

I can't lose
because this is my destiny!

With that, I was ready. We hurried to the SUVs and made our way to the state capitol, where the Oklahoma Supreme Court is located. I was mostly silent during the seven-minute drive, thinking about the task at hand. At the capitol, I shared a hug with Eric, then it was time for the long walk through security and to the courtroom, with Tyrone and me ahead of the pack. Mia followed me like a Hollywood director filming a long tracking shot as I greeted Mother Randle and finally entered an impressive but relatively snug courtroom filled with many familiar faces from Tulsa and across the state and nation.

As I had before entering Judge Wall's courtroom two years earlier, I retreated to the restroom to gather my thoughts and go through my pregame rituals of prayer, affirmations, and pronunciation and enunciation drills, and when I went back into the courtroom I was locked in.

The justices entered, and I stood and introduced the co-counselors at my table: Eric Miller of Loyola Law School; Randall Adams and Michael Swartz of SRZ; Jana L. Knott from Bass Law; and Kymberli Heckenkemper of SSL. The rest of the team sat just behind us, and everyone was armed with note cards ready to pass to me as necessary. The defense introduced themselves, then it was time. I got up and looked into the faces of the justices, and I couldn't help thinking, *Wow. I'm here. I'm this little Black boy from North Tulsa, from Greenwood, and I've got these nine white justices in front of me who will carry our fate.* Then I said, "Thank you, Mr. Chief Justice, and may it please the Court," and it was on.

I jumped into my two-minute introduction to the case: "The survivors alleged that Defendants blighted the localized discrete Greenwood neighborhood through offensive and criminal acts causing property damage that is ongoing and requires abatement. And this Court has held for over 113 years that blighted property can cause a public nuisance and there is no statute of limitations on a public nuisance. Second, the District Court's reasoning for dismissing the survivor's case because they failed to state a specific remedy is contrary to the well-established precedent of this Court."

I was hoping the justices wouldn't interrupt me and prepared for questions when I finished.

"The facts of this case fit squarely within the common law property-based limitations that have shaped Oklahoma's public nuisance statute for more than a century. The District Court unlawfully imposed on survivors a heightened pleading standard that has never been adopted by a court in Oklahoma. Survivors adequately plead a public nuisance claim pursuant to the definition provided by the Oklahoma Supreme Court in their recent decision in Johnson & Johnson on November 9, 2021."

Because my energy is always so high, my game plan was to start at what I consider to be a low energy level. I finished my introduction, expecting to get some questions but not actually stopping.

Nothing. I moved on quickly, thinking, *I am going to get some questions soon.*

Nothing. I looked those six men and three women in the face, and I realized that they were looking back at me, focused and concentrating.

About four or five minutes in, I really hit my stride and successfully married the trial and appellant skill sets, and a full but more refined version of attorney Damario Solomon-Simmons was now on full display. I was charismatic and concise, which I had not been during my early moot sessions.

One of the key points I made to the court was that the passage of time does not erase a public nuisance. As I told the justices:

> One I would like to talk about is Meinders vs Johnson, which is a Court of Civil Appeals case, which is obviously not binding on this Court, but I think it's very persuasive because in that case you had a public nuisance that oil and gas exploration that actually started in the 1920s and the case was not brought until the late 1990s and not resolved until 2006. And the Court of Meinders vs Johnson stated, "It does not matter when the actual pollution starts," and it's the same here. It does not matter that the massacre happened in 1921. What matters [is] that the public nuisance, the property is still blighted, there's still vacant properties. The public nuisance is ongoing, causing the Greenwood neighborhood to suffer [in] its health, safety, comfort and repose, or feel less secure in their life and security—that comes directly from the statute at 50 OS1.

I then gave the justices another example:

> We also cited a case called Briggs vs. Freeport-McMoRan Copper & Gold. This was a very interesting case because it involved a smelting plant in Blackwell, Oklahoma[,] that was in operation from 1916 and ceased operations in 1972, and yet a lawsuit

by the Plaintiffs [was] brought in 2015, and the Western District in that case allowed [it past] a motion to dismiss. They overruled a motion to dismiss based on the fact that the Plaintiffs were able to say that the pollution, the public nuisance was ongoing and that's where we are at this stage in this litigation. We haven't done any discovery. We haven't had [an] opportunity to do any fact finding that we need to do for this case to move forward, and we believe if we had that opportunity, we could prove the allegations that we state in our petition.

But one of the biggest differences between my moot performance and my supreme court argument came when the justices finally asked me questions.

Justice Dustin Rowe came out of the gate first. "Public nuisance actions are typically brought by public officials, not private individuals, and in order for a private individual to bring a public nuisance action, it must be shown that the individual has a special injury different from that suffered by others, and here we had a large number of victims. How are these Plaintiffs' injuries different in kind or special from the other victims of this event, this Massacre?"

In my early moot sessions, I fumbled this sort of question badly. I stammered my answers, couldn't pull from relevant case law, and when I started speaking, I had no idea where I would end up. But all my hard work and prep had paid off. When Justice Rowe lobbed me that "softball" (because we had prepared for that very question), I felt like I hit it out of the park.

"Thank you, Justice Rowe," I began. "These particular plaintiffs, who are both 109 years old, are the only two living survivors of the Massacre, so no one else in the world has the injuries that they have today. That's number one. Number two, this Court has said that special injury in your case McKay vs City of Enid, it's a 1910 case, [']the special injury to['] meaning harm that is different in kind from the public at large. It doesn't mean necessarily that some other people may not share the injury of the damage, but again, there's no one else in the world that shares this injury because they're the only two that's still living today."

Other questions came in, and I handled them just as smoothly. I could feel the gravity of where I was and what I was doing. I had nine white justices in front of me. I had a couple of hundred people from my community behind me. I had some portion of the country watching on a live stream. With all that, I had to stay on my argument. I had to stay within my time. I had to keep eye contact with all nine of these people and watch for facial cues. I had to watch the clock as it went from green to yellow to flashing yellow to red.

I did it all.

I finished, and the defense's turn came. They had split their presentation between different attorneys, which Jana had said was a huge mistake. She was right. Their argument was disjointed, terrible. Attorney Garry Gaskins was the first to speak, and this is part of what he said:

> Plaintiffs' claims against the governmental entities are obviously precluded by sovereign immunity. As of 1921 when the Tulsa Race Massacre occurred, there was no Governmental Tort Claims Act, or any statutory mechanism to waive sovereign immunity. In 1958, this Court said, "It is fundamental that the state cannot be sued in any manner or upon any liability, constitutional, statutory, or contractual, unless there is express consent thereto."

In other words, the perpetrators of the Massacre argued they could not be held liable because at the time of the Massacre, established jurisprudence said governments could not be sued. That was the doctrine of sovereign immunity. But as I explained to the justices, that principle does not apply here. Public nuisance claims have always been treated differently. From statehood forward, Oklahoma courts have consistently allowed equitable relief—injunctions, abatement, and declaratory relief—against cities and state entities, even when damages were barred.

I told the court:

> We cited several cases in our briefs, there's three I would like to highlight. First is Markwardt vs City of Guthrie. This is a 1907 case where this Court held that abatement could be held . . . Public injunction relief could go against the City of Guthrie . . . we cited Finlay's vs Oklahoma City, it was a 1942 case. What's very interesting about that case is that the Plaintiff bought action for injunctive relief and monetary damages, but this Court dismissed the monetary damages before sovereign immunity, but allowed the equitable relief to move forward. We cited a case from 1981, Gay Student Alliance vs Oklahoma Board of Regents . . . those Plaintiffs were asking for monetary damage and equitable relief. Again, this Court dismissed the monetary damages portion of the case because of sovereign immunity, but allowed equitable relief to move forward, because equitable relief is different than monetary damages.

I pressed further with the plain language of the statute itself: "If you look at 51 OS 153(A), it says the state shall be liable for losses if a private entity would be liable for money damages. And 51 OS 152.4 defines a claim as a written demand to recover money as compensation. That evidences the clear legislative intent—the Governmental Tort Claims Act (GTCA) is only about money damages. It has nothing to do with equitable relief. And what we are asking for is equitable relief."

That was the point the defense wanted to blur. They wanted the court to believe immunity was absolute, that cities and state agencies could never be touched. But the law says otherwise.

After several other attorneys spoke, the defense concluded, and I had five minutes to rebut. This is where Jana's expertise was invaluable. She said, "Focus on three things we want to rebut, get them out, and sit down." That's what I did, and then I made what I suppose you could call my closing argument:

> As we plan our petition, over a third of the homes and businesses destroyed through the Massacre were never rebuilt, and many of those people have never been heard from again. Eight thousand people were made homeless overnight. And I want to say one last thing. One hundred and seventeen years ago, the founders of the great State of Oklahoma wrote these powerful words in the Constitution, Article two, section VI, "The courts of justice of The State shall be open to every person, and speedy and certain remedy afforded for every wrong and for every injury to person, property, or reputation; and right and justice shall be administered without sale, denial, delay, or prejudice." Yet these Plaintiffs have been waiting for almost 103 years for their opportunity to be in court to prove what happened to them and their community. We're simply asking that this Court give us the opportunity to be remanded back to the District Court to prove our claims.[6]

When I sat down, something happened that had never happened before in my career. In fact, I have never heard of it happening anywhere. The courtroom broke into spontaneous applause. Yes, the spectators in Judge Wall's courtroom had given me a standing ovation in 2022, but that had been *before* I argued. This applause came after I concluded, like a warm wave of love washing over me.

Going in, I felt confident that we had three votes. Based on the questions asked, I felt confident that we could get two more. But I was a little concerned. After the arguments concluded, Justice Yvonne Kauger, the oldest justice on the court, said, "No matter what happens, I want you to know you've done a great thing here." Laypeople might think that was encouraging, but lawyers know that's an old trick, a way of saying, "You did a good job, but I'm still going to rule against you." I didn't need her to placate me. I needed her vote.

Everything about the session had been extraordinary. Justices don't say things like that from the bench. The Oklahoma Supreme Court is never packed with Black people from North Tulsa. Court attendees don't applaud at the end of arguments. When it was done, all I wanted to do was get to Mia. She made it through the crowd, and I wrapped her in a big hug and just started bawling.

We exited the courtroom and then greeted the survivors and supporters who had come to join us. National supporters like Barbara Arnwine (with her booming voice) and Tamika Mallory were there. Congresswoman Sheila Jackson Lee hadn't been able to make it,[7] but she called. Everybody was coming up to me wanting to shake my hand or hug me. People were crying tears of joy and hope. The consensus feeling was "There is no way they can rule against us after that."

We gave a quick press conference with local and state elected officials (including Oklahoma State Representative Monroe Nichols, who was gearing up to run for mayor of Tulsa), my legal team and Justice for Greenwood staff, and community supporters standing with us. Everyone believed we were going to win.

We went back to the hotel, and the rest of the day we celebrated a job well done. My team and I had done some brilliant, brave lawyering to get us here. Everybody felt like we should survive to fight another day. All we could do now was wait.

I was only five years old when the Tulsa riot occurred, but I remember the awful feeling of not having a home to go to. For our house, which my parents owned, was burned down. We lost everything in that riot. There was so much grief in our family. Everywhere we looked in our Greenwood District, there was nothing but ashes, ashes, ashes!*

—Archie Jason Franklin, Massacre survivor,
as told to Eddie Faye Gates

Detainees are marched through downtown Tulsa on June 1, 1921. The original photograph by James Sidney Swinney is in the Department of Special Collections, McFarlin Library, the University of Tulsa.

CHAPTER 12

SUSPENDING DISBELIEF

We were headed back from Oklahoma City, Tyrone behind the wheel and me in the passenger seat, my phone buzzing with calls. Outside the window, spring in northeastern Oklahoma unfurled: wide green fields, trees just filling out, ponds glittering. More than once, I caught myself fantasizing about stopping to fish, just to steal a moment of peace. No time, though.

I was deep in conversation with members of my Black Creek Freedmen litigation team. In September 2023, we won a landmark trial to restore my clients' Muscogee (Creek) Nation (MCN) citizenship,[1] but the nation appealed. Now, in April 2024, I was knee-deep in the briefs before the MCN Supreme Court. After two decades of not touching appellate work, suddenly I was living and breathing it. There was a lot at stake: Black Creeks were not just members of the Muscogee (Creek) Nation but co-founders of Greenwood itself.

Then came another call, this one from the staff for California Congresswoman Maxine Waters. She had stood with the Massacre survivors and descendants for years, and she had long fought for Black Creeks—those descended from people enslaved by the Creek Nation and those the government had simply labeled "Black" and denied their rights. Now her staff informed me that she would be filing an amicus brief in the Massacre case and inviting other members of Congress to join her.[2] An amicus brief is a powerful gesture that lets outsiders tell the judges that the outcome of a case is bigger than what happens in the courtroom.

This amicus wasn't born overnight, either. It took more than two decades of consistent advocacy to Representative Waters and other members of the Congressional Black Caucus to elevate both the Massacre and the Black Freedmen issues. For the congresswoman and her colleagues, the brief was also a signal to the Muscogee (Creek) Nation: *We are watching.*

But as we approached Tulsa, I felt that seductive call to rest—to fish, to walk, to hold hands with my wife and talk about trivial things, to breathe deep and be at peace—come over me again. I had earned a break, and I knew Mia wanted me to stand down for the sake of my health. But this wasn't the time. Win or lose at the Oklahoma Supreme Court, things were coming to a crisis point. My profile was higher than ever, so the cause of reparations was more public than ever. In six months, there would be an election to determine whether the nation embraced open authoritarianism and white supremacy as a governing principle.

Most important, I had to quietly prepare for a possibility I didn't want to think about but that as an attorney I had to think about: *What would we do if we lost at the supreme court?* I had spoken confidently after the hearing and meant every word, but privately I knew we were fighting an uphill battle. If the court ruled against us, we had a few cards to play, but our case would be, for all intents and purposes, dead. If that happened, how would I carry on the fight? *Could* I carry on the fight? How would the survivors, the descendants, and the community find reason to hope?

Those questions weighed heavily as we swung into Tulsa. Fortunately, I had the busiest few months of my life ahead of me as a distraction. The spring of 2024 became a blur of birthdays, boardrooms, and the rooms where decisions are made.

It was May 20 when Mia and I traveled to D.C. for another round of meetings, starting with Kristen Clarke at the DOJ. Later, I huddled with members of the Congressional Black Caucus—including my fraternity brother Georgia Congressman Hank Johnson and my friend (and rising star) Texas Congresswoman Jasmine Crockett—about the DOJ investigation and the appeal. And as always when I was in D.C., I joined Roland Martin at *#RolandMartinUnfiltered* to make sure our story hit the grassroots.

At one point, Roland asked me, "Y'all are still waiting from the Oklahoma Supreme Court, correct?" I laid out the key issue: time. "We need five out of the nine justices to come back with a yes vote," I said. "And they're not telling us if we won the case; we're just asking to let us move forward to a trial and discovery. . . . Time is of the essence. We do know that the Oklahoma Supreme Court takes a recess at the end of June all the way to September, so hopefully, fingers crossed and praying every day, we get a decision before June 30."[3]

On the plane home, Mia and I finally had time to talk. I pulled up a list of goals I had written back in 2019 and read them aloud while Mia listened and nodded:

- Reprioritize survivors and their descendants.
- Reinvigorate the push for Congress to pass the John Hope Franklin Tulsa-Greenwood Race Riot Claims Accountability Act.
- Recenter all discussions of the Massacre, locally and nationally, around reparations.
- Prove the Massacre stunted the economic growth of Tulsa's Black community.
- Push the Tulsa County Grand Jury and/or the DOJ to open a criminal investigation into the actions and omissions of the defendants and others involved in the Massacre.
- Create and support an entity specifically designed to ensure that descendants of the Massacre's survivors receive the resources and services they need.
- Secure reparations, including direct payments to survivors and descendants, modeled after the Marshall Plan.

When I finished, Mia leaned back, folded her arms, and said, "You wrote this five years ago. Every one of those points is still breathing because you refused to let them die. And that fight isn't over. I am so proud of you." Her words steadied me. The court might drag its feet. The politics might shift. But the blueprint had held.

Circle Cinema, a classic old movie house located in Whittier Square in downtown Tulsa, has been a vital part of the city's cultural scene since 1928. On May 31, 2024, the 103rd anniversary of the Massacre, it lit up for the premiere of *Greenwood Is Still Burning*, a documentary directed by Gavin Hartigan, co-executive-produced by me, and made possible by our partnership with Lush Cosmetics.

For one night, Hollywood came to Tulsa as the lobby buzzed with survivors' families, descendants, and supporters. My parents came (the first time in my adult life both of my parents were at an event to support me at the same time), and I got to rock my tuxedo with a purple bow tie! As the lights dimmed and the first images hit the screen, I felt the power of story—the way film could reach places legal briefs never could. It wasn't just about capturing history; it was about making sure Greenwood's fire still burned in the conscience of this country.

Since Judge Wall's dismissal, doubt had crept in—there's no sugarcoating it. But Bryan Stevenson's words echoed in my head: "The longer this goes on, Damario, there is the victory." That became my anchor. I couldn't guarantee a victory, but I could guarantee a fight! When I looked around the theater lobby and saw so many others who were part of this crusade, I couldn't deny that things had changed for the better.

Thirty years ago, hardly anybody outside North Tulsa even knew about the Massacre. Textbooks skipped it. Politicians ducked it. Now survivors had testified before Congress, live on international television. The Department of Justice was at the table. The long-taboo word *reparations* was part of conversations on Capitol Hill. That didn't happen because America suddenly grew a conscience. It happened because we kept pushing and refused to let Greenwood be forgotten again.

I would never say it to anyone, but I knew we could lose. In those dark moments, the people were my lifeline. The descendants who turned grief into advocacy, the students who packed auditoriums to hear the story, the pastors, professors, and partners who lent their voices—they were what I believed in. Even if the court slammed the door on us, the fight would go on in the streets, in legislatures, in churches, and with every new generation.

Another flight, this time to meet Mia in Phoenix for Lush's annual conference, and then I was ready for poolside. My phone was off; no agenda, no interviews. I savored the dry, baking heat of the desert sun, the smell of chlorine and sunscreen, the spray of the misters, and the quiet joy of just relaxing with my wife.

Eight o'clock the next morning, I turned my phone back on. I went through my texts. Nothing urgent. I saw an email with the subject line "Media Inquiry—Randle v. City of Tulsa (No. 121, 502)" from a reporter for *Legal Insurrection,* asking me if I wanted to comment on my case being dismissed.

Surely if our case had been dismissed, I'd have been buried in media requests. I disregarded it as an old message. Then my personal phone rang. It was Emma Weinberg, my paralegal. "I'm sorry to bother you, but we just got an order from the Oklahoma Supreme Court."

The court had dismissed our case, 8–1.[4]

The justices wrote, "Even after the initial violence subsided, local officials engaged in actions that exacerbated the harm. State and local officials participated in the mass arrests and detention of Greenwood residents, and black detainees could only be released upon the application of a white person. . . . Though Plaintiffs' grievances are legitimate, they do not fall within the scope of our State's public nuisance statute."[5] The court agreed that Oklahoma and Tulsa had tried to exterminate Greenwood. They just didn't think the law could do anything about it!

What do you do when something comes to an absolute end, when there are no more options, no more speeches? It's got to be like an ER doctor losing a patient. You try to come to terms with the reality that there's nothing else you can do. I just sat there and thought, *What do I say? What do I tell the team? What do I tell the survivors? What now?*

Mia has come to know "that look" on my face all too well, and when I told her the news, she just wrapped her arms around me for a silent embrace. There really wasn't anything to say.

The rest of the day became about putting one foot in front of the other. I scheduled a Zoom with my team, and we read the order together, absorbed it together, got angry together, grieved together, and discussed what we would do next. Then I had to call the survivors and their families, who were both disappointed and confused by the decision. After that, I had to get ready for the media, because by now reporters were burning up my phone.

I should have been poolside with my wife, gearing up for a day of relaxation and fun, but instead I was holed up in a hotel room, curtains pulled shut, lamps dragged across the floor to create makeshift lighting. Once again, Mia had turned into my publicist and producer: moving furniture, testing camera angles, adjusting lampshades so I looked halfway decent on TV. When the MSNBC interviewer came on, I was finally able to let out my anger and frustration.

"We will file a petition for rehearing, but make no mistake about it, we understand the only thing that will help Mother Randle—and the fifty million Black people who trust and believe in the system—is for the Biden administration to step in and stand with Mother Randle," I snapped. "Now that we have been failed by the courts, now that we've been failed by Congress, we're calling upon President Biden to fulfill his promise to these survivors, to this community, and to Black people throughout this nation.

"It is time for the administration to show up not just for the two living survivors of the Tulsa Race Massacre, Mother Randle and Mother Fletcher, not just for Greenwood, but for all of Black America who want justice and reparations!"[6]

After I don't know how many interviews, I pulled myself together and went over to the Lush conference. I did my presentation, but everybody was deflated. Everyone was asking me what we were going to do next, and I didn't know.

The next morning, I was back in that hotel room, tie knotted, lamps still angled like spotlights, doing a round of national morning shows, including one with my friend Sara Sidner on CNN. I went through the motions, but my heart wasn't in it anymore. What cut the deepest wasn't just the public nuisance claim rejection but that the court had thrown out our unjust enrichment claim, too. That was a purely factual argument. The City of Tulsa and the white power structure had been unjustly enriched by the destruction of Greenwood and the theft of its wealth. That was undeniable. But they denied us anyway. The vote wasn't even close. Only Justice James Edmondson stood with us, and I will always thank him for that.

All that work, all that sacrifice, all that great lawyering—and still, the door slammed shut. Once again, "and justice for all" didn't apply to Black people.

I walked along an enormous sandstone-colored wall 43 feet tall and 155 feet long. Sweeping my eyes down its length, I could see 122,000 surnames carved into its face, names that had been adopted by the 4.7 million formerly enslaved African Americans listed on the 1870 U.S. census. I walked along that wall, silent and reverent, until I found Solomon, Ransom, Brown, and Hobson—the names of my ancestors who had been bound, sold at public markets like cattle, imprisoned on Southern plantations, and forced to work nearly to death in subhuman conditions: beaten, starved, raped. Nearby, Mia found Fleming and Jones, the names of her enslaved forebears. Stark and silent, the wall brought those horrors to the present without explanation or equivocation. *Here it is, deal with it.* This wasn't just a memorial; it was time travel.

I was still hurting from the court decision, so Mia and I had flown to Montgomery, Alabama, for the public dedication of the Equal Justice Initiative's Freedom Monument Sculpture Park, a memorial that's one of several incredible monuments—collectively called the Legacy Sites—developed to preserve the memory of enslaved people and the fight for civil rights and justice and truth-tell about the atrocities Black people have endured in this country.

It was a trip I didn't realize I so desperately needed.

But it was the Legacy Museum that broke me. If you visit (and you should), you will feel it when you walk in. It was built on the site of a former cotton warehouse where kidnapped Black men and women had been forced to labor under the threat of whip and knife. I wandered from softly lit room to softly lit room, from sickening photos of emaciated children in the holds of slave ships, to life-size sculptures of proud Black people—my people!—in shackles and chains, to exhibits that brought home the savagery of lynching. But when I finally got to the wall of glass jars containing the ashes of enslaved men and women, that's when the tears started to stream down my face.

I wasn't the only one weeping, but my weeping was different. For me, this was even more personal. This wasn't just about my enslaved ancestors. This was about my country. The country that had inflicted such agony on my people for so long, the country that I was now asking to do the right thing after it had refused again and again to do so. Finally, the weight of the Oklahoma Supreme Court defeat pressed down on me and nearly drove me to my knees.

Would this country ever do what was right? Could it? Was I wasting my time? Why even bother? But even as I was asking myself the question, I knew the answer.

Because someone has to.

I had come to Montgomery to heal my wounded spirit, and that meant seeing Bryan Stevenson (who had spearheaded the effort to build the Legacy Sites) in person. I had looked forward to visiting him ever since I first emailed him for guidance and help in January 2020. His positive response changed my life, and since then he has become the big brother I never had. To this day I don't make a major legal or strategic decision without consulting him. He made the most difficult and expensive work of my life possible, connecting me to resources and relationships I could not have acquired on my own.

I watched him give a moving speech for the dedication that day before hundreds of people from across the country: elected officials in sharp suits, celebrities trailed by fans, activists with slogan T-shirts, musicians with guitars slung across their backs, philanthropists eager to be supporting the Equal Justice Initiative. When he finished, the crowd buzzed with energy as people pressed forward, each determined to get Bryan's attention. Everywhere I looked, someone was angling for a handshake, a photo, or a word of encouragement. It felt like a revival, a family reunion, and a political summit all at once.

A line formed for well-wishers and autograph-seekers, and I slipped into it, my heart pounding. I wanted to jump the line to visit with him and get our picture together, but I held myself back. Every couple of minutes, I turned to Mia, whispering, "Is the phone ready? Make sure you're ready." I couldn't risk missing this moment.

As I inched forward, I caught snippets of conversation: someone thanking him for saving their relative from death row, another calling him a hero, another begging him to visit their city. Cameras flashed. People clapped him on the back, leaned in for photos, pressed books and papers into his hands. Bryan gave each of them time—listening, nodding, offering a soft smile, a word of grace. Watching him, I was struck again by how he carried the weight of being America's moral compass but still gave each person his full presence.

I couldn't stop fidgeting and shifting from foot to foot. What do you say to your hero? The man who helped you in your time of greatest need? But by the time I reached him, I knew exactly what to do. I wrapped him in a bear hug and told him I loved him. It was the first time we had seen each other face-to-face since he became my Phil Jackson.

Bryan looked at me and said calmly, "It's all right. We're just getting started."

In that moment—overlooking the Alabama River, surrounded by monuments to the enslaved and the free, holding on to my mentor and brother—I believed him.

My visit with Bryan renewed my vigor. Time to get off the mat and practice another part of Willful Resilience: having a plan B. I worked with my team to file a petition for rehearing—basically asking the

Oklahoma Supreme Court to reconsider its decision. It was a Hail Mary pass, especially after an 8–1 decision. But we had to file, not because we expected a victory but because it was our responsibility to exhaust every legal remedy available. To stop short would have been to abandon our clients and the cause.

The team came together from across the country for a press conference in the Greenwood Cultural Center's Survivors Room. Muriel Watson (Uncle Redd's daughter) flew in from Denver to stand in her father's place. In the front row sat Mother Randle, 109 years old, her body frail but her mere presence uplifting.

When I stepped to the microphone, I spoke plainly. "The courts failed us in 1921 when lawsuits languished and were dismissed without trial. They failed us in 2005 when the federal courts closed their doors. And once again, they have failed us by denying Mother Randle and Mother Fletcher even a hearing. We filed this case in 2020, and yet once again the court system has failed the survivors, descendants, the Greenwood community, and all of Black America who still wants to believe in this country's promise of equality under the law."

But this filing wasn't just symbolic. In our petition for rehearing, we laid out why the court should rehear the case and reverse its decision. For decades, Oklahoma law said unjust enrichment was proven if one party unfairly kept money that, in equity and good conscience, should not be retained. Yet for the first time in state history, the court had added a new requirement: fraud, abuse of confidence, or unconscionable conduct. That standard had never been applied before, and the defense had never argued it. It wasn't hard to see that our case had been targeted.

We argued that the court had wrongly dismissed our public nuisance claim. Eric Miller reminded the crowd, "The Oklahoma Supreme Court rewrote its own public nuisance statute to keep these women out of court. They ignored their own precedent. Our petition lays out exactly how they twisted the law to justify this dismissal. This cannot stand."

While cameras clicked and reporters scribbled, I closed by invoking the promise made in that very building just three years earlier. "In this very room, my clients met with President Joe Biden," I said. "He told them he would see that they get justice. He told the nation he stood with the survivors. Now that the courts and Congress have failed, we are calling on him to keep that promise. We are calling on the Department of Justice to investigate, to stand with this community, and to ensure that America does not fail Greenwood again."

The DOJ was our last hope for any sort of meaningful legal action. We had no path to appeal to the U.S. Supreme Court, and we were all sick of moral victories. We were tired of empty goodwill gestures and commissions and panels and memorials. We were fed up with platitudes, commemorative medals, and hearing people say, "No matter what happens, I want you to know you've done a great thing here," and then voting against us. We wanted reparations.

People who love fantasy and science fiction talk about "the suspension of disbelief." To get into the story, you've got to make yourself believe in things you know are impossible. To be a Black civil rights attorney in Oklahoma, I have to do the same thing. The only way I can fight for Justice for Greenwood, the Black Creeks, and so many others is to believe against all evidence that if I prepare harder, work longer, and push further, I can win. That belief is what fuels me when I'm running on empty, what keeps me in the fight even when the game is rigged from the moment I sit down. That belief (call it self-delusion if you want to; there's a fine line) carried me through the chaos of the summer of 2024.

On July 19, my good friend and ally Congresswoman Sheila Jackson Lee died of cancer. The loss hit hard. But after that, the coming election dominated my attention and my schedule. In August, I flew to Chicago for the National Association of Black Journalists convention, where Trump spewed venom at my friend and journalist Rachel Scott. Next, Martha's Vineyard, where I participated in a reparations town hall. Then on to the main event, the Democratic National Convention, where my "cousin," Kamala Harris, would accept the party's nomination for president.

As I boarded a flight to Chicago, I wanted to believe in the electricity that was building for Kamala in part because the prospect that the country might elect the convicted felon and racist Donald Trump for a second time was too horrifying to consider. But Kamala knew our plight. She had met the survivors. She was a compassionate person. I believed she would help our cause . . . and hoped desperately that I wasn't gaslighting myself.

Ever been to a party convention in a presidential election year? Try it sometime. I had been to the Super Bowl and thought I knew about high energy, but that was nothing compared to the excitement at the Democratic National Convention! I held a "Kamala" sign on the convention floor and did live analysis on Roland Martin's Black Star Network. I visited with dozens of elected officials and national leaders.

I got fired up during Michelle Obama's mic-dropping speech,[7] the best of the convention, especially when she said, "For years, Donald Trump did everything in his power to try to make people fear us. See, his limited, narrow view of the world made him feel threatened by the existence of two hardworking, highly educated, successful people who happen to be Black. I want to know—I want to know—who's going to tell him, who's going to tell him, that the job he is currently seeking might just be one of those Black jobs?"

The building nearly shook off its foundation.

I was sold. The convention had us all feeling like there was no way anyone could stop this train, certainly not Donald Trump and his Project 2025 fantasy.

Everywhere I went in Chicago, I promoted the screening of *Greenwood Is Still Burning* to leaders, cornered elected officials, and built new alliances. At a screening of the documentary presented in collaboration with the Emmett Till and Mamie Till-Mobley Institute, I met Texas Congressman Al Green, who's been fighting racism since before I was born. After the film, I offered him the chance to speak, but he declined. When was the last time you saw a politician say no to a microphone? Instead, he said, "I'm so moved, my brother. I'm going to do everything in my power to help you."

Right there, he took out his phone and called his chief of staff. "I know you're on vacation and I'm sorry to bother you, but this is very important," he said. "We've got to get the DOJ to do something about Tulsa. These women are 110 years old." In that moment, I saw what public service could be. Representative Green has been on our team ever since.

But amid all the excitement, there was one sobering moment. I was at a reception at a high-end hotel called theWit when I saw the high-level Democratic operative who made it possible for us to collaborate with the Emmett Till and Mamie Till-Mobley Institute and hold the screening. He looked me in the eye and said, "As much as I am working to make it happen, this country is not going to elect a Black woman."

Deep down, I knew he was probably right and his words stayed with me all summer and into the fall.

In September, Jana's email hit my phone: "The Court denied rehearing today. Edmondson dissented. Darby didn't vote for whatever reason."

That was it. The door had slammed shut. I wasn't surprised, but the decision still landed like a slap in the face. By September 11, the ruling was public, splashed across headlines. Everywhere I went, people pulled me aside, offering condolences and thanking me for my "service." It was kind, even uplifting, but it felt like people were eulogizing the fight. I knew better. We weren't done yet.

A few weeks later, I was proved right. I was in my home office when the phone buzzed with a call from a trusted national journalist. I answered, knowing it couldn't be bad news, because I wasn't away on vacation with my phone turned off, trying to enjoy myself. The caller lowered his voice and said, "You can't tell nobody, but the DOJ is going to open an investigation into the Massacre. I just found out."

I screamed so loud that if Mia had been home, I would've given her a heart attack. I jumped up and ran around the house like an athlete who had just won an Olympic gold medal, pumping my fists. After years of having doors slammed in my face, filing motions and getting denials, and being told that nothing could be done, finally, the federal government was about to take Greenwood seriously!

Trouble was, I had no one to share this moment with! I called Mia, my voice cracking, barely able to get the words out. Then I called Tyrone. (So much for "You can't tell nobody.") Each time I repeated the news—"The DOJ is opening an investigation!"—it felt more real. For the last two years, I had fought this fight on fumes, suspending disbelief just to get out of bed some days. Now disbelief gave way to joy.

The following Monday, Barbara Bosserman called and got right to the point. "The department will not be conducting an investigation," she said. "We will do a 'review and evaluation.'" She explained that the DOJ would make the public announcement later that day and planned to have their work completed by the end of 2024.[8]

My exultation evaporated. It felt like this was political theater designed to give the Biden administration street cred with Black voters going into the election. The end of 2024 deadline alone told me that. No real investigation has a predetermined endpoint. True federal investigations can take years, and they conclude when everyone has been interviewed, all the evidence has been reviewed, and the prosecutor or grand jury decides if an indictment should be issued. But that wasn't going to happen.

I held another press conference in the Survivors Room at the GCC. The lights glared, cameras clicked into focus, and reporters craned forward with notebooks open. "Chief, Tiffany, LaDonna, Muriel—come stand with me." They joined me at the podium. Beside me were descendants, caretakers, leaders—living links to Greenwood's past and future.

"Good afternoon. I am Attorney Damario Solomon-Simmons, and I have the great honor of representing this community of Tulsa, which suffered through the 1921 Race Massacre. Today, I bring news. This morning, Assistant Attorney General for Civil Rights Kristen Clarke announced that the United States Department of Justice will, for the first time, open a review and evaluation of the Tulsa Race Massacre under the Emmett Till Unsolved Civil Rights Crime Act—the Cold Case Act."

Everyone absorbed it. Then came the explosion of applause. Spectators hugged and lifted their hands to heaven. "One hundred and three years later," I said, leaning into the mic, "the federal government finally knocks on Tulsa's door."

I named those who had helped make this day possible: my mentor Bryan Stevenson and the Equal Justice Initiative, Damon Hewitt and the Lawyers' Committee for Civil Rights Under Law. Angela Rye, Tiffany Cross, Roland Martin, and Karen Hunter. The Raben Group, Human Rights Watch, and Rashad Robinson of Color of Change. Our allies in Congress—Representative Maxine Waters, the late Sheila Jackson Lee, the late John Conyers, Representative Hank Johnson of Georgia, and Congressman Al Green of Texas, who was with us on the phone.

Congressman Green's voice filled the room. "This was a criminal abomination," he said. "It left people homeless, penniless, and remediless. And let us be clear: had this been done to white Americans, the courts would have awarded compensatory and punitive damages. Black victims deserve no less." Applause and murmurs of "Amen."

I returned to the podium. "This moment did not fall from the sky. It came because we never stopped asking, never stopped pushing, never stopped demanding." I looked out over the faces in that room—descendants, activists, neighbors, students—and felt the atmosphere thicken into something more than hope. It was resolve.

I raised my voice. "When we fight—"

They shook the walls. "We win!"[9]

About two weeks later, we hosted Barbara Bosserman and Walter Henry in Tulsa for meetings with Mother Randle, descendants, and members of the community, a tour of important Massacre-related sites, and information gathering. They interviewed LaDonna Penny, Mother Randle's granddaughter, who told them about the trauma and fear her grandmother still experienced about events that took place more than a century earlier, and how she finally convinced Mother Randle to share her story in 2019.

They interviewed Michael Penny, grandson of Massacre survivor Jurel O. Penny, a World War I veteran who went to the courthouse on

May 31, 1921, to help defend Dick Rowland from the white mob. He spoke about how his grandfather was detained by the Oklahoma National Guard, leading to a long discussion about the Guard's role in the Massacre. He shared the words of his grandmother, who said, "Greenwood was heaven. You didn't have to deal with Jim Crow. You could be a person."

Via Zoom and in person, they interviewed Dr. Vivian Clark-Adams, attorney Jim Lloyd, and Professor Jimmie White, who had all served on the Oklahoma Commission to Study the Tulsa Race Riot of 1921 and helped write the seminal 2001 report. They spoke about being warned to stay away from the issue of the Massacre being a conspiracy to steal land, and about receiving death threats—including a phone call historian Eddie Faye Gates received where the caller said, "If you want to find the bodies, look under the Sears parking lot and under the overpass of I-244 and Denver." They spoke about the efforts to stop the search for the bodies of Massacre victims, and Jim talked about his yearslong effort to locate the "disappeared" records of the 198 original lawsuits filed by B. C. Franklin.

Following the interviews, Representative Green joined us, and we took the DOJ officials to meet Chief Amusan, who led them on a walking tour of Greenwood and shared some of its history. We visited Paradise Baptist Church, one of only thirteen remaining pre-Massacre entities, whose four walls are covered with giant panoramic photos of the aftermath of the Massacre, showing the scale of the destruction and the meager housing the survivors had to make do with. We went to the city-owned Oaklawn Cemetery, where unmarked graves of Massacre murder victims had been found—a solemn end to the day.

But right before the interviews started, Barbara took me aside and said, "The Department of Justice will not have subpoena power as part of this review." This left me stunned, thinking, *This is some B.S.* No subpoena power meant this was nothing more than a fact-finding excursion with no teeth. Without subpoena power, the DOJ could not compel witnesses to appear and testify or compel the production of documents by the City of Tulsa or any other entity. What were they planning to do, ask nicely?

On the second day, Barbara and Walter found out just how pissed the people of Greenwood really were about this. They met with several more descendants, who told them how disappointed they were about the lack of subpoena power and made it clear what the descendant community wanted: a true investigation and prosecution of the responsible parties. What we got were a few interviews and a promise that we would receive the DOJ's comprehensive report by the end of 2024.

After the officials went back to D.C., my team sent them a letter on behalf of the survivors, descendants, and everyone involved in the fight for Justice for Greenwood:

> Although our Clients appreciate the Department's visit to Tulsa, they were discouraged after hearing that the Department would not use its subpoena power to obtain documents from key entities or individuals, failed to transcribe or record witness interviews to establish a more certain record, and ignored information pertaining to recently discovered mass grave sites which house the desecrated remains of Massacre victims. . . . Our Clients believe that they were used in a box-checking exercise, which not only discredits their pain, but once again heightens their disbelief in the power of the American justice system to do right by its Black citizens. Our Clients want to know: Is this the America this Department of Justice wants?[10]

We did not receive a reply.

PART FIVE

WILLFUL RESILIENCE

We do more than face disappointments and setbacks with a brave face. Willful Resilience brings together strength, intelligence, faith, and unity to not only withstand hardship but maintain hope and come out swinging on a new day. Communities that seek justice will face resistance, and they must become stronger, smarter, and more united after each challenge.

Throughout our fight, we demonstrated this principle through coalition building, accumulating sustainable community power for long-term victory, exploring new ways to obtain justice, and never, ever giving up.

We could see what they were doing. They took everything they thought was valuable. They smashed everything they couldn't take. My mother had [opera singer Enrico] Caruso records she loved. They smashed the Caruso records.*

—Dr. Olivia Hooker, to *The Washington Post*

Mount Zion Baptist Church burns as witnesses watch from Elgin Avenue. The original photograph is in the Department of Special Collections, McFarlin Library, the University of Tulsa.

CHAPTER 13

GREENWOOD IS STILL BURNING

Injustice plus time does not equal justice.

—*REVEREND MARLIN LAVANHAR*

On the morning of November 5, Mia and I drove to my church, one of the thirteen surviving institutions from the Tulsa Massacre, now serving as a polling site. We pulled up around 6:30 A.M., thirty minutes before the polls opened, and there were already at least one hundred people in line. As we parked and joined the crowd, we spotted dozens of familiar faces—friends, family, clients, community members. Everyone carried the same expression: hopeful but nervous, and if they were being completely honest, probably scared of what might happen, just like Mia and I were.

After casting my ballot, I went to my home office and buried myself in work, trying to keep my mind off what was coming. When night fell and the polls started closing, Mia and I withdrew to different spaces. She went into the bedroom, deliberately avoiding the news broadcasts, asking me just to tell her when Kamala had won. I stayed in the living room, locked onto the television, unable to look away as Trump won state after state. When Wisconsin fell, I turned the TV off and sat in the silent house, wondering what had gone wrong.

I knew what the election of Trump meant. I knew what was coming. I had been talking with Mia about it for months, saying that we should be thinking about moving out of Oklahoma. I knew that if the American people elected an open white supremacist after knowing exactly who and what he was, not only would no place be truly safe for Black people, but Oklahoma would be one of the worst places to be.

I couldn't stop myself from imagining catastrophe. What would Trump mean for North Tulsa? Would he encourage and even fund white gentrification of Greenwood out of spite? I had given everything I had to fight for Tulsa. Would a newly empowered Proud Boys force me to leave for my own safety? Nothing seemed too extreme at that moment.

I went into the bedroom, heart pounding, almost frantic, words spilling out before I could catch them. "Mia, we can't stay here. I'm serious this time."

Softly, she said, "Damario." She was waiting for me to calm down. But I couldn't.

"Mia, Trump carried all seventy-seven counties in Oklahoma. All. Seventy. Seven." I spit the words out like poison. "MAGA controls the statehouse, the senate, the governor's office, the whole federal delegation. They've tried to ban the teaching of Black history that makes white children uncomfortable. The education secretary stood up and said the Massacre wasn't even about race. If that's what they'll do under Biden, imagine what they'll do under Trump!"

I had already taken steps. I bought a couple more guns. Upgraded our security system. Put cameras everywhere. But even as I did those things, I knew it might not make any difference if MAGA decided it wanted to carry out a sequel to the Massacre. "If we stay," I told her, "I don't know if I can keep you safe."

She just looked at me, her face filled with concern. Then she got up off the bed and silently hugged me. In saying that out loud, especially to Mia, I felt the shame of thinking about abandoning my family and friends in Tulsa. This was my home. I wasn't going anywhere, and neither was she.

When I found the strength to check my phone, I saw that former Oklahoma State Representative Monroe Nichols, whom I had supported for years and who had stood with us after the supreme court oral argument, was winning his bid to be the first Black mayor of Tulsa. I tried to be happy about that. Monroe's campaign was having a watch party at the Greenwood Cultural Center, and I had planned to go up there, but as the national election results were coming in, I was just getting more down.

But once Monroe won, I knew I had to go to the GCC and pay my respects.

When I walked in the door, what a difference! I had felt like the world was ending, but at the GCC the mood was festive. Music was playing and there were balloons everywhere. The crowd was diverse—men and women, Black and white, all different ages—and everybody was pumped. Just what you want in your community. I put on a brave face, told our mayor-elect, "Congratulations, Mr. Mayor," and stayed for an hour. Then I went home and crawled into bed for two days with a headache, body aches, fatigue, and fever.

In law school, one of the things that they tell you is not to take outcomes personally. So after a couple of days of feeling sorry for myself, I did the only thing I could do: I went back to work. For years, I had been thinking about a reparations framework called Project Greenwood, which was the basis for our public nuisance abatement plan. I decided this was the time to fully develop it as a stand-alone initiative. What else could I do? The courts, Congress, and the Department of Justice failed us. It was time to consider a new strategy. But first, I went to a birthday party.

Five days after the election, the daylight streamed into Fixins Soul Kitchen, casting a glow on a room filled with love and reverence. Family, friends, and community leaders gathered to celebrate Mother Lessie Benningfield Randle's 110th birthday. Platters of fried chicken, collard greens, cornbread, and peach cobbler lined the tables, while vases of lilies and hydrangeas brightened every corner. It felt less like a restaurant and more like a family kitchen.

I reminded the crowd of the extraordinary history in the room. "I have the great pleasure to be the attorney for Mother Randle, who—while we're all here today—turned 110 years old. For all of you, she is your mother, your grandmother, your auntie, your cousin, your friend. To be in her presence is a blessing, almost like standing in the presence of God. Think about this: she was born in 1914. And here she sits with us, vibrant and strong. This is not just a family celebration. It is a historic occasion for Tulsa and for the entire nation." The applause that followed was punctuated by music and laughter as rich as the food on the tables.

Representative Al Green presented Mother Randle with a flag that had flown over the U.S. Capitol to commemorate her life and legacy. "As one of the last living survivors of the 1921 Tulsa Race Massacre, your courage and resilience serve as a testament to our collective history," Representative Green told Mother Randle. "I would say you are 110 years young, because we are looking forward to having you for at least 110 more years."[1]

Since the Democratic National Convention, Representative Green and I had been working quietly on a reparations bill, but we agreed that the birthday would not be the time to unveil it. But as he looked into Mother Randle's eyes, the plan changed. Overcome by the moment, to my complete surprise he said, "Mother Randle, I am going to introduce legislation on the floor of the House seeking twenty million dollars for each of the living survivors of the Tulsa Race Massacre."

Later, he explained that being in Mother Randle's presence compelled him to act. He wanted her to hear the promise with her own ears, and he hoped declaring it publicly might inspire others—especially Tulsa's Mayor-elect Monroe Nichols, who was seated nearby. I leaned over to Monroe and said, "Hey, man, we need to do something. She's 110 years old." He looked at me and promised that he would, and that he would do it quickly.

As the room erupted in applause, I looked back at Mother Randle—her red and black jacket gleaming in the sunlight, her smile serene and unshakable. I knew she wouldn't speak, but she didn't have to. Her expression of pride and peace said it all. This was more than a birthday party. It was a convergence of joy, justice, and history.

But even as the applause rang out, my thoughts turned to the world outside. It was a day for joy, and the joy was real. But I knew coming to justice would be harder than ever in a nation that had just chosen Donald Trump to be its president for a second time. That's the rhythm of this struggle: We celebrate and we resist, sometimes in the same breath.

Monroe's election gave me hope that we would be able to do something for the survivors and descendants, even if not on the same scale as we could have done had we won our lawsuit. Tulsa had never had a Black mayor, and one of the reasons I and others in the Black community had supported his candidacy with such passion was because we believed if he got into power, he would take swift action on reparations. He wouldn't behave like every other Democratic politician, who said the right things about equity and justice before votes were cast but offered nothing but empty words after being elected. We wanted a Democratic leader who would wield power and take care of his base—like a Republican.

Monroe was set to be inaugurated on December 2, so I had a meeting with him shortly before to talk about reparations and what we hoped he would do. He gave me his word again and said, "I will get this done."

I went to his inauguration and the next day flew to D.C. to meet with Linda Wilson, executive director of Fund II Foundation, the charitable organization founded by the third-wealthiest Black man in America, Robert Smith. After the state supreme court dismissed our suit, Smith posted on LinkedIn how he'd been personally impacted by the dismissal because his family was from Oklahoma, and they had to leave because of the Massacre. "Members of my family left Oklahoma for Denver after the attacks, so this event is deeply personal for me," he wrote. "The decision by the Court stands as a stark reminder of the ongoing struggle for #justice and recognition faced by Black communities in the U.S."[2] I had never heard the story about Smith's family before, but Linda and I laid the groundwork for a good relationship between our organizations.

Naturally, while I was in D.C. I took the opportunity to meet with the DOJ one more time. I reminded them that on January 20 at noon, their department would cease to exist. Anticipating a Trump purge, people were resigning and looking for new jobs. What was the timing for their report? All I got was, "We are still working on it." I tell you, if I had any hair, I would've torn it out by the roots a long time ago.

I sent a letter to Mayor Nichols formally requesting that he work aggressively to make reparatory justice a top priority for his administration.[3] In it, I also laid out the Project Greenwood framework for a comprehensive reparations program, some of which I knew the mayor had the power to do with a series of executive orders:

1. **Victims' Compensation Fund.** Financial restitution would be provided to the last living survivors. Compensation would also extend to descendants of victims such as physician A. C. Jackson and World War I veteran C. L. Daniel, who were murdered by the mob.
2. **Descendant Business Support Program.** This program would provide business resources to Massacre descendants.
3. **Descendant Scholarship Program.** Verified descendants residing in Oklahoma would be eligible for dedicated scholarships to pursue higher education opportunities.
4. **Surviving Entity Grant Program.** The twelve churches that survived the Massacre would receive grants to help them continue their vital service to the Greenwood community.
5. **Descendant Employment Preference Program.** Qualified descendants would receive preferential employment consideration for City of Tulsa jobs.
6. **Descendant Contracting Preference Program.** The city would establish a program granting Massacre descendants preferential status in bidding on city contracts.
7. **Immunity from City Taxes, Fees, Assessments, and Utility Expenses.** Survivors and descendants have paid millions in taxes and city fees, despite Tulsa's role in the Massacre. They

would receive exemptions from these payments for a defined period.

8. **Audit of City-Owned Land in Greenwood.** The city would audit its landholdings in the Historic Greenwood District to determine if they were unlawfully acquired.
9. **Return of Land.** Following the land audit, any property acquired by the city due to the Massacre would be returned to the original families or, if infeasible, those families would be compensated for the land at fair market value.
10. **Build Level 1 Trauma Center Hospital.** A Level 1 trauma center and urgent care facility, named after Dr. A. C. Jackson, would be established in North Tulsa.
11. **Official Holiday on June 1.** To ensure the history of the Massacre is preserved and the violence never repeated, the city would establish June 1 as an official holiday.
12. **Release of Hidden Records.** Thousands of Massacre-related documents currently withheld by the city would be released to the public.

It wasn't everything we were owed, but if we could get even some of Project Greenwood enacted, it would still be a historic win. I even offered to draft all the documents for Mayor Nichols—executive orders, a public presentation, press releases, legal documents, the public trust, you name it—to make following through as turnkey as possible.

On December 11, I explained to the mayor that Project Greenwood's harm-based eligibility framework is designed to withstand legal challenges—essential in the anti-Black MAGA 2.0 era. By attaching reparative benefits to the harm of the Massacre, not the race of the victims, Project Greenwood aligns with the Supreme Court's Fourteenth Amendment equal protection interpretation standards and precedents, which require narrowly tailored remedies. It also sidesteps Oklahoma's bans on race-based preferences. In a time when race-conscious policies are under assault, this harm-centric model is the way forward.

I assured the mayor that implementing Project Greenwood would bring conciliation and healing throughout Tulsa. He was supportive. "I want you to go through everything we've discussed here with my team. We'll meet again on December twentieth and let you know that day what we're going to do."

Mia was asking me to take the holidays off, but by now you know I didn't. Instead, my team and I prepared a presentation on Project Greenwood. Eric Miller flew in from L.A., and Jana Knott came in from Oklahoma City. We created everything Mayor Nichols would need to implement Project Greenwood. All he would have to do to grant historic reparations would be to sign his name a few times.

On December 20, we met with Mayor Nichols; his future deputy mayor, Krystal Reyes; his communications director, Michelle Brooks; and his government affairs director, Shane Stone. We made our presentation. Mayor Nichols listened carefully and said, "This is very impressive. Some of this stuff I know we can get done. I will let you know by next Friday [December 27] what we'll do. Give me a week."

Now my radar was pinging. This was unnervingly familiar language. Mayor-elect Nichols had told me back in November that he was going to take care of the survivors immediately. Now he was Mayor Nichols, and we were talking about December 27. I could hear the unmistakable sound of a can being kicked down the road.

Damn.

I was supposed to be enjoying Christmas. SolomonSimmonsLaw was closed. Justice for Greenwood was closed. But instead of enjoying the holiday, all I was thinking about was how I could get the mayor to commit to Project Greenwood. Meanwhile, the DOJ had told me they would issue their report before the end of the year, but they hadn't. I spent that holiday preoccupied and irritable. I was afraid that once again, the people and entities we were counting on to do the right thing were going to let us down, as they had so many times before.

December 27 came. Nothing from the mayor or the DOJ. New Year's came and went. Finally, on the evening of January 8, I received a text from Kristen Clarke. She informed me that the report was almost complete, and that she was coming to Tulsa on Friday, January 10, to discuss it in a community meeting. But first, Kristen said, "I want to meet with Mother Randle and Mother Fletcher to present the report to them personally."

We did not want her meeting with our clients without knowing in advance what the report said. Mother Randle and Mother Fletcher were 110 years old. It was January. The weather was freezing. Their caregivers would have to spend hours getting them ready to go into the harsh winter during cold and flu season, and for what? Not to mention, I already had oral arguments scheduled for Friday, January 10, in Oklahoma City. So, when the DOJ declined our request to provide us with a copy of the report to review, we declined the meeting.

But the folks at the DOJ kept pushing, and it seemed to us like the real motivation was securing positive PR and a photo op with the survivors. After several more tense communications, they finally agreed to reschedule their community meeting for Saturday, January 11. But we weren't done. "Kristen, we need to review the report before I, my team, or the survivors and their families will agree to participate."

They refused to provide us with an advance copy.

On January 10, the DOJ released the report to the news media under embargo (meaning the press couldn't release it to the public until the department gave the green light). I only found out because a local reporter I knew texted me asking, "Do you want to comment on the report?"

"I haven't seen it yet," I texted back.

"I'll send it over, but don't tell anyone." Moments later, the document was in my inbox.

Seeing the report, I felt immensely proud. We had pushed for four years to persuade the federal government to get involved, and now we had something to show for all that work. It was extremely well written and well researched. But the more I read, the more I realized it contained mostly information we already knew.

Then I read the part of the report where the DOJ actually *harmed* our cause. The department had found that prosecution for the Massacre was a practical impossibility because the perpetrators were all deceased and the relevant laws had not existed in 1921. We disagreed with that finding, because all the governmental entities that had perpetrated the Massacre were still "alive," but it was a valid part of the criminal analysis under the stated scope of their "review and evaluation." But when they made the unbelievable claim that the City of Tulsa was not legally responsible for the Massacre and no civil liability could have existed, they went way outside their lane.

Calling their logic tortured was too kind. According to the DOJ, the United States Supreme Court had held that a local government can only be held liable for constitutional violations when an injury is a direct consequence of the execution of that government's policies. So, because the City of Tulsa had not passed laws or publicly adopted policies authorizing the Massacre, and because there was no evidence that city officials had planned the Massacre in advance, the City of Tulsa was absolved of liability.

Apparently, the fact that the Tulsa Police Department (a city entity) deputized and armed white men on May 31, 1921, empowering them to commit mayhem and violence with impunity, didn't matter. By publishing a civil finding that was outside their scope of work, the DOJ had sabotaged us. In all my years of working on Massacre reparations and reviewing the work of courts, attorneys, and commissions, no one (apart from the biased reports published by the perpetrators immediately following the Massacre) had ever suggested that the City of Tulsa was not responsible! Now the U.S. Department of Justice had. I knew this would be used against us.

When my team read the report, they were as furious as I was. Immediately, we demanded that the DOJ amend its report. We finally arranged a Zoom call, but now some DOJ personnel were flippant, even arrogant. At one point, one of their lawyers said, "If you just read it carefully—" and I could see half my team's eyes bulge and faces contort. It took all my restraint not to shout, "We've been reading this shit for more than twenty years! That's why we know you're wrong! We know this better than you do!"

To her credit, Kristen calmed things down and said she would have her team carefully consider our concerns. The next day, they came down to Tulsa and held their community meeting, but just a handful of people showed up. The survivors weren't there. Justice for Greenwood wasn't there. The entire community was angry that Biden's DOJ had refused to hold the entities responsible for the Massacre accountable.

I issued a public statement: "President Biden and his DOJ have now joined the Tulsa County Court System, the Oklahoma Supreme Court, the Oklahoma State Legislature, the United States Supreme Court, and the United States Congress in failing the survivors and descendants of the Massacre over the last 103 years. Our last best hope is that the City of Tulsa will fulfill its promise to repair the harm it caused."[4]

To Kristen and her team's credit, on January 17, the DOJ issued an amended report that corrected the record.[5]

After Trump's inauguration, the mayor gave an interview to a Black journalist from *The Washington Post,* Karen Attiah (who was subsequently fired in 2025 for writing the wrong thing about the killing of activist Charlie Kirk), and proved our concerns about the original DOJ report justified. "I currently have a tort claim on behalf of survivors on my desk," he said, "and, frankly, the federal government makes it really hard for me to settle that court claim, because the federal government has said the city of Tulsa is blameless."[6]

Now I was worried. We wanted the mayor to use the power vested in him to immediately take tangible actions that, while they might burn some of his political capital, would materially improve the lives of the Greenwood descendants. We began to exert what pressure we could to compel him to act.

Project Greenwood had its soft public launch on February 1, the first day of Black History Month, at the first-ever State of Black Tulsa Summit, where people from all over the city came together to learn about how we could rebuild North Tulsa. The next week, I held a big press conference where I introduced the Project Greenwood framework to the nation. Mayor Nichols issued a statement in which he publicly blessed Project Greenwood:

> Project Greenwood reflects the unshakable resolve of the last living massacre survivors and descendants to address the generational impact of Greenwood's destruction and move Tulsa forward. I look forward to implementing significant elements of the plan in partnership with Justice for Greenwood and other stakeholders. In the coming weeks, I will share the framework my Administration will use to heal the open wounds left by the Massacre and create a stronger, more unified Tulsa for all.[7]

I suggested to the mayor that Black History Month would be the perfect time to make a big reparations announcement. I knew we were pushing him hard (maybe too hard), but no matter what I did, I could not get him to act. I was becoming concerned that he was getting cold feet because of pushback from Tulsa's white power structure.

It was time to sit down and talk with the mayor. Angela Rye, Linda Wilson, and I met with him at his office in city hall to push for swift action. He reiterated that he supported Project Greenwood and would do something for the survivors as quickly as he could. "I can do the small business support, the scholarships, the grant program for surviving churches, and the city contracts," he said. "I'll release the records and establish the June 1 memorial holiday." He could do most of that simply by signing an executive order.

We again pushed him to meet every Project Greenwood demand, and to do it during Black History Month. But he pushed back. "I can do the holiday in February," he said, "but the rest will have to be announced in March." Black History Month came to a close with no announcement from the city.

By March 8, my team and the survivors were getting restless and worried. Even Mother Randle and Mother Fletcher, who had mostly gone back to their quiet lives since the end of our court case, were concerned. We had all seen this movie before, but there were limits to what we could do. Monroe was a friend, and I had supported him in every way I could, but now that he was mayor, many Black voters had adopted a "hands off the mayor" policy. It reminded me of when Barack Obama had been elected president. Many in the Black community were so grateful just to have him in office that they were uncomfortable making demands, holding him accountable for his promises, or God forbid, criticizing him. I saw the same thing happening with Mayor Nichols.

On March 9, I sent him a text: "I have a client meeting coming up and my people are frustrated and pressing me hard for answers."

He replied, "Frustrated? With me? I get they are frustrated. I've only been in the office less than a hundred days. It's been 104 years. I'm working on this as hard as I can." He then told me there would be an announcement on March 16, but he didn't tell me what it was.

On March 16, Mayor Nichols announced that he was accepting Project Greenwood's recommendation to make June 1 an official city holiday.[8] I was excited to see a dream I had first put into writing more than twenty years earlier as a law student come to fruition. I also believed that a holiday, in conjunction with other substantive reparations, was important to ensure that the Massacre and its impact were never erased from history again.

However, I had hoped for more. In making the announcement, the mayor also said that on April 6 at Morning Star Baptist Church (another surviving church supported by Justice for Greenwood) in North Tulsa, he would hold an event where he would throw his support behind a "complete framework and path forward" for addressing the Massacre.

We prepared for the April 6 event, letting the community know about it and inviting them to join us there. Then, abruptly, on April 3, the event was canceled. June 1, the 104th anniversary of the Massacre, was the new date. I was beginning to feel like Charlie Brown trying to kick the football, only to have Lucy pull it away again and again. To us and everyone who had put their faith in us, Greenwood was indeed still burning, but true justice seemed very far away.

It looked like the world was on fire.*

—Alice Andrews, Massacre survivor and pianist,
as told to Eddie Faye Gates

A group of men attend the State Funeral Directors and Embalmers Meeting held in Tulsa. They were photographed in front of the Jackson Funeral Home on East Archer Street in the Greenwood District. Collection of the Smithsonian National Museum of African American History and Culture, Gift of Princetta R. Newman.

CHAPTER 14

WHEN WE FIGHT, WE WIN

By now, you might have noticed that I'm intense, even obsessive, about the things I care about. (Folks who know me are rolling their eyes and saying, "Really, Damario? Tell us more.") But I'll tell you something: Fighting wears on you. It grinds you down in ways that are hard to describe. Waking up each morning with the weight of history on your chest, carrying the pain of your people in your bones, and bracing yourself to go another round with systems built to outlast you—it takes a toll on body, mind, and spirit. It's not healthy to live with your fists clenched.

After years of doing exactly that, I was drained. It was getting harder to bench-press that disbelief over my head. The oppressive knowledge that MAGA was now in control of the country made it even worse. Yes, we had a few small victories we could point to, like the DOJ report, but they weren't enough considering the price so many of us had paid in sweat, lost time with our families, stress-related health issues, and more. The community needed a win, something to show us that the fight hadn't been in vain. We needed a decisive breakthrough.

Then, against all odds, we got one.

I won't lie to you. When Mayor Nichols canceled his April 6 announcement and pushed it back to June 1, I was furious. I felt betrayed. After all these years, I knew the telltale signs: vague promises, calls for patience, endless excuses. But it was worse for the delay to be coming from our first Black mayor, a man I had supported, donated to, and endorsed, and whose win I had celebrated. It never left my mind that I had two 110-year-old survivors waiting for *someone* to stand up and take responsibility for the horror and loss they had experienced.

But I had to be cautious. By becoming the first Black man to win his office, Mayor Nichols had also become royalty to a lot of people in the Black community. During his first months in office, every time he walked into a room full of Black folks, he got a standing ovation. Also, Monroe was raised by a powerful, brilliant Black woman whom I respect, an educator who has worked for the cause of equity and justice for decades. He's a brother for real. Lastly, for him to make history and become mayor by beating a popular sitting white county commissioner and local news anchor was a testament to his political acumen and strong community relationships. I had to give him space and be careful how I publicly engaged him.

But I was tired of waiting. I'd spent most of the last five years waiting for a court, Congress, or the DOJ to do *something* transformative. The longer I held off with the mayor, the more uneasy I felt. Also, I had vouched for Monroe—not just to the community and the descendants but also to influential leaders in my network like Roland Martin, Ariel Investments founder John Rogers, and Angela Rye. I had told them, "We can trust this guy. He's going to do what he says." Every day without visible progress left me exposed and second-guessing whether I'd spoken too soon. By April 2025, I felt like I had no choice but to push the mayor to act, respectfully but publicly.

I told nearly everyone I met, "Contact the mayor. Here's his official email." I took my pressure campaign to Los Angeles for screenings of *Greenwood Is Still Burning* at Loyola Law School and then with the NAACP's Hollywood chapter. I went to New York to speak at an event that Lush Cosmetics organized called the Resist Ball, which celebrated the company donating $100 million to grassroots causes. On the panel, I talked about Project Greenwood. I talked about resilience. I talked about the survivors. I pushed hard but in a way that I believed would not be interpreted as unreasonable.

Not surprisingly, Mia, always levelheaded, spoke up with sage advice. "Let him do whatever he is going to do," she said to me at home one evening. "You've done everything you could possibly do. You've presented Project Greenwood to him and got his public endorsement. You've got to relax. I cannot have you dying over this. You remember last year, when you went to the hospital with a heart event? You got to chill out. You can't make him do anything, and you do not want to destroy your relationship with him trying."

Tyrone said the same thing. Of course, they were right. Mayor Nichols was our first real ally to be elected mayor, and I believed that he wanted to do right by the survivors and the community. But he was also a newly elected leader and a politician. If I was perceived to push him "too hard," I risked alienating him and many of our mutual supporters. Also, I wasn't well. I was grinding my teeth in my sleep. I'd developed hemorrhoids. The delay seemed to be literally eating away at me.

My inner linebacker did not want to back off, but for all the reasons my wife gave me, I did. The experience reinforced that professionalism—and the duty of representing others—isn't about my comfort, it's about doing what it takes to win. I had to work hard to find a balance, because even though I consider Monroe Nichols a friend, *Mayor* Nichols is a politician, and at the end of the day, politicians are conduits to distribute what my friend SiriusXM host Karen Hunter calls "rights and resources." Politics is about who gets what, and when, where, and how they get it. That doesn't mean I don't like politicians, but at the end of the day, they're like the media: a tool I can use to accomplish my justice goals.

The day after the Lush event in New York, I was back in Tulsa for a panel featuring my friend Tamika Mallory, a bestselling author and one of the sharpest, most fearless voices in racial justice. But my day had already gone sideways. My flight from New York was delayed, I missed my connection, and in the scramble to deplane, grab my carry-on, and rush to the gate, I lost my phone. By the time I slipped into All Souls Unitarian Church and slid into my chair onstage, with Tamika and Dr. Tiffany Crutcher between me and Mayor Nichols, I was disheveled, sweaty, and grumpy.

But my mind wasn't on the panel. It was on a meeting I'd had with Mayor Nichols a couple of weeks earlier concerning the Black Creeks, with my clients present. The mayor was working on a policing agreement with the Muscogee (Creek) Nation, and I asked him to tell the Creek Nation that he wouldn't work with them until they stopped discriminating and restored the citizenship they had unlawfully stripped from my clients and thousands of other Black Creeks.

"I can't do that," he stated. That refusal stuck with me like a stone in my shoe, and now here we were on the same stage, separated by two powerful Black women but connected by unfinished business.

Also, I didn't know what was going to happen on June 1—or if anything was going to happen at all. Every smile I offered the audience felt heavy, every nod rehearsed. I had to sit within eyesight of the mayor, trying to look cool while inside I wanted to shout, "WTF, man? What's taking so long? Mother Fletcher turns 111 tomorrow. What are you waiting on?"

Tamika spoke with her usual fire. Then Mayor Nichols leaned into his mic and said something about speaking up for the downtrodden, even when it's not popular. My head almost exploded.

I spoke next. "We need politicians to actually do what they say they're going to do." Everyone in the room seemed to gasp at the same time. I could almost hear them thinking, *Is Damario going to do it? Is he going to call the mayor out?* Part of me wanted to go further and tell Mayor Nichols exactly what was on my mind. But then I saw his mother sitting in the front row. It's one thing to call out white officials who have spent decades blocking justice. But this was our new Black mayor, and his mama, a woman I respect immensely, was right there. As I met her gaze, I steadied. Things shifted.

Who was I mad at? It wasn't Mayor Nichols. It was *inaction and delays*. People with power had fed us a diet of excuses and roadblocks for two decades. I was starved for action by those in power, and the mayor had the power to act. Truthfully, I didn't just want action for the survivors and the descendants; I wanted it for myself. This fight had defined much of my adult life, and I did not know how much longer I could continue it without some kind of transformative result. Kamala said, "When we fight, we win." Well, we had been fighting for more than twenty years. Where was our win?

All that went through my head in a split second, and I knew I had to make a choice. I could make this all about me and my need to win. I could rip the scab off in front of the audience, name a long train of complaints, and leave everyone bloody. But this wasn't about me. My duty was to protect the fragile seed of hope that still waits inside our people. The moment didn't call for spectacle and ego. It called for humanity. That's what I chose . . . barely.

"That's why we're happy and blessed to have Mayor Nichols," I continued, "somebody we know will stand up for us." I felt the tension in the room drain like water from a bathtub, and the audience broke into applause. I had saved the moment; my Justice for Greenwood people told me the same afterward. But inside, I knew this was a temporary peace. My patience was wearing thin, and I didn't know how much longer I could hold back.

The next day, we celebrated Mother Fletcher's 111th birthday at Fixins. It was a beautiful, sunny Saturday afternoon, and the restaurant was packed and buzzing with joy because she was in the building. Mother Fletcher spent the day greeting people, taking pictures, laughing, and eating like she had no plans of slowing down. I watched her enjoy chicken wings, catfish nuggets, collard greens, mac and cheese, and—true to form—two slices of cake. That's a serious appetite for somebody 111 years old!

I presented her with a massive bouquet of flowers and led the whole restaurant in singing "Happy Birthday"—the Black version, of course. The place erupted in clapping and cheering when we finished, but Mother Fletcher grabbed my arm and said with a grin, "We forgot to say, 'and many more'!" Then, just as I was laughing, she looked at me and Tiffany Crutcher, seated next to me, and said matter-of-factly, "You know, I want to live at least five more years."

It was a moment full of love, joy, and living history. As he had for Mother Randle, Congressman Al Green presented Mother Fletcher with a U.S. flag that had flown over the nation's Capitol and promised again to introduce reparations legislation in their names. It was like a family reunion. But even amid the celebration, people kept pulling me aside with the same question: "What do you think the mayor's going to do?" Outwardly, I stayed cool, but inside I wanted to snap, "Why are you asking me? I don't know."

Two weeks later, JFG launched our second annual genealogy series, "The Story of Us: Connecting Generations"—part of a three-day gathering from May 29 to 31 to commemorate the 104th anniversary of the Massacre. Descendants and community members sat shoulder to shoulder with trained genealogists, tracing names, unearthing records, piecing together stories that stretched from the Massacre to the diaspora.

On May 31, our workshop became part of the Black Wall Street Legacy Festival, one of the most exciting, life-affirming events on the annual calendar. How can I describe it? Starting at sunrise, Greenwood was alive again! The day opened with the "Ride to Remember" at Oklahoma State University's Greenwood lot, with cyclists pedaling through history in honor of the lives and legacies torn apart in 1921. By midmorning, Fulton Street Books & Coffee was packed for the Black Wall Street Legacy Festival Summit, where voices rose in panels and conversations that demanded justice, including one on the DOJ report featuring my friend and partner Eric Miller.

By 5:00 P.M., Greenwood Avenue was a festival of color, music, food, and joy. Vendors lined the block, music poured from speakers, and the smell of barbecue wafted through the air. Families unfolded lawn chairs, kids climbed onto shoulders, and neighbors greeted neighbors with handshakes and hugs. Community love rippled through the crowd like an ocean current.

By 6:00 P.M., the Divine Nine Block Party had the lawn rocking with a DJ, and the crowd swelled to more than ten thousand people, everyone buzzing with energy, anticipation, and pride. Yes, that was roughly the same number of people who had once called those streets home. They had also communed outside, surrounded by the smells of cooking food and the warmth of their shared community. It was a beautiful but sobering moment.

More than a century earlier, this district had been built on community, enterprise, and love. Now that same spirit lived again as people shopped with Black vendors, supported local Black businesses, and created space for joy, justice, and remembrance all at once. That's what it means to ThinkGreenwood. To honor our ancestors through Community Love, to live with a Freedom Mind State and strive for Ownership, to concentrate our Education and Wealth, and to embody the Willful Resilience that has carried us this far. On that night, you could feel it all—the past and future, struggle and triumph—alive in the streets.

Before the headliner took the mic, I stepped onto the stage. This was my home, and these were my people, and I was ready! A roar surged from the crowd as I led them in my signature chant: "*Justice for Greenwood! Justice for Greenwood! Justice for Greenwood!*" The sound boomed down Greenwood Avenue, rattling my chest. I stood still for a moment, eyes closed, just letting it wash over me. Then I reminded them who I was—not just a lawyer or an activist but a son of Greenwood and North Tulsa. I laid out my bona fides, invoking the schools that raised me—Hawthorne, Carver Middle, and the great Booker T. Washington High. That mattered. I wanted the crowd to know I was theirs, that this fight was ours, and that the story of Greenwood was not just history—it was a living call to action.

"The very fact that we were gathered here, in these numbers, on this sacred ground, is proof that we are still here!" I said. "We're still fighting. Still building. Hold on and keep pressing, because Greenwood's story was never meant to end in tragedy. It was meant to bend toward justice!" The people went wild.

I ended the way I began, with thousands of voices chanting back at me: *"Justice for Greenwood! Justice for Greenwood!"* The sound shook the night, echoing down the block like a promise. Then the music came. Tobe Nwigwe lit up the stage, the bass pounding, people dancing under the stars. I partied and danced with them. The bass rattled my eardrums. It felt so good to let go and move with my people! But as I danced, I felt conflicted. Greenwood is a crime scene. It's sacred ground soaked in blood. Was this resilience, a way of honoring our ancestors who refused to be broken? Or was it irreverence, turning a burial ground into a dance floor?

W.E.B. Du Bois spoke of "twoness" for Black people—living as both Black and American. That night I felt my own twoness, the pull between joy and resilience and remembrance and sanctity. I couldn't resolve it. I just held both in my body, moving to the beat, lost in the sounds, the colors, the smells, and the fellowship.

Everywhere I turned, someone leaned in: "Do you know what's going to happen tomorrow? Do you know what the mayor is going to say?" I didn't, but I did know one thing. By tomorrow, the waiting would end—one way or another.

June 1. The Greenwood Cultural Center was filled to overflowing. The air buzzed with a sound I knew all too well: the rustle of dozens of audience conversations. Hundreds filled the hall—descendants in their Sunday best; community elders sitting proud with canes, walkers, or wheelchairs; supporters pressed shoulder to shoulder. Community booths lined the walls, including one for Justice for Greenwood. Reporters, city officials, business leaders, church groups—it felt like the whole community had turned out. This was the moment everyone had been waiting for: the mayor's long-awaited announcement on reparations.

I entered with my team—Mia at my side, Tyrone and Chris Harvey, my videographer, just behind—walking only a few steps in front of Mayor Nichols and his entourage. Almost immediately, I was pulled into hugs and photos. People whispered in my ear, "We're proud of you, Damario." One person squeezed my hand and said, "Your grandma Mama Brown is smiling down on you today." I carried those words with me to the stage.

Five chairs were set at the front for State Representative Ronald Stewart, State Senator Regina Goodwin, City Councilor Vanessa Hall-Harper, Michelle Burdex of the Greenwood Cultural Center, and me. When my turn came, I began steady, voice firm. "Family, let me be clear—this is not the end. This is only the beginning. Whatever the mayor says today, it is not the finish line. It is the starting point of the work we must do together."

I paused, scanning the rows of faces.

"We're going to have to support him. We're going to have to push with him. And we're going to have to hold him accountable. Because Greenwood's promise is bigger than one speech. It's bigger than politics. It's about justice. This community raised me, and that's why I fight. I fight because Greenwood still matters. I fight because our survivors and descendants are not relics of the past—they are living witnesses, and they deserve repair in their lifetimes."

The energy swelled as I leaned forward and called out:

"So let's say it together—Justice for Greenwood!"

The chant thundered back: *"Justice for Greenwood!"*

Again: "Justice for Greenwood!"

Again: *"Justice for Greenwood!"*

The assembly came to its feet as one, the sound rattling the walls, people clapping, shouting, and chanting in unison. It wasn't just a response—it was a promise.

As I stepped back, Reverend Jamaal Dyer leaned into the mic with a grin: "Damario got a little preacher in him." The room broke into laughter and applause, and the ovation only grew stronger. I stood there, taking it in, knowing in my bones what so many had told me was true: Mama Brown was smiling down. Next came the mayor:

> Imagine a city without the massacre. Imagine if Greenwood would have continued to thrive uninterrupted. Imagine what

> that would have meant for our economy. Imagine what it would have meant for outcomes for our children. Imagine what it would have meant for public safety. And most importantly, imagine the trust and faith we would have built in each other over these last 104 years.
>
> There is not one Tulsan, no matter their skin color, who wouldn't be better off today had the massacre not happened or if generations before us would have done the hard work to restore what was lost.
>
> Instead, the massacre was hidden from history books only to be followed by the intentional actions of redlining, a highway built to choke off economic vitality, and the perpetual underinvestment from local, state, and federal governments.
>
> Given all of this, our city remains resilient. Our community has been working to bind the wounds left open for ten decades. We've worked to recognize and remember, but now it's time to take the next big steps to restore.[1]

My heart leaped. It was one of the best speeches I have ever heard. Then the mayor unveiled his "Road to Repair" plan. At its center is a historic plan to raise $105 million by June 2026 to create the Greenwood Trust, a charitable trust that will distribute funds for various initiatives, including:

- $24 million to support housing and homeownership opportunities for descendants
- $60 million to be invested in cultural landmarks and businesses within the Greenwood District
- $21 million to create the Legacy Fund to pay for the development of trust-owned land and the acquisition of land for the benefit of Massacre survivors and descendants, create a college scholarship fund for the children of descendants, and provide small business loans and organizational grants to descendants who own or desire to start businesses.

The mayor also pledged to release more than forty-five thousand pages of records (part of another case[2] I have been leading since 2021), which will allow attorneys, historians, and scholars to learn new information about the events of 1921, and the continuing harm. He also committed to continuing the search for additional mass graves at Oaklawn Cemetery and other locations, and of course, to honoring the previously established Tulsa Race Massacre Observance Holiday on June 1.

"Hallelujah" spilled from my mouth. Tears welled up in my eyes, and I bowed my head in prayer thanking God and my ancestors.

We did not get everything we wanted. We didn't get preferential hiring and city contracts for descendants. We didn't get compensation for land stolen from Greenwood residents. Most important, we didn't get direct cash payments to the survivors or descendants who lost generational wealth. Still, after more than a century of denial, finger-pointing, delays, and lies, the City of Tulsa finally took official, tangible responsibility for the harm it inflicted on Greenwood and its people—*my people.* That in itself is historic. But it goes deeper.

For the first time, Tulsa put reparations on paper. That precedent matters. This plan cracks the wall of resistance that has stood for more than one hundred years and forces the city to stop hiding behind hollow apologies and stall tactics. No longer can Tulsa's power players simply run out the clock and wait for our survivors to pass away.

Nationally, this changes the conversation. The Road to Repair marks one of the first times a U.S. city has formally acknowledged a racial massacre with a reparations framework—proof that the fight for repair is not just theoretical, not just symbolic, but actionable. And that means lawyers, activists, and descendants everywhere can point to Tulsa and say: *If it happened here, it can happen anywhere.* It gives us a platform to keep pressing, to keep building, and to keep widening the cracks until full repair is not only possible but inevitable. That's why there's a photograph of Tiffany and me grinning from ear to ear next to the mayor after his speech. We knew we had secured a real victory.

Yes, there was still work ahead—those words could be carved on my gravestone—to ensure that the Road to Repair was built with transparency and accountability, truly benefiting survivors and descendants. But after generations of loss, anger, and despair, we finally had something to celebrate. We had it because Mayor Nichols showed the courage to do what no Tulsa mayor had ever done: put himself in the line of fire to do what was right and long overdue.

This wasn't just about Tulsa, either. In an era when MAGA 2.0 is dismantling racial justice across the country, the Road to Repair has become the Tulsa precedent. It happened in Oklahoma, a place with no statewide elected Democrats and no statewide Black officials, where all seventy-seven counties are "red." In a city once known for racial terror, Tulsa took a step—imperfect but undeniable—toward repair. That step made reparations real, not theoretical.

Two days later, the mayor and I joined a national interview on #RolandMartinUnfiltered. It was powerful to sit—virtually—side by side, speaking to a national audience about what had just happened. I made sure to give the mayor his roses. "If you get a chance, go listen to his speech," I told Roland. "It was one of the best speeches I've ever heard. . . . He laid out the case not only for why this should happen but what it will look like, not just for us as descendants in the Greenwood community, but for Tulsa.

"If we are fully implementing this plan, and as the mayor said, this is just the start of a plan, but once we fully implement it, this will be a model that communities around this country can actually make happen for their community," I continued. "We're excited to continue to work with the mayor. We know it's going to be a lot more work to put everything together, and I'm asking everyone that's listening tonight, connect with us, connect with Mayor Nichols, connect with Justice for Greenwood. We need to raise this money. We need to make sure that this plan has the success it should have."[3]

I also told the truth: There was more to do. Survivors still deserve direct cash payments. Families still deserve restitution for the homes and businesses burned to the ground. North Tulsa still needs a hospital with a Level 1 trauma center. These are not luxuries—they are necessities rooted in the facts. I further explained that we have to make sure the Greenwood Trust is fully funded, structured correctly, and governed justly, and that it delivers for the people it was created to serve. Survivors and descendants must remain at the center.

That's why the other big task ahead of us is expanding the JFG survivor and descendant certification process through our WeAreGreenwood Genealogy Project to ensure that benefits go where they belong. About one hundred descendants are already certified and have their documentation in order—they're ready. For those who aren't there yet, the WeAreGreenwood Genealogy Project will continue to walk families through the process at no cost, helping them gather records and stories so that no rightful descendant is left behind when the Road to Repair benefits begin to flow.

Even better, another unexpected piece of good news came around the same time: The U.S. Senate unanimously passed a bill, the Historic Greenwood District–Black Wall Street National Monument Establishment Act,[4] championed by Dr. Crutcher and Oklahoma Republican Senator James Lankford,[5] among others. The bill would designate the Historic Greenwood District as a national monument.[6]

About a month later, as promised to Mother Randle and Mother Fletcher, Representative Al Green introduced the Original Justice for Living Survivors of the 1921 Tulsa/Greenwood Race Massacre Act (H.R. 4228) on June 27, 2025. The bill would order more than $20 million to be paid to these two courageous survivors.

But for me, the best outcome of all might be the effect of our work on the survivors. If you recall, Mother Randle still suffered from the trauma she experienced as a young girl back in 1921, sometimes having sleep problems and nighttime panic attacks. But her granddaughter LaDonna Penny told *The Black Wall Street Times* that since people began to share her story and advocate for her, Mother Randle has found peace and healing. "Since we started this journey she's gotten a lot better. When we started she wasn't able to sleep," LaDonna said. "I'm happy that my grandmother's still here to see 110."[7]

So am I.

Then, in July, the Muscogee (Creek) Nation Supreme Court issued a unanimous ruling restoring citizenship to my clients, Rhonda Grayson and Jeff Kennedy, descendants of "Creeks of African Descent," and other similar so-called Creek Freedmen. We celebrated with a big press conference where we raised our hands in victory, knowing that even in the midst of the federal MAGA takeover, justice was winning big in Tulsa, Oklahoma. Together, these two breakthroughs mark twin landmark milestones in the struggle for racial and reparatory justice.

The Creek decision does more than correct a legal wrong. By restoring citizenship rights to more than one hundred thousand Black Creeks, the court not only returned housing, healthcare, scholarships, and political representation to an entire class of Black people, it also restored dignity and respect to Black Creeks and halted the attempted erasure of our history and our contributions to the Muscogee (Creek) Nation.

The ruling, just like the work that eventually became the Road to Repair, creates a replicable blueprint. Any community can marry historical research, strategic litigation, and community organizing into a proven playbook to demand redress. And it carries profound meaning for Greenwood, where many victims, survivors, and descendants of the Massacre were Black Creeks—including some of the children of Mother Randle.

For me, the victory further reinforces that justice, though delayed, cannot be denied if you keep fighting for it. Part of the ongoing harm of the Massacre was the weakening of the Black Creeks' political and economic power that allowed for further marginalization of Greenwood. These twin victories reverse those evils and lay a foundation for Greenwood and North Tulsa to rise again—bigger, better, and stronger.

Following both wins, I took some time to enjoy what I had accomplished. I attended the National Bar Association 100th annual convention in Chicago, and the membership was kind enough to recognize me with a standing ovation. I was humbled and overjoyed when I learned that I'd made the "Centennial Lawyers of Distinction" as one of the top one hundred Black lawyers of the last one hundred years. The list includes some of the most accomplished lawyers in history: Justice Thurgood Marshall, Judge Constance Baker Motley, Johnnie Cochran, Congresswoman Sheila Jackson Lee, Ben Crump, and Vice President Kamala Harris.

Since then, encouraged by Mia and my friends and finally feeling at peace after all the years of battling, I've taken time to slow down a little and live something that looks suspiciously like an actual life.

Unfortunately, the chance to truly rest like I deserve to will be hard to come by, because everything I care about is now under attack under Trump 2.0. With white supremacy resurgent, state-sanctioned racial violence rising, and basic civil rights enforcement dismantled, the road toward racial justice and reparations has only gotten harder. Across the country, MAGA is erasing history, blocking school curriculums, gutting federal protections, and mocking even the idea of repair.[8]

Indeed, this road is long but not hopeless. It may be dimly lit, but the taillights of our ancestors in front, and the headlights of our children behind, will guide us to the destination. The odds, obstacles, and opposition are real, but we will not bow, we will not break, we will not surrender, and we will not retreat.

We draw strength from those who came before us: the Black Creek founders of Greenwood, survivors like Mother Randle, elders like my grandmother Mama Brown, and collective ancestors like Harriet Tubman. Their sacrifices paved this road, and their faith demands we keep walking it.

But this road does not belong to Tulsa alone. Every Black community in America can claim it. Every descendant and ally can travel it. The fight for Greenwood is the fight for Detroit, for Birmingham, for Harlem—for towns like Rosewood, Florida, and Elaine, Arkansas, which suffered their own massacres—and for every place where Black people built, resisted, and dreamed yet face continued harm. Our story is your story, and our victory can light the way for yours if you follow some of lessons I've learned along the way.

First, win the moral argument and tell your story to the persuadable. After the survivors testified before Congress, I was emboldened and gratified to see how America lined up to support them. The more we told their story, the more it found its way to new ears. Power already knows the harm it has caused. Tell your story to the people who can still be moved, the ones who will show up and act, make calls, write letters, pack meetings, donate, and refuse to look away. That means building strong ties with media and storytellers who will help keep your cause alive.

Second, build trust and nurture relationships. Without trust, you don't have a movement. We didn't just file lawsuits; we built a relationship with survivors, descendants, and the larger community. You need people you can rely on, because this fight will cost you friends, business, and opportunities. Stay true to your values, act honorably, and share your story, and allies will come—sometimes from completely unexpected places. When they show up, whether it's Bryan Stevenson or a neighborhood pastor, honor them. Movements thrive when partners and allies feel respected.

Third, keep your movement alive in the public square. Silence kills causes, but be strategic and disciplined with your communications. People are busy, and if they don't hear about you, they'll assume your organization folded or your case was dismissed. I'm sure you've noticed that I never pass up a chance to do an interview, speak on a panel, or appear on a podcast. That's not about my ego; it's about survival. The other side wants to wear you down. That's why they delay and file motions; they want you to be silent and quit. Survivors testifying before Congress drew national coverage, but that only happened because we had kept Greenwood alive in the public imagination for years.

Fourth, ask for the moon. Small visions don't sustain big fights. Most people thought my goals for Greenwood—from the lawsuit to the DOJ investigation to Project Greenwood—were impossible. But bold visions inspire people, and fighting like hell to make them real turns the impossible into the undeniable.

Fifth, understand what politicians are and the job they're elected to do. They are elected to distribute resources and shape policy, not to save you. Mayor Nichols's embrace of Project Greenwood created opportunities, but it also allowed him to keep an important promise. We got some unprecedented reparatory measures; he got to be a hero to the Black community.

Sixth, don't let the work consume your personal relationships. I could not have done this without Mia. It's as simple as that. I would be dead, all my staff would've quit, or both. Don't sacrifice the people who love and support you on the altar of any cause.

Finally, prepare yourself for the cost. In this work, you will lose more than you will win. You must carry disappointment without letting it break you. That means protecting your mental, physical, and spiritual health—eating well, drinking plenty of water, resting, exercising, and tending to your soul. It also means asking for help when you need it and forgiveness when you fall short. People don't need perfect leaders; they need real ones.

The way forward is not a mystery. Greenwood has already shown us how to do this. The same principles that built and sustained it through terror and tragedy, and built our movement from the first lawsuit filing to our historic win, can be the blueprint for repair and renewal across this nation. They are more than a strategy—they are an inheritance. They are the gift of our ancestors to every community still waiting for justice, and my gift to you.

I call this set of principles ThinkGreenwood.

We could hear bullets hitting against the house. It was an awful experience that I will never forget. Our home and everything we owned was burned to the ground. Dad rebuilt us a home at 1144 N. Elgin St., but it wasn't as nice as that home we had on [201 N.] Detroit. That is why I believe I am owed reparations. My family lost a lot. Things might have been different for me had that riot not happened.*

—James Durant, Massacre survivor and veteran educator,
as told to Eddie Faye Gates

Two young men and six women and girls pose in a row on the steps of a brick building in this black-and-white photograph postcard. Collection of the Smithsonian National Museum of African American History and Culture, Gift of Princetta R. Newman.

CHAPTER 15

THINKGREENWOOD

It was late 2021, and I was spending most of my time on Zoom calls with my team discussing the speeches I would have to give, the presentations we would need to make, how to influence the press coverage of the lawsuit, fundraising, and how to rally the network of descendants. It was a busy time. But as we were working, I started to think about how we had gotten to this point.

There I was, working with a united, passionate team of people of all races, genders, and backgrounds, all committed to justice for Greenwood. Behind us stood a community of descendants and North Tulsans, like Dr. Tiffany Crutcher, Chief Amusan, and Terry Bradford, ready to raise money, take to the streets, and rally behind the cause. Behind them stood an army of national attorneys, journalists, politicians, academics, and activists like Bryan Stevenson, Joy Reid, Roland Martin, Tiffany Cross, Barbara Arnwine, and Angela Rye. Finally, behind everyone stood three centenarian survivors—people who could have easily said, "Leave me alone, I want to enjoy the final years of my life in peace," but instead volunteered to go to court, travel to Washington, D.C., and go on television to be the faces of our cause.

That League of Extraordinary People did not come together in a vacuum.

As my extended team worked, an idea kept nagging at me. While the fight for reparations on a national level would go on, the outcomes in Tulsa, Palm Springs, and other locales suggested that the most promising avenue for obtaining reparations for traumatized populations might involve activism at the local level. But how could I teach Black leaders and communities to build what we had built in Greenwood?

The more I thought about it, the clearer the answer became. *If you want to build something like what we have, you can't start today.* You have to go back to the Greenwood that existed before urban renewal. From there, you have to go back to Greenwood before the Massacre. But Greenwood didn't spring from the dust, either. It was born because of ideas that had existed in the minds of Black people for hundreds of years. To understand that, you have to go back in time to the all-Black towns of Oklahoma, and from there to the Black Creeks, and other Black Indians of the Five Tribes. There's a common thread, an enduring set of principles, linking our ancestors to the community that surrounds me today.

As I was building a presentation to tell the story behind our historic lawsuit, that idea kept creeping back into my mind. Finally, it hit me: The presentation had to be built around those fundamental ideas! If anyone outside Tulsa was going to understand what made Greenwood so special—and what makes our community so special today—we had to show them why Greenwood was special. That was the thought process that led to the five principles that I call ThinkGreenwood:

1. **Community Love.** Loving ourselves, our neighbors, and our communities. Building spaces where everyone is valued, protected, and empowered. Honoring our elders, investing in our youth, and lifting one another as we climb.
2. **Freedom Mind State.** Self-determination. We lead our lives, build our institutions, teach our history, grow and protect our wealth, and tell our stories on our own terms.
3. **Ownership.** We own our lives, stories, businesses, land, and ideas. But this is not just about assets. It is about reclaiming our minds, bodies, and futures from white supremacy, racial capitalism, and Euro-American norms that elevate individualism over the collective good.
4. **Wealth Circulation.** We pool our resources, invest in our own

institutions, and practice cooperative economics rooted in intergenerational learning. We circulate both dollars and wisdom, understanding that real wealth includes money, health, time, knowledge, and the freedom to live without constant extraction.

5. **Willful Resilience.** We don't simply endure hardship. Each time we're challenged, we emerge stronger, smarter, and more united.

ThinkGreenwood is a framework for Black power and reparatory justice that draws from the history and legacy of Greenwood, the historical events that made Greenwood possible, and most of all, the people who brought Greenwood to life. It combines legal advocacy, genealogy, history, community organizing, political and narrative advocacy, and economic justice to create sustainable pathways toward racial justice and collective prosperity. Through the devastation of the Massacre, the insult of "urban removal," decades of civic malice and racist public policy, and even the threats of MAGA, Greenwood's principles of self-determination, collective economics, and mutual support remain just as strong as the day O. W. Gurley broke ground on Greenwood's first buildings back in 1906.

ThinkGreenwood is my gift to every Black town, neighborhood, and community in this country where people seek to repair past harms and give themselves and their children a fair chance at a better life. It's a blueprint for Black Power in the modern era that any group can use to build the same indomitable foundation that's enabled Tulsa's community to stay strong and united through decades of setbacks and disappointments.

Let's break those principles down.

COMMUNITY LOVE

Above all else, Greenwood was one of history's greatest love stories. When Dick Rowland became the target of a lynch mob, it would have been easy for A. J. Smitherman and Greenwood's other wealthy, successful Black residents to close their eyes and look the other way. After all, they had a lot to lose: their property, their freedom, even their lives. But the leaders of Greenwood didn't turn their backs on him. More than one hundred Greenwood men risked everything to protect a nineteen-year-old from an angry white mob. Why? Community Love.

In Greenwood, the love was simply part of the social fabric: *We look out for one another. We cherish one another.* In today's language, we might say that Greenwood was a place where everyone was valued, protected, and empowered.

Community Love goes beyond "love thy neighbor" into radical love, protection, and mutual support for all the members of our communities. That's where Community Love starts. Who are you working on behalf of? Who are you trying to help? It's surprisingly easy to let the fight consume you and forget who and what you're showing up for. Once you know that, subordinate your own goals and wishes to those of that group of people or community. This is the "servant leadership" that Dr. Carter G. Woodson, "the Father of Black History," advocated for in his 1933 masterpiece *The Mis-Education of the Negro*. You lead and find your purpose by serving others above all else.

Community Love also means helping the people you serve move past anger and revenge to justice, healing, and a productive path forward. If a population has spent many years being disenfranchised, disrespected, and disinvested in, they are experiencing the effects of trauma. They might not be as educated on all the issues as you are, but they know they're suffering. So part of Community Love is care—self-care and care for one another. We look after everyone's physical and mental health. We encourage leaders to take breaks (something I am just learning how to do after all this time). We find ways for people to communicate what they're feeling and find support from others who share the same experiences. We keep everyone informed, and we're honest about what can realistically be done and what's not possible right now.

In the Greenwood community, our solidarity—our family connections stretching back generations to Black Wall Street and beyond—has kept us strong and united through the many ups and downs of this fight.

Another foundational piece of Community Love is communication—really, *over*-communication. You keep everyone involved and feeling heard by defining what it means to be part of the community you serve and by keeping them up to speed on everything that's happening. I created the WeAreGreenwood Program to do that. The descendant diaspora is the heart of what we do, so we built a program that asks, "Who is a descendant? What does it mean to be a descendant? How do we work and organize descendants and find out what they want?"

Without WeAreGreenwood, we might never have figured out that what a lot of people wanted more than anything was acknowledgment. Yes, they wanted to be compensated financially for what had been stolen from their families, and we didn't accomplish that with what Mayor Nichols did—at least, not yet. But through the press, the courts, and the city's actions, we got massive national and international recognition for the harm that Tulsa's Black citizens have endured. The world said, "We see you. You have suffered. You deserve justice." That matters. If the JFG team had stayed in our legal cocoon, we might have focused only on monetary outcomes and ignored people's hunger to be seen.

Finally, Community Love is about coalition building. We don't just have lawyers on our team. We have activists, pastors, politicians, journalists, teachers, and most important, regular folks from the community. If you use support, communication, and openness to build a coalition, then your fight is no longer just your fight. You can pass the baton when you're ready, as I will do one day. No one person is carrying all the weight on his or her shoulders, because no one person needs to or can sustainably bear that burden. When everyone shows up, it stops being a burden.

Have conversations with as many different people in your community as you can. Try to find common ground. Try not to blindside people while understanding that sometimes it's necessary to work in secret or to make split-second decisions without consulting anyone. But the people you have relationships with who do not agree with you on an issue? Show them love. Show them respect. Let them know the work isn't personal. This makes operational unity possible even amid disagreement over strategy or tactics.

We've long been fed the racist myth that Black people are more divided than other groups and that we're our own worst enemies. But the facts say otherwise: Black Americans often show the deepest levels of connection and unity of any group, anchored by our racial identity and shared history.[1] However, you don't need everyone to march in lockstep—you need a critical mass united by a common goal. History shows that when Black folks have a clear purpose and a glimmer of hope, we don't hesitate to move together. You don't need unanimity—you need enough of us united by purpose.

WE ARE NOT OUR OWN WORST ENEMY

You cannot be your own worst enemy when you have a real enemy. An open enemy. A 500-year enemy. The enemy is the system known as white supremacy. That system has been organized, funded, protected by law, and reinforced by culture. One of its most effective tricks is getting Black people to speak about ourselves the way it speaks about us. That language is not "keeping it real." It is surrender disguised as honesty. Having a real enemy does not absolve us of responsibility; it prevents misplaced blame while we do the hard work of growth and self-determination.

FREEDOM MIND STATE

The people who built Greenwood had a Freedom Mind State. They came to live where they chose, work as they chose, and build what they could with their sweat and ingenuity. They didn't seek only the freedom to live as they pleased but also freedom from the poison of white supremacy and racism that assaulted them practically everywhere else they went.

In his essay about the 1965 Selma to Montgomery march, "From Alabamy, with Hate," the great writer Harlan Ellison quotes a young Black resident of Montgomery, who says, "We live in a state of perpetual caution."[2] That's how Black people were forced to live in post-

Reconstruction America. It wasn't just Jim Crow segregation, lynchings, and massacres that wore on Black folks but the innumerable daily humiliations and constantly living on edge, knowing that one wrong look or word to a white person could get you beaten or lynched, leaving your family to starve.

The Freedom Mind State was about living without fear in a place where Black people could determine the course of their own lives and succeed or fail according to their gifts and hard work. For fifty years before the founding of Greenwood, Oklahoma's Black Indigenous population had already been living mostly free of white oppression.

When O. W. Gurley made his first land purchase, he envisioned a place that would offer a fresh start for Black people seeking to escape oppression in the Deep South. Like Gurley's original vision, the principle of a Freedom Mind State demands that Black communities commit to leading our lives untethered by outside views and limited expectations. It requires that we build up and preserve institutions that nurture our autonomy and our ambition, teach our full history without a filter, and keep control of our narratives.

The foundations of a Freedom Mind State begin with the insistence that we, both as individuals and as a community, must have control over our lives, our resources, our property, and our stories. Whether it is resisting unfair gentrification or fighting for a living wage, the struggle is never only personal—it is collective. My ancestors in Greenwood understood this. They demanded more than survival; they demanded freedom: to speak their truth, worship in their own churches, build wealth for their children, and live without fear of destruction. Those are the freedoms they fought for, and those are the freedoms I carry forward.

As you build your movement, think about the freedoms that you want to *gain* for the people you serve. For instance, the movement to get justice for the people of Greenwood was to a great extent about freedom from want. Tens of thousands of descendants around the United States had been robbed of the generational wealth that would otherwise have been passed down to them by parents and grandparents, denying them everything from the chance to own successful businesses to the ability to live in better homes.

But the Massacre was just the beginning of the decline of North Tulsa. Before the Massacre, any Greenwood resident could see a world-class physician or dentist whenever they needed to, and there was a centrally located hospital. After urban renewal and decades of intentional neglect and disinvestment, Black Tulsans lived in a healthcare desert, a food desert, and a commercial desert. One of our goals was to repair these harms with our comprehensive abatement plan now known as Project Greenwood.

But we also wanted to help give our people freedom from fear, including the fear of coercive, aggressive policing. In 2016, the year Terence Crutcher was killed, Oklahoma had the third highest rate of police killings in the United States. Of those killed, 20 percent were Black—almost three times the 7.8 percent Black population of the state.[3] The Tulsa Police Department's 2023 annual report revealed that while Black people made up about 15 percent of the city's population, 48.2 percent of verified police uses of force were against Black suspects.[4] As expected, Tulsa's usual "nothing to see here" attitude held sway.

Former Tulsa Police Chief Drew Diamond said the quiet part out loud at a public hearing on the racial disparities in Tulsa's policing: "In the data out there now . . . if you're in south Tulsa and you're White and you're stopped, it will take a few minutes. You may get a ticket; you may get a warning. In north Tulsa, statistically, that stop will take twice as long. And it takes twice as long because you're going to get asked some questions. Is this really your car? Where are you going? Where have you been? That's right. And so, at the end of the day, that doesn't happen to folks on the other side of town. . . . I will tell you that this is on the Mayor and the Police Chief and the City Council. This is fixable."[5] I was a signatory on a letter the NAACP Legal Defense and Educational Fund sent to the city after this report came out, demanding changes in Tulsa's policing.[6]

I could go on and on, but you get the point. Tulsa's Black community has endured the same racial discrimination in policing—the humiliations, the fear, the needless arrests and incarcerations, the tragic deaths—as every other community in the United States. One incident from the late 2010s illustrates the kind of fear I'm talking about. A Black teacher driving home from North Tulsa with her young daughter was stopped by police. One police cruiser became multiple cruisers, followed by an amplified voice shouting, "Step out of the car with hands visible!" The woman obeyed, leaving her now-terrified daughter in the car as she walked to the curb with several officers' guns trained on her. The second grader rolled down a window and screamed, "Please don't shoot my mom!"

Allegedly, the woman's car matched the description of a car that had been reported stolen. Of course, hers was not the stolen car, a fact the officers could have discerned by running her license plate. If they had done that, she could have gone on her way without incident. But because they saw a Black face, they immediately threatened to use deadly force against an innocent woman while her child watched.

Eventually, the woman was allowed to leave, but the encounter had traumatized her and her little girl. She changed her driving habits so she could avoid going through North Tulsa. Her daughter experienced anxiety, panicking if she saw a police car and telling her mother that she was afraid to go to the police in an emergency because she was worried they would shoot her.[7]

A Freedom Mind State begins with the old Negro spiritual "Oh Freedom" and its defiant declaration: "Before I'd be a slave I'll be buried in my grave." That cry was more than a song—it was a worldview. It proclaimed that dignity and freedom are worth more than life itself, and that survival without justice is no survival at all. My ancestors carried that spirit through Greenwood, and I carry it now. It is the foundation of every fight I take on. That conviction is urgent today as civil rights protections are dismantled, Black history is under attack, and anti-Black rhetoric is celebrated at the highest levels of government. Since January 2025, the Trump administration has gutted antidiscrimination enforcement, weakened civil rights agencies, and stripped resources from Black history preservation—replacing truth with erasure.

That's why we held town halls, spoke in churches, and sent weekly emails to our network, helping our people understand what they've lost and are still being denied. Too many learn to survive by accepting injustice as normal. Our job is to show them things were better—and can be again.

Truth-telling is survival. As Dr. Carter G. Woodson warned: "When you control a man's thinking you do not have to worry about his actions. . . . He will find his 'proper place' and will stay in it."[8]

The builders of Greenwood refused that prison. Twice they rose from the ashes to build wealth, culture, and dignity under Jim Crow, confronting injustice without compromise. Today, as rights slip away and history is distorted and erased, their legacy is our blueprint: stand firm, speak truth, resist without compromise. When the mind is free, the hands can build anything.

STAY FOCUSED

Keep a tight focus and don't get too far outside the scope of your expertise, resources, and mission. That's a hazard in working with a dejected, downtrodden people where there are so many issues. You want to fix everything, and you can't. Our demands to Tulsa were consistent and very specific. If there are areas you want to tackle that fall outside the boundaries of your organization, ally with another group that you can support to address them.

OWNERSHIP

Economic power and economic justice remain major motivators for modern-day Black people and leaders. But within the ThinkGreenwood framework, ownership extends beyond material assets. Of course, owning our businesses, land, intellectual property, and investments is critical to freedom, control, and self-sufficiency. That's why fighting for equity and reparatory justice (two different things) within the legal, financial, educational, and insurance systems must be a core aspect of any justice movement's agenda.

However, Ownership goes beyond that to what I call *identity* ownership. This Ownership calls for reclaiming our minds, bodies, and futures from white supremacy and exploitative systems. It's acknowledging Black culture as the source of our power. Both forms of ownership must co-exist and work together to realize Gurley's vision in a modern era.

The material version of Ownership has direct solutions, many of which we have pursued in our reparations demands under Project Greenwood. From the return of or compensation for stolen land to the restoration of justified insurance claims, promoting the ownership of business and assets is often a matter of two things. First, the systems must be in place to enable and protect that wealth and to properly administer and manage our assets, including estate plans, business structures, and related holdings.

Second, the mindset of Ownership—both individual and collective—must be present in the community. That's not easy when for decades we've seen businesses flee, credit denied, capital stripped away, and chances to own land or industry stolen. Yet Black people have always been investors, builders, and entrepreneurs. A strong movement lifts that up and connects people to the tools to chase their dreams. But Ownership must also be collective. True community power comes when we hold assets together, control institutions together, and build wealth together. That's why we need cooperatives, credit unions, land trusts, and cultural institutions. They root Ownership in community, in our tradition of stewardship, ensuring that what we build today is held in trust for generations to come.

BLACK-OWNED BUSINESS

A Black-owned business is not the same thing as a business owned by a Black person. The distinction is about more than semantics—it's about purpose, power, and accountability. A business owned by a Black person measures success by profit margins only. But a true Black-owned business is rooted in the collective well-being of the people it serves. Its purpose is not solely to extract profits but to circulate them. It exists to employ, empower, and uplift; to keep dollars, dignity, and decision-making within the community.

The other aspect of Ownership is more personal. As you've read, my journey was filled with disappointments, betrayals, health issues, and more. One of the things that kept me going was my ownership of my identity as a keeper of my family's legacy, a son of Greenwood and a part of the community. *This is who I am, this is where I come from, these are the people I come from. This is the community I come from.* When I felt discouraged or exhausted, I would think about my proud legacy—how so many men and women endured so much to make it possible for me to do what I was doing—and I would feel unstoppable again.

As a community, and as a movement, you must own your history. You must own your story, collectively and individually. You must own your ability to make sure that the people you serve are taken care of. You must own your self-care. As you've read, I have pushed myself beyond the bounds of good sense more than once in service of the cause. I try not to do that anymore, and neither should you. Own your care—again, as individuals and a group. Rest. Eat well. Breathe. Spend time away from the work. It will be there when you get back.

The goal, I think, is *sovereignty*. It's a fantastic word. Frantz Fanon, in his writings about the revolution in Algeria, talked about the difference between real sovereignty and flag sovereignty. Many of the countries in Africa and Latin America have what he called *flag sovereignty*. Sure, they have their own flag, but they're not sovereign in the sense of being self-sufficient economically, in control of their resources, their land, or free from colonial-era systems. There's no independent vision of what the country can be. In a sense, they're still under the thumb of colonization.

Real sovereignty means that you—as a community, a city, a country, or a people—possess and control everything you need: wealth, property, ideas, stories, and culture. It is the power to decide your own future and the unwavering belief that such self-determination is your absolute right. Malcolm X put it plainly: "The Black man should control the politics and the politicians in his own community. . . . We should control the economy of our community."[9] That is the essence of sovereignty. It must be spoken often, taught deliberately, and woven into the fabric of our daily lives.

Greenwood was the embodiment of that vision. It was a place where Black people controlled a substantial portion of the politics, the businesses, the land, and the culture, as well as the means of sharing and passing them along to others. It was not overly dependent on permission from outsiders and was built on the conviction that we have both the right and the responsibility to govern ourselves. That's why its destruction was not only physical but psychological, aimed at breaking the belief that such a community could exist. Because after years of loss, disappointment, and humiliation, even the proudest people can grow weary. They begin to anticipate defeat, stop imagining victory, and forget that hope is not a luxury—it is a discipline. Greenwood teaches us that sovereignty is possible—but it must be claimed, protected, and passed on.

It's our job—your job—to be that hope. Teach Ownership, demonstrate that it's possible, and lay out the pathways by which it can become a reality.

GET INVOLVED IN POLITICS

You don't have to run for office, but your movement must have someone inside the political system where you operate. Politics is a battle over power—over who decides who gets which resources and rights, when they get them, and how much they will receive. If you are not represented in that fight, you will lose by default.

Many of these decisions are made in daytime meetings most people can't attend—so find someone who can be in the room. Politics is more than voting. Build allies in the political sphere, starting with regular folks who get things done: aldermen, city council members, county commissioners. And remember, no politician in their official capacity is your friend! They are mechanisms to deliver the rights and resources your community needs to survive and thrive. If you're fortunate enough to find an elected official who cares more about the cause than their reelection, use that relationship strategically and relentlessly.

WEALTH CIRCULATION

Booker T. Washington High School was the crown jewel of Greenwood in its heyday. In 1926, as people were rebuilding after the Massacre, the community built George Washington Carver Middle School. So, education was always an important part of the community. Kids grew up formally educated together. After they graduated, they fanned out all over the nation, going to HBCUs, getting master's degrees and Ph.D.s, and then came back home to teach, start businesses, and share what they had learned. They had everything so many of our communities and families lack today: connection, a sense of duty, and the support and infrastructure to learn and succeed.

Education and close-knit people are force and wealth multipliers. Having both makes your community and your movement stronger. As the businesses, land, and communal culture of the Greenwood District multiplied, so did the prosperity of its residents. Today, the idea of creating generational wealth for our families and communities, as well as garnering support for Black-run entities, has become popular again. This is vital to reparatory justice. A strong, wealthy community has the ability to support the law firms, co-ops, nonprofits, houses of worship, schools, and other bodies that do the important work with donations, expertise, and other resources.

The ability to build thriving businesses or launch organizations that fight for civil rights, economic justice, and political power doesn't just appear out of thin air—it's taught and modeled. Traditional schooling won't show a passionate young Black woman how to write a winning fundraising letter, run for city council, or organize a protest march. That's *our* lane. That's the work of true practical education—teaching the skills that turn vision into power. As Dr. John Henrik Clarke put it, "Education has but one honorable purpose, and that is to train people to be responsible handlers of power. Everything else that goes for education is a waste of time."[10] Our job is to make sure our community gets *that* kind of education—no permission slips, no gatekeepers, just power in the hands of our people.

Through Justice for Greenwood's Legacy Protection Program (LPP), we don't just teach families how to protect their assets, we deliver the legal services to do it. That means drafting wills and estate plans, handling probate cases to clear title, and resolving ownership issues that keep families from fully controlling their property. Alongside the legal work, we provide "wisdom education," connecting elders, professionals, and community leaders with the next generation to share practical skills, cultural knowledge, and hard-earned lessons. By combining direct legal action with financial, practical, and intergenerational education, we make sure wealth and property stay in the family—and in the community—for generations to come.

Today, Wealth Circulation also demands mastery of technology. Just as Greenwood once sent its children to HBCUs and graduate schools to return with knowledge that built institutions, we must now send them into the world to master data, digital platforms, and emerging technologies. Artificial intelligence in particular is reshaping every sector—law, business, healthcare, finance, even organizing itself. If Black communities fail to understand and implement AI, we will be locked out of the next economy. But if we embrace it, we can scale our enterprises, strengthen our institutions, and safeguard our legacies. Greenwood mastered the tools of its time; we must master the tools of ours.

The old Greenwood may have come to an end after the Massacre and urban renewal, but while it existed its people had the place of love and prosperity and the haven from want and fear that they had dreamed of. Such a place can be created, using these five principles. Greenwood was a real place and an enduring idea. It was built on these principles. If it was done once, it can be done again, all over the country. These principles live within people like you. ThinkGreenwood is really all about possibilities.

INVEST IN THE COMMUNITY

Justice for Greenwood also runs a Legacy Fund that financially supports survivors, descendants, and community organizations working to preserve and uplift Greenwood and its memory. The Legacy Fund gives money to descendants and Massacre survivors' organizations, and that keeps the money within the Greenwood community, where it can continue to do good. To date we have invested more than $700,000, but the impact of this giving is triple that amount. So, even if your organization only has a small amount of money, try to give it back if you can, in ways that multiply the good it can do.

WILLFUL RESILIENCE

This principle begins with enduring hardship in the face of oppression and loss, but it doesn't end there. Willful Resilience ties together strength, intelligence, and unity. It means that after each challenge, we as a community come back to the fight stronger, wiser, more prepared, and more filled with love and hope. Justice for Greenwood embodies this idea through our litigation and our uncompromising advocacy campaigns that helped us win the Road to Repair concession and Black Creek citizenship victory.

I won't lie to you. This can be a tough principle to live up to, especially in the face of repeated disappointments and defeats. After Judge Wall dismissed our public nuisance case, I felt like I had nothing left. When the Oklahoma Supreme Court ended our chances of any court victory, that took an even greater toll. But after a brief period of despair and hopelessness, I got back into the fight. That's what Black people do. We endure. We regroup. We find new avenues to keep pushing. We have plan B already booted up. We don't quit. Every time we're challenged, we emerge stronger, smarter, and more united.

But there are two bigger ideas behind Willful Resilience. The first goes back to what Bryan Stevenson and I talked about many times, which is that continuing the fight equals winning. And no, that's not a trick to make losing hurt less. As Black freedom and liberation battles of the past have shown us, the path to victory is a winding one. Sometimes, the value of one lawsuit or campaign is that it establishes a precedent that will play out in the next lawsuit, or the one after that. Sometimes, you keep pushing just to keep your story alive long enough for it to have an effect on public opinion. Remember, you don't know what tomorrow will bring. There's a straight path from our keeping Greenwood and reparations in the courts and news for as long as we did to the outcome we got from Mayor Nichols.

Sustaining the fight means "expanding the battlefield," having backup plans and being willing to put them into action before plan A proves to be a dead end. Long before the state supreme court ended our lawsuit, my team and I were pressing the Department of Justice to open an investigation. It took three and a half *years* to make that happen. Long before Monroe Nichols was elected mayor, I, Tiffany Crutcher, and others in the movement were building community power and political literacy that became key to him defeating a popular former white TV anchor and sitting county commissioner.

Whatever your initial plan might be, don't get complacent. Develop backup strategies. If you never have to employ them, that's a miracle, because the history of Black freedom and justice movements is one of crushing defeats coming long before eventual victories. After all, the Tulsa Race Massacre is one part of a five-hundred-year war against Black people in this country. The first goal is to not die, to not lose completely.

The other principle of Willful Resilience is learning how to appreciate the wins you can get. We would all love to achieve something as sweeping as the 1964 Civil Rights Act or *Loving v. Virginia,* but those happen once in a lifetime. I would have been thrilled to go to trial in our public nuisance case, tell the stories of Mother Randle and Mother Fletcher to a jury, and walk into the sunshine having won billions of dollars for the survivors and descendants, but that wasn't to be. Instead, we took the wins we could get because something is always better than nothing. Discuss the "spectrum" of wins with your community and emphasize that accomplishing something less than the entire jackpot does not necessarily equal settling. It's just the beginning of the fight. "This is all we can get *today*. We will come back tomorrow and fight for more."

Celebrate those wins, even the small ones. When Judge Wall's courtroom went crazy in May 2022, we hadn't won the case. We'd simply been allowed to keep our lawsuit alive a little bit longer. But that didn't matter to the Greenwood folks who showed up. We all needed a reason to rejoice, so when it became clear we would live to fight another day, the chants of "Justice for Greenwood" were as cathartic as they were celebratory.

Once, while at Riggs Abney, I settled a case for $100,000 and told David Riggs that we should have gotten $125,000. He said, "Celebrate the settlement, then move on to the next case. Every case you don't lose is a win."

Resilience comes in two stages, too. First, manage expectations. Be clear that whatever your pursuit, it will be a process. It will take time. For a while, you may take two steps back for every step forward. Second, allow yourself and your community to mourn the losses, but do it together. Don't pretend the disappointment or racist decision didn't happen. Be angry and outraged . . . together. Be sad and hopeless . . . together. You'll recover and rise again together, too.

ON ANGER AND RAGE

I've tried not to have this book reflect it, but during this fight and in general, I spent a lot of time angry. Black people in this country know anger and rage. It's an understandable response not only to the violence, hate, and hypocrisy but also to the indifference and neglect of the institutions that were supposed to protect us. As you pursue your own brand of justice, it's okay to feel rage at the setbacks, double-talk, and lies. Lord knows I have. Righteous anger can even help make your coalition stronger. But be careful not to let anger and rage define your movement. Rage is stressful and frightening; our goal is to inspire and motivate others to stay the course and spread hope. Not one of the Think-

Greenwood principles says a word about anger. That's all the proof you need.

THE FIGHT GOES ON

There was a time when I believed that anything besides a comprehensive reparations program that included direct cash payments was a failure. In fact, I would have treated anything less than such an outcome as selling out and betraying my people. But I'm wiser, if more world-weary. Doing this work and then writing this book has given me a new perspective on the value of what my team accomplished. We creatively used our litigation and advocacy campaigns, including the public nuisance suit, to keep the story of Greenwood alive and the issue of reparatory justice in the public eye for more than five years. As a result, millions of Americans who had never heard of the Tulsa Race Massacre of 1921 are talking about it today.

Justice for Greenwood is now a nationally recognized human rights and racial justice organization that has accomplished more in five years than many organizations have in fifty-five years. Because of our efforts, each survivor has received nearly $1 million from private sources. We've lifted them out of poverty and arranged for their care in top-tier nursing homes for the rest of their lives. They've become civil rights heroes and been celebrated, respected, praised, and honored throughout the world.

We identified and exposed the still-operating insurance companies that wrongfully denied Massacre victims' claims. We built a strong nationwide Greenwood descendant network. We caused the Oklahoma National Guard and the City of Tulsa to issue apologies for the first time in one hundred years. We caused the U.S. Department of Justice to issue their first-ever report on the Massacre and then caused them to amend that report. We ensured that the Massacre would never officially be referred to as "the Tulsa Race Riot" again. We made it clear that while the "Black Wall Street" business aspect of Greenwood was important, the real lesson and star of the story is the community the people of Greenwood built.

We taught the world that Greenwood was co-founded by Black Creeks and that without their contributions Greenwood would not have become the most prosperous, organized, and successful Black community in U.S. history. That makes our win for the Black Creek Freedmen in 2025 just a little bit sweeter.

None of this is the full justice and reparations I have pursued since 1997. But it's not nothing, either. I finally understand that when it comes to remedying injustices that predate the United States, success is not an all-or-nothing proposition, as Bryan and Mia are always reminding me. Sometimes you lose the case but win the narrative battle. Sometimes you change minds. A Gallup poll from 2002 found that only about 14 percent of Americans supported the idea of paying financial reparations to Black people for enslavement. Fifty-five percent of Black people were in favor of reparations, but only 6 percent of white Americans were.[11] But in 2021, a Pew Research poll found that overall support for reparations was up to 30 percent, Black support was 77 percent, and white support had grown to 18 percent.[12]

Don't look at the raw numbers. Look at the change. Overall support more than doubled in nineteen years. Support among white people tripled. That's progress. History shows that we will lose ground during the Trump presidency, but it also shows that with hard work, we can regain it. When the mountain moves even a few feet, you celebrate, because moving a mountain is *hard*.

Bryan Stevenson agrees. "I always have felt like this is a marathon," he said in our interview. "A lot of people started running fast after George Floyd, because all of these corporations were giving money. So, people started sprinting as if somehow that moment was going to allow us to achieve a victory. I was excited. We'd never gotten a corporate penny donated to the Equal Justice Initiative, and this money started coming in, but I realized it wasn't going to last. They weren't doing it because they believed in racial justice. They were doing it because the atmosphere had shifted, the politics had shifted, and it became necessary for them to do something performative.

"I kept asking, 'Is this a moment or is this a movement?'" Bryan went on. "Because movements are hard to build. Movements are not reactions to things. They are proactive. They can begin as a reaction to something, but then we have to have the discipline to build. So, it never felt to me like this marathon was all of a sudden going to turn into a sprint and we were going to win. These issues are too deep. These are four-hundred-year-old problems, and we're not going to solve them in a four-month period of recognition. We can do a lot to advance things. But for all the narratives, there's always a counternarrative. For me, we have to do what we realized we had to do before George Floyd, which was to create a new era of truth and justice, truth and restoration, truth and repair, truth and redemption."

Before we part ways, a few thoughts and suggestions. First, as we strive for justice, let's not forget to look after ourselves. No one can fight forever. I tried and ended up in the hospital. Part of being effective is knowing when to step aside for a while and forget about the fight. Allow yourself and others to rest, relax, and recreate without guilt. Rest, relaxation, and time away from the work protects our creativity, sharpens our analysis, and fuels the sustained, disciplined action our liberation demands. By pausing, we change the expectation that Black resilience equals unbroken toil. In reclaiming rest, we reclaim our power.

Second, forge alliances with as many people of good faith and goodwill as possible. I've tried to mend fences with many Tulsans with whom I've had conflict because of how I prosecuted this issue. I sat down with them and said, "We need to work together. We need as much unity as we can get." I've even swallowed my pride and apologized where appropriate. I told them that whatever mistakes I made—and I made plenty—I made them in service of the mission to secure justice and reparations. Are there things I would do differently if given the chance? Yes. But everything I did while fighting for justice for Greenwood I did in good faith. When you're trying to move mountains, you do whatever you think will budge the mountain another few inches.

This book will come out around the time of three milestones: the 105th anniversary of the Tulsa Race Massacre, the 160th anniversary of the Treaty of 1866 (signed by my ancestor to end the enslavement of Black people in the Creek Nation), and the 250th anniversary of the signing of the Declaration of Independence. Each anniversary comes at a time of trial and trouble, both for Black people in America and for our country itself. That does not mean they are not worth marking. On May 31, visit justiceforgreenwood.org to commemorate the Massacre and celebrate what was great about Greenwood with us.

On June 14, visit justiceforblackcreeks.com to learn more and join us in honoring the Treaty of 1866. And on July 4, read Frederick Douglass's 1852 speech "What to the Slave Is the Fourth of July?" His words should sting, because the truth they reveal remains: Black people have never fully enjoyed liberty and justice. Therefore, commit to honor the Declaration's promise by doing all you can to ensure that the United States finally delivers full equity and repair to Black communities.

Finally, remember that Greenwood was born in an era that historian Rayford Logan named "the Nadir," the violent virtual re-enslavement of Black people following Reconstruction between the late 1870s and 1930s. During that time, Black people endured rampant violence, were stripped of our voting rights, and felt the smothering grip of Jim Crow. And yet out of that storm emerged a thriving community rooted in the ThinkGreenwood principles.

Today, I see an ominous echo of the Nadir in what I call "the MAGA Delusion." Open white supremacy is operating in the highest echelons of government, business, law, media, and higher learning. This resurgence is unprecedented in my lifetime, and it's terrifying. In this age, lies are sold as truth, history is rewritten to protect white power, and reality is distorted by relentless attacks on anything that does not worship rich white male interests. From school boards to courtrooms, it's a calculated push to make us not only forget that America has *never* been great for Black people but to literally *unlearn right from wrong,* to silence any pursuit of justice, and to dismiss the essential work of repair.

Trump's unapologetic rhetoric, swift power grab, and defiance of both norms and the rule of law are an effort to re-create the "Whites Only" world my grandparents lived in and my parents were born into. His actions, and those of his allies, have ripped the blindfold off my generation and those behind us to show us just how cruel, vile, and greedy racism is. Now more than ever, it's clear that tragedies like the Massacre can and will happen again if we're not intentional about building a more just and unified community. We have no time for illusions—the fight of our lives is here.

I interviewed Joy Reid, who was fired by MSNBC while I was writing this book, and who remains a friend and ally, and she spoke forcefully about the wake-up call this generation is experiencing. "Our generation only experienced the tail end of the horrors that our near ancestors experienced," she said. "We didn't get it full-on. By the time we were in our twenties, it was the 1990s. It was the golden age of the American economy. We were getting money, we were flush. It was Bill Clinton in there, playing the saxophone. He was going on *Arsenio Hall*. That's why we vote so poorly. Most Black folks my age thought of Trump as the guy talked about in hip-hop songs. He was the bling guy. We were the money generation.

"We didn't quite believe our parents about how bad it was, because we weren't experiencing it like that," Joy went on. "Well, now, this Trump era is showing you exactly how Tulsa happened. Now you can picture the kind of people who would go into a place like Black Wall Street and burn it to the ground. They're the same kind of people who are on X-Twitter, justifying lynchings and calling Amy Coney Barrett's adopted Black children 'nigglets.' Look at people's vicious, violent reactions to Barack Obama becoming president, and the surge in hate speech and hate crimes. There were never more threats to an American president than Obama got, [plus] the mocking of Michelle Obama as an ape and a monkey.

"I think the benefit of Trumpism and MAGA is that it's demonstrating to Gen X—who can then explain to Gen Z and Gen Y, our kids—that this is real," Joy concluded, "and that the kind of people who lynch folk are the same kind of people who right now just say, 'I'm MAGA.'"

This awareness is unnerving, but it should also be energizing. It should galvanize us to passionately resist historical erasure, aggressively push for reparatory justice. Just as Greenwood thrived during America's original racial Nadir through those five core principles, we can revive these principles today. We can re-create Greenwood throughout the country—in our small towns, our big cities, and everywhere in between—while also creating the means to protect those communities. Then (and only then) will America finally be great and redeemed . . . for the first time in our history.

Greenwood is not a distant tragedy. It's our blueprint for justice. It's within all of us. If we ThinkGreenwood, live Greenwood, and remember Greenwood, winning is certain.

Justice for Greenwood!

Justice for Greenwood!

Justice for Greenwood!

Left to right: Tulsa Race Massacre survivors Hughes Van Ellis, Lessie Benningfield Randle, and Viola Fletcher were marshals at the Tulsa Centennial Parade in 2021. Courtesy of Damario Solomon-Simmons.

EPILOGUE

THE ROAD AHEAD

In 2026, history collides with itself. This nation will celebrate 250 years since its founding. We will mark 160 years since the Creek Treaty of 1866, which promised the Black citizenship still denied in practice. We will remember 105 years since Greenwood burned.

These anniversaries expose what America so often tries to bury: True freedom for Black people has never been a full reality, only something demanded, fought for, and defended, generation by generation. Nothing has been freely given. Everything has been contested. Every right, every institution, and every gain has been secured at the cost of blood, risk, and sacrifice.

So, as America congratulates itself, we must ask, What exactly is it celebrating? A quarter millennium of "democracy," or false promises? A republic of liberty, or a nation that has never extended liberty fully to its Black citizens? The answer is in Greenwood's ashes, in the chains of slavery, in the laws of Jim Crow, in the prisons filled with our people. It's in the danger barreling toward us now.

Under the MAGA Delusion, racial animus is not hiding anymore. It is policy. We are no longer dealing with dog whistles. We are facing open fascism. But the danger also brings with it a strange clarity. The mask is off. America can no longer pretend to be "a shining city on a hill." The "racism is dead" self-congratulation and ridiculous post-racial thought pieces that appeared after the election of Obama have been exposed as liberal self-delusion. We're faced with the brutal truth of what this nation has always been. That truth is not comfortable, but it is liberating.

Because if people of good faith and conscience across this nation face this reality, we hold in our hands a rare chance. We can redeem this nation not by restoring a false dream but by creating the country we want to see. The MAGA Delusion is not just a threat. It is a test.

Some will tell us the answer is to "get back to normal." But let's be clear: Normal has never been liberty and justice for all. Normal is stop-and-frisk, mass incarceration, stolen land, redlined neighborhoods, and schools that erased the histories of "others" while glorifying individualism, capitalism, sexism, racism, and homophobia. Normal is a media machine that sold us lies and a political class that managed decline instead of daring to repair. Normal is the Black leader of the House Democrats voting to honor a known Republican bigot under the guise of bipartisanship mumbo jumbo while refusing to endorse the Democratic nominee for the mayor of New York until it was clear he would win the general election. Anyone promising a return to the way things were either does not understand the moment or is an enemy of justice.

This is why the coming midterm elections cannot be treated as horse races between Republicans and Democrats. We cannot afford recycled candidates repeating recycled scripts. We need new, bold politicians unafraid to challenge both the status quo of the last century and the open white supremacy of today—leaders who reject the falsehood that government "of the people, by the people" should not be first and foremost about serving the people. We need leaders rooted in community, not corporations. And we need journalists and ethical media that tell the truth, amplify our struggles, and refuse to normalize autocracy.

When voices that traffic in anti-Black stereotypes and rhetoric go unchallenged, their words do not remain abstract. They legitimize policies that show up in classrooms, courthouses, and city budgets. Platforming is power, and power in the hands of hate *always* turns to violence. That is why hosts and platforms have a duty to fact-check in real time, label opinion as opinion—not fact—confront lies with evidence, and bring in experts who can defend truth. Anything less is not dialogue but propaganda.

Nowhere is this clearer than in how we treat anti-Blackness compared to antisemitism. I am against all forms of bigotry and discrimination. Of course, the fight against antisemitism is urgent and necessary, but so is the fight against anti-Blackness. Both deserve the same vigilance. Yet popular culture continues to recycle anti-Black stereotypes, slurs, and narratives. Anti-Black policies are debated as if they were legitimate public discourse, while those who push them are given microphones, even by outlets that claim to serve our people. Meanwhile, even the perception of antisemitism meets immediate, coordinated condemnation. Why do we allow anti-Blackness to masquerade as opinion? Why do we tolerate it as dialogue? Why do we tolerate it at all?

Hate is hate. Bigotry is bigotry. We can't be selectively outraged. If we are serious about building a just and equitable society, we must stop sanitizing bigotry with labels and treating truth and "I believe" as equals and hold all forms of hatred to the same standard—especially anti-Blackness, which is woven into the fabric of American culture. We have the power to do so, as the immediate anti-Disney backlash that followed the short-lived silencing of Jimmy Kimmel at Trump's behest shows. We can withdraw clicks, views, and dollars from outlets that platform hate, no matter who owns them. Yet where was the anti-MSNBC backlash when Joy Reid was fired? We can build our own media infrastructures of podcasts, Substacks, and more that refuse to dignify bigotry as debate. Our ancestors built their own newspapers, presses, and schools during the first Nadir; now it's our turn to protect truth and defend dignity.

We must also prepare ourselves for discrimination, injustice, and violence the same way our grandparents and ancestors did: with organization, endurance, and resolve. Our ancestors built HBCUs, churches, newspapers, fraternities, sororities, and Black towns in the face of lynching, dispossession, and legalized hate. During the first Nadir (1877–1930), they built flourishing infrastructures of wealth creation and cultural enrichment. Again, it's our turn. We must call out political double-talk, even from friends. We can't applaud "dialogue" with racists as progress. As one elder told me plainly, "When you are in the fight of your life, you can't be afraid to fight."

Justice and reparations won't come from thoughts, prayers, or appeals to conscience. They will come through disciplined, visionary, collective work. When I think about how to move forward, I close my eyes and commune with ancestors and heroes like Harriet Tubman, Nat Turner, Malcolm X, Dr. King, Thurgood Marshall, Fannie Lou Hamer, W.E.B. Du Bois, Dr. Carter G. Woodson, John Brown, and Representative Thaddeus Stevens—and closer to home, Mama Brown, Daddy Brown, Jake Simmons, Jr., and Cow Tom. For me, they are not distant figures; they are present, alive in the struggle, pressing their charge into my hands. They thunder the same command: *Do the work, protect the wins, build what cannot be taken away.*

They do more than remind me. They instruct me. They direct me. They pour courage into my spirit and fire into my voice. They remind me that we are not wandering without a map. We have one. They wrote it for us. My task is to carry their directives forward and to share them with you. Their words are not whispers of the past. They are marching orders for the future.

This "Council of Ancestors" is blunt. It says, "Do not wait your turn. Take your place. We are counting on you to carry what we carried, to finish what we could not finish. You are the ones we dreamed of, the ones who must dream beyond us."

Here is what you, the reader, must know in this year of anniversaries, this season of danger:

- You are not crazy. This moment is as dire as it feels.
- You are not alone. Our ancestors walk with us, and our children rise beside us.
- We have what we need. We have the history, the community, the road map, and the will.
- We will fight for our rights and our dignity, no matter the odds.
- We will protect the wins and defend them against every attack.
- We will repair what was broken.

- We will redeem America not for what it has claimed to be but for what it must become.

Redemption will not fall from the sky. It must be built and earned by us, with us, through all of us. Between the light of our ancestors and the fire of our children, we already have all we need not just to survive but to redeem this nation.

ACKNOWLEDGMENTS

This was the hardest part of the book to write. Not because I don't know who to thank but because I have been loved, taught, and carried by a village so expansive that no page could ever hold them all. I'll do my best to highlight those most connected to my Justice for Greenwood work. If I leave someone out, charge it to my head and not my heart.

To my mama, thank you for fighting through disability, racial discrimination, and single parenthood to shower me with love, books, and prayer and inspiring me with your grit, toughness, and perseverance. I get my refusal to quit from you.

To my maternal grandparents, Mama and Daddy Brown, you turned 243 East Woodrow into a house of love and service. I never felt safer or more loved than in that magical home.

To my father, Ahmad Shadeed, my paternal grandmother, Johnnie Mae Austin, and my Uncle Don Simmons, who made sure I understood the Simmons legacy, our Black Creek roots, the story of Cow Tom, and the call to serve that compels me today. To my in-laws, Udell Winston and Aubrey Winston, thank you for loving me like a son.

Outside of my wife, the most important person to the success of the work discussed in this book is attorney Bryan Stevenson. Bryan didn't just give me advice; he walked with me through the hardest moments. He has been my coach, adviser, lead strategist, and compass.

I have also been blessed with sisters and brothers in this struggle:

Angela Rye has been my sister in the fight, speaking hard truths, opening doors, and showing up when it mattered most.

Dr. Tiffany Crutcher has been with me at every step, determined and fearless, turning grief into power and standing with me in every battle.

Tiffany Cross gave us more than coverage, she gave us a lifeline, using her platform to lift survivors onto the national stage when the world wanted to look away.

Eric Miller has been my brother in the struggle for Greenwood for more than twenty years. When I called him in 2019 and said I was ready to file a new case for reparations for the Tulsa Race Massacre, he didn't hesitate.

Karen Hunter, through her SiriusXM Urban View 126 platform, gave our movement constant exposure and reach.

Attorney Bill Zabel mobilized his firm, joined my board, secured major donors, and made it possible to sustain the Justice for Greenwood work at the heart of this book. I am deeply grateful for his belief in me and in this mission.

To my brother and JFG board member Jerome Clark—your calm, steady counsel was instrumental in helping me withstand the pressure of this work.

Roland Martin and the Black Star Network made Greenwood's cry for justice impossible to ignore.

My fraternity brother and best friend of more than thirty years, Jeff Trevillion Jr., has walked with me through this journey, offering reasoned counsel rooted not in what I wanted to hear but in what I needed to hear.

My therapist and spiritual coach Dr. Siri Sat Nam, whose wisdom and spiritual guidance have been medicine for my soul.

Chief Egunwale Amusan has, for more than twenty years, helped me carry Greenwood's story with courage and clarity.

To the Congressional Black Caucus, especially Representative Maxine Waters, Representative Sheila Jackson Lee, Representative Al Green, Representative Hank Johnson, Representative Joyce Beatty,

Representative Barbara Lee, Representative Jasmine Crockett, Representative Brenda Lawrence, and Senator Lisa Blunt-Rochester. I thank you for standing with me, pushing legislation, elevating Greenwood, and encouraging members to personally support our work when it mattered most.

To Mayor Monroe Nichols, who, by adopting substantial aspects of Project Greenwood and other policies in his "Road to Repair," showed real leadership and proved that moral courage in public office not only matters—it is essential if we are ever to redeem this nation.

To my Justice for Greenwood team that supported me through this battle: Yolantrice Collins, DJ Mercer, Sadae Williams, Jericka Handie, Chad Clayton, Shaun Prewitt, Greta Smith, Jasmine Henry, Nicka Smith, Gail Jackson, Angela Walton-Rajii, and Kate Richey. Special thanks to Tyrone Lynn, my chief of security and senior adviser, who not only kept me safe but sharpened my vision.

I give props to my SolomonSimmonsLaw team: Emma Weinberg, Kathy Daniels, Kym Heckenkemper, Beatriz Mate-Kodjo, Jourdan Johnson, and Jill York; Spencer Bryan and Steven Terrill of Bryan & Terrill Law, PLLC; Jana Knott of Bass Law; Maynard Henry; Cordal Cephas and Lashandra Johnson of Johnson Cephus Law, PLLC; Adjoa Aiyetoro; and the amazing team of lawyers at Schulte Roth & Zabel (now called McDermott Will & Schulte after a 2025 merger), especially Sara Solfanelli, Michael Swartz, Randall Adams, Erika Simonson, McKenzie Haynes, Oscar Saunders, and Danny Greenberg. For more than four years, you stood with me and with Greenwood, bringing your skills, compassion, and relentless effort to this fight. You also pulled in so many others at your firm, including Angie Garcia, Amanda Barkin, Brandon Faske, Ted Keyes, Keni Ukabiala, Sedinam Anyidoho, Lea Dyce, Ashley Cardenas, Donna Izzard, Victoria Harris, Shaya Schapira, and Scott Kareff.

I honor my clients, the survivors and descendants whose courage forced America to see what it tried to forget by courageously serving as plaintiffs in our public nuisance and related litigation during this campaign: Mother Viola Fletcher, Mother Lessie Randle, Hughes "Uncle

Redd" Van Ellis, Laurel Stradford, Ellouise Cochrane-Price, Tedra Williams, Don M. Adams, Don W. Adams, Jon Adams, Stephen Williams, Historic Vernon AME Church, and the Tulsa African Ancestral Society.

I thank my national allies in this work, including Sherrilyn Ifill, Janai Nelson, and the NAACP Legal Defense Fund; Barbara Arnwine of Transformative Justice Coalition; Rashad Robinson and Amanda Jackson of Color of Change; Nicole Austin-Hillery, Gerry Johnson, and Dreisen Heath of Human Rights Watch; the Equal Justice Initiative; Carleen Pickard and Seth Laxman; the Lush Cosmetics team; Robert Raben and Edgar Burch of The Raben Group; Linda Wilson of Fund II Foundation.

Lukas, Ben, Kaitlyn, and the Inheritance Juicery family, who gave me unconditional love and support. I couldn't have done this without you.

I thank all the media voices who refused to be silent about Greenwood and who consistently lifted up our narrative, especially Joy Reid, Karen Attiah, Dr. Jason Johnson, Jesse Washington, Lurie Daniel Favors, Kaitlyn Kennedy, April Ryan, Niele Anderson, Sabina Ghebremedhin, Audra Burch, Nehemiah Frank and *The Black Wall Street Times,* and Clay Cane.

To my book team: Ricky Anderson, my trusted attorney; Tim Vandehey, my writing collaborator and friend; and Chelcee Johns, my editor. You carried this project across the finish line. And to Idea Architects, especially Rachel Neumann and Wenonah Hoye—your contributions are appreciated.

Likewise, these early endorsers gave this project wings by lending their names, reputations, and platforms: Resmaa Menakem, Brittany Packnett Cunningham, attorney Ben Crump, Reverend Al Sharpton, LaTosha Brown, Shaun King, Dr. Darrick Hamilton, Ryan Haygood, attorney Areva Martin, Etan Thomas, attorney J. Wyndal Gordon, and attorney Lee Merritt.

To my business and financial team at First Oklahoma Bank, Brian Connally of Connally & Associates, and my trusted FCFO Pam Riddle.

Lastly, at the center of it all is my wife, Mia. You are my love, my partner, my greatest defender, my top adviser, my safe harbor, my truth-teller, and the steady heartbeat of my life. For more than twenty-five years you lived this work with me, through every doubt, deadline, and fight. You carried burdens no one will ever know and reminded me who I was when I forgot. This book is not mine. It is *ours*.

NOTES

PART ONE

* Lessie Benningfield Randle, Deposition Transcript, *Randle v. City of Tulsa,* Case No. 121502 (taken remotely, October 14, 2020).

CHAPTER 1: CROSSING THE TRACKS

1. Booker T. Washington visited Oklahoma twice, and both times he stayed with the Simmons part of my family on our Muscogee (Creek) Nation land.
2. "Mob Lynches Taxicab Slayer; Roy Belton Hanged to Post Near Scene of Murder—Goes to Death Calmly—Crowd Subdues Sheriff," *The Tulsa Tribune,* p. 1, August 29, 1920.
3. "The Victory of Greenwood: A. J. Smitherman," 2017, https://thevictoryofgreenwood.com/2020/01/15/the-victory-of-greenwood-a-j-smitherman/?v=0b3b97fa6688.
4. Tim Madigan, *The Burning: The Tulsa Race Massacre of 1921* (New York: St. Martin's Griffin, 2021), 70.
5. One of the primary engines driving Greenwood to greatness, Booker T. Washington High School was founded in 1913, when its legendary principal, E. W. Woods, walked five hundred miles from Memphis, Tennessee, to Tulsa, Oklahoma, to head the new high school for "coloreds." Booker T. was the first high school of any kind (not only the first Black school) below the Mason–Dixon line to obtain the prestigious and essential Accreditation Certificate from the North Central Association of Colleges and Schools in 1926. In fact, Booker T. Washington High School had a curriculum in 1921 that would rival any at the nation's best high schools today.
6. "Bootblack" was often used as a derogatory term to describe Black men. At the Oklahoma Constitutional Convention in 1906, future Oklahoma congressman William "Alfalfa Bill" Murray remarked that Blacks would never be the equals of whites and always remain "bootblacks, barbers, and farmers."
7. My great-aunt Lorene Asher worked at Renberg's for decades and retired in the late 1980s. I now own her old property, one of many examples of how my life and family and this story are interwoven.
8. These are the same people who today ask, "Why do Black people run from the police?"

9. "Loot, Arson, Murder!," *The Black Dispatch,* June 10, 1921, p. 1.
10. "Tulsa Race Riot of 1921," Tulsa City-County Library, https://www.tulsalibrary.org/tulsa-race-riot-1921.
11. "The Tulsa Race Massacre," Oklahoma Historical Society, https://www.okhistory.org/learn/trm6.
12. Equal Justice Initiative. "Lynching in America | EJI Report," 2019, https://eji.org/reports/lynching-in-america/.
13. This number only accounts for those that can be verified. Most experts believe thousands more took place throughout the rural areas of this country during that time period.
14. Jan Davidson, "When White Supremacists Overthrew a Government," *American Experience,* October 23, 2024, https://www.pbs.org/wgbh/americanexperience/features/when-white-supremacists-overthrew-government/.
15. Only after their deaths was it discovered that Loney had been shot in self-defense as he prepared to shoot L.D.'s father in cold blood. Also, it's likely that L.D. was only twelve years old.
16. "On This Day—May 19, 1918: Mary Turner, Pregnant, Lynched in Georgia for Publicly Criticizing Husband's Lynching," Equal Justice Initiative, https://calendar.eji.org/racial-injustice/may/19.
17. Madigan, *The Burning,* 91.
18. Ibid.
19. Madigan, *The Burning,* 102.
20. Written Testimony of Viola Fletcher, United States House of Representatives Subcommittee on the Constitution, Civil Rights, and Civil Liberties, Wednesday, May 19, 2021.
21. "Passing" refers to the practice in which individuals with mixed or light-skinned Black ancestry present themselves as or are perceived as white.
22. R. Halliburton, *The Tulsa Race War of 1921* (San Francisco: R and E Research Associates, 1975), 1.
23. John A. Gustafson, Chief of Police; Wm. McCullough, Sheriff; V. W. Biddison, District Judge, Western Union Telegram, Tulsa, OK, June 1, 1921.
24. There is a lot to talk about when it comes to Dr. Jackson. First of all, his family left Memphis, Tennessee, when his father, a Civil War veteran named Townsend Jackson, was threatened with lynching after he smoked a cigar in the white part of town. The family resettled in Guthrie, Oklahoma. Second, Townsend came to Guthrie to replace a county jailer, Jerry Emerson, who had been murdered by an escaping prisoner. Jerry Emerson is my wife's great-great-grandfather. Finally, today I represent the estate and descendants of A. C. Jackson. I'm not a distant observer of the ongoing tragedy of Greenwood and Black Tulsa; it runs through my veins.
25. Juanita Delores Burnett Arnold, "Oral History Accounts of the Tulsa Race Riot of 1921 by Black Survivors," Tulsa Reparations Coalition, https://tulsareparations.z19.web.core.windows.net/index.html.
26. B. C. Franklin, "The Tulsa Race Riot and Three of Its Victims," unpublished manuscript, collection of the Smithsonian National Museum of African American History and Culture, August 22, 1931.
27. Oklahoma Commission, "Tulsa Race Riot: A Report by the Oklahoma Commission to Study the Tulsa Race Riot of 1921," 2001, https://www.okhistory.org/research/forms/freport.pdf.
28. *The Black Dispatch,* June 10, 1921.
29. Affidavit of Lolita Buckner Inniss, testimony on Tulsa Race Massacre of 1921, December 3, 2021, paragraphs 17–19.
30. Alex Albright et al., "After the Burning: The Economic Effects of the 1921 Tulsa

Race Massacre," Working Paper No. 28985 (National Bureau of Economic Research, July 2021), https://ssrn.com/abstract=3880218.

31. Mary Childs, "Black Economist's Research Finds a Blindspot on a Theory of Innovation," *Morning Edition,* NPR, June 25, 2020, https://www.npr.org/2020/06/25/883233406/black-economists-research-finds-a-blindspot-on-a-theory-of-innovation.
32. Due to the City of Tulsa's segregation laws, almost all Black Tulsans lived in the Greenwood community until the 1960s. What we now know as North Tulsa was an all-white community until the forced removal of Black residents from Greenwood to North Tulsa. Today, the vast majority of Black Tulsans live in North Tulsa by the design of the perpetrators of the Massacre and its continued harm.

* B. C. Franklin, "The Tulsa Race Riot and Three of Its Victims," unpublished manuscript, collection of the Smithsonian National Museum of African American History and Culture, August 22, 1931.

CHAPTER 2: THE GREATEST BLACK TOWN IN AMERICA

1. Although the physical chains were removed, bondage was still evident through other restrictive and oppressive tactics employed by those in opposition to African freedom. The restrictions and frustrations that accompanied chattel slavery remained a sad reality for the masses of African Americans. See John Hope Franklin and Alfred A. Moss, Jr., *From Slavery to Freedom: A History of African Americans,* 7th ed. (New York: Alfred A. Knopf, 2000).
2. Hannibal B. Johnson, *Acres of Aspiration: The All-Black Towns of Oklahoma* (Austin, TX: Eakin Press, 2004), 14.
3. In 1865, Congress passed an act to establish the Freedmen's Bureau, which would be in force for one year. The purpose of the Freedmen's Bureau was twofold: (1) to provide for the needs of the formerly enslaved so that they could eventually become independent and self-sufficient and (2) to gain Black political support for the Republican Party. The bureau continued to operate until 1872. Its most lasting achievement was founding and helping Black colleges.
4. Black codes were laws that categorically denied the rights of African Americans during the early years after the formal ending of chattel slavery. See Kwame Anthony Appiah and Henry Louis Gates, Jr., *Africana: The Encyclopedia of the African and African American Experience* (New York: Oxford University Press, 1999), 249.
5. The practice of sharecropping entailed Black workers living and working on the land of a white landowner, often their former slave master, using tools and other necessities provided on credit by a merchant. In return, the worker was required to pay the landowner and the merchant a portion of the crop produced. At year's end, however, records would be produced purporting to show that the cropper had little or nothing coming to him.
6. David Zuber, "Trail of Tears (1831–1850)," BlackPast, February 10, 2022, https://www.blackpast.org/african-american-history/concepts-african-american-history/trail-of-tears-1831-1850.
7. In addition, in May 1868, Cow Mikko traveled by train to Washington, D.C., to testify before the U.S. Senate Committee on Indian Affairs to ensure that Creek Freedmen received their per capita dividends promised in the Treaty of 1866. His testimony secured the payments to Creek Freedmen.
8. "OK Tribes Reconstruction Treaty," August 2, 2022, https://www.doi.gov/ocl/ok-tribes-reconstruction-treaty.
9. Department of the Interior, Census Office, Extra Census Bulletin, *The Five Civilized*

Tribes in Indian Territory: The Cherokee, Chickasaw, Choctaw, Creek, and Seminole Nations (Washington, D.C.: United States Census Printing Office, 1894), 7.

10. Perryman was a blood relative of mine. His uncle Mose Perryman was the grandfather of Jake Simmons, Sr.
11. "Treaty with the Creeks, 1866 - Tribal Treaties Database," n.d., Treaties.okstate.edu. https://treaties.okstate.edu/treaties/treaty-with-the-creeks-1866-0931.
12. Michael Eric Dyson, foreword to *Acres of Aspiration,* by Hannibal B. Johnson, vii.
13. See Franklin and Moss, *From Slavery to Freedom,* 105–11, 278–79.
14. Some clarity on the usage of "African American," "Native Blacks," "Africans," and "Black." "Africans" refers to people of African descent. "Native Blacks" were descendants of African explorers to America or Indigenous Blacks who had never been enslaved.
15. Larry O'Dell, "All-Black Towns," in *The Encyclopedia of Oklahoma History and Culture,* Oklahoma Historical Society, https://www.okhistory.org/publications/enc/entry?entry=AL009.
16. "Emma Evans Gurley: A Pioneer of Black Wall Street," Black Wall Street USA, 2024, https://blackwallstreet.org/emmagurley.
17. Alexis Clark, "Tulsa's 'Black Wall Street' Flourished as a Self-Contained Hub in Early 1900s," *History,* September 4, 2019, https://www.history.com/news/black-wall-street-tulsa-race-massacre.
18. According to the Oklahoma Historical Society, there are thirteen all-Black Oklahoma towns still in existence: Boley, Brooksville, Clearview, Grayson, Langston, Lima, Red Bird, Rentiesville, Summit, Taft, Tatums, Tullahassee, and Vernon.
19. *Before They Die!*, directed by Reginald Turner, St. Clair Bourne, Michael Hausfeld, John Rogers, and J. Denise Clement, 2008, beforetheydie.org.
20. The school was named after the inspirational Paul Lawrence Dunbar (1872–1906), one of the first Black poets to get national recognition for his work.
21. DeNeen L. Brown, "'We Lived Like We Were Wall Street,'" *The Washington Post,* October 11, 2018, https://www.washingtonpost.com/history/2018/10/11/we-lived-like-we-were-wall-street/.
22. Leeanna Keith, *The Colfax Massacre: The Untold Story of Black Power, White Terror, and the Death of Reconstruction* (New York: Oxford University Press, 2009).
23. "The Fourth," *The Memphis Daily Appeal,* July 6, 1875.
24. Shayla Moon, #WHYDOIVOTE, LinkedIn, November 2024, https://www.linkedin.com/posts/shayla-moon_whydoivote-honor-vote-activity-7257003187939733504-mW2Q/.
25. *The Encyclopedia of Oklahoma History and Culture,* "Segregation," Oklahoma Historical Society, https://www.okhistory.org/publications/enc/entry?entry=SE006.
26. Scott Ellsworth, "The Tulsa Race Riot," https://tulsareparations.z19.web.core.windows.net/TulsaRiot.htm.
27. Steve Gerkin, "Beno Hall: Tulsa's Den of Terror," *The Pickup,* May 27, 2025, https://thepickup.com/beno-hall-tulsas-den-of-terror.
28. Lee Roy Chapman, "The Nightmare of Dreamland," *The Pickup*, November 21, 2024, https://thepickup.com/the-nightmare-of-dreamland.
29. "The City of Tulsa Was the Klan and Mob in the 1921 Race Massacre," *The Black Wall Street Times,* April 29, 2022, https://theblackwallsttimes.com/2022/04/29/the-city-of-tulsa-was-the-klan-and-mob-in-the-1921-race-massacre/.
30. Steve Gerkin, "Beno Hall: Tulsa's Ku Klux Klan Klubhouse," Center for Public Secrets, July 6, 2023, https://www.centerforpublicsecrets.org/post/beno-hall-tulsa-s-ku-klux-klan-klubhouse.

* Faye Eddie Gates, *Riot on Greenwood: The Total Destruction of Black Wall Street* (Austin, TX: Eakin Press, 2021).

CHAPTER 3: URBAN REMOVAL

1. "5,000 Negroes Held in Fairgrounds Camp," *Tulsa Daily World*, June 2, 1921, https://chroniclingamerica.loc.gov/lccn/sn85042345/1921-06-02/ed-1/seq-2/.
2. "Confirmed Deaths: A Preliminary Report," 2025, https://tulsareparations.z19.web.core.windows.net/Deaths.htm.
3. I. Marc Carlson, "Martial Law Orders," The Tulsa Race Massacre, June 14, 2017, https://tulsaraceriot.wordpress.com/2017/06/14/martial-law-orders/.
4. "An American Pogrom: Reckoning with the 1921 Tulsa Race Massacre," Museum of Jewish Heritage—a Living Memorial to the Holocaust, April 30, 2021, https://mjhnyc.org/blog/an-american-pogrom-reckoning-with-the-1921-tulsa-race-massacre/.
5. Black Wall Street USA, "The Last Holocaust Survivor Speaks. Olivia J. Hooker Is the Last Surviving Black Wall Street Tulsa 1921 Holocaust Survivor at 95 Years Old," Facebook, 2017, www.facebook.com/blackwallstreetusa/videos/the-last-holocaust-survivor-speaks.
6. Victor Luckerson, "Everything They Owned Burned, and They Still Can't Get Restitution 102 Years Later," Opinion, *The New York Times*, July 28, 2023, https://www.nytimes.com/2023/07/28/opinion/tulsa-race-massacre-reparations.html.
7. "Cannot Enforce Fire Ordinance," *Tulsa Daily World*, September 2, 1921, https://www.docsteach.org/documents/document/cannot-enforce-fire-ordinance.
8. Buck Colbert Franklin, *My Life and an Era: The Autobiography of Buck Colbert Franklin*, ed. John Hope Franklin and John Whittington Franklin (Baton Rouge: Louisiana State University Press, 2000), 197–98.
9. "Wess & Cathryn Young: Survivors of Tulsa 1921 Race Massacre," Voices of Oklahoma, Oklahoma Historical Society, August 21, 2019, https://voicesofoklahoma.com/interviews/young-wess-cathryn/.
10. Lee Roy Chapman, "The Nightmare of Dreamland," *The Pickup*, November 21, 2024, https://thepickup.com/the-nightmare-of-dreamland.
11. *Gilliam, N.L., vs. T.D. Evans et al.*, Case #23312, June 29, 1921.
12. *Holloway, W.S., vs. T.D. Evans et al.*, Case #23372, May 31, 1923.
13. *Harrison, Belle, vs. T.D. Evans et al.*, Case #23373, May 31, 1923.
14. Spreadsheet, "Insurance Claims and Lawsuit Filed as a Result of the Massacre, Including Policy Numbers and Settlement Info," prepared by SolomonSimmonsLaw.
15. Andre Perry, Anthony Barr, and Carl Romer, "The True Costs of the Tulsa Race Massacre, 100 Years Later," Brookings, May 28, 2021, https://www.brookings.edu/articles/the-true-costs-of-the-tulsa-race-massacre-100-years-later/.
16. Case filing, J. L. Northington vs. Westchester Fire Insurance Company of New York, Tulsa County District Court, May 22, 1922.
17. "To Appraise All Loss by Negroes," *Tulsa World*, June 3, 1921, p. 1, https://chroniclingamerica.loc.gov/lccn/sn85042345/1921-06-03/ed-1/seq-1/.
18. Maurice Willows, "Disaster Relief Report," in *1921 Tulsa Race Riot: The American Red Cross—Angels of Mercy*, ed. Bob Hower (Lucky Eight Pub, 1998), 145.
19. "Realtors Start Task of Listing All Losses," *The Tulsa Tribune*, June 3, 1921.
20. "The Tulsa Race Massacre," Oklahoma Historical Society, n.d., www.okhistory.org/learn/trm.
21. "Dallas Offers Assistance," *Tulsa World*, June 4, 1921.
22. Roscoe Dunjee was an important figure in the Oklahoma civil rights movement, a gifted writer, an orator, and a member of the NAACP's national board of directors.
23. Sadly, the Williamses could never truly be made whole after the Massacre. Loula's

mental health deteriorated, and by 1925 she was in an asylum. They lost their two other theaters before Loula's death in 1927.

24. "New Dreamland Theatre at Tulsa, Oklahoma," *The Black Dispatch,* September 14, 1922.
25. Carlos Moreno, "Volunteer Spotlight: Using Data to Reveal an Untold Story," Code for America, February 22, 2022, https://codeforamerica.org/news/volunteer-spotlight-using-data-to-reveal-an-untold-story/.
26. Eddie Faye Gates, *They Came Searching: How Blacks Sought the Promised Land in Tulsa* (Austin, TX: Eakin Press, 1997), 112.
27. "Bad Niggers," editorial, *Tulsa World,* June 4, 1921, 4.
28. T. D. Evans, editorial, *Tulsa World,* June 14, 1921.
29. "It Must Not Be Again," editorial, *The Tulsa Tribune,* June 4, 1921, p. 8.
30. Suzette M. Malveaux, "A Taxonomy of Silencing: The Law's 100 Year Suppression of the Tulsa Race Massacre," *Boston University Law Review* 102 (2022): 2173–236, https://scholar.law.colorado.edu/faculty-articles/1587.
31. Janine Jackson, "Tulsa: 'A Cover-Up Happens Because the Powers That Be Are Implicated,'" FAIR, June 9, 2021, https://fair.org/home/tulsa-a-cover-up-happens-because-the-powers-that-be-are-implicated/.
32. "The slums are the handiwork of a vicious system of the white society; Negroes live in them but do not make them any more than a prisoner makes a prison." Dr. Martin Luther King, Jr., "The Crisis in America's Cities," *The Atlantic,* February 2018, https://www.theatlantic.com/magazine/archive/2018/02/martin-luther-king-jr-the-crisis-in-americas-cities/552536/.
33. Dr. Bate was the first African American admitted to the Tulsa County Medical Society, and was a leader in the Greenwood and Black North Tulsa community for many years. See Dr. Charles Bate interview by Cherie Poyas for the Junior League of Tulsa, May 6, 1980, Tulsa City-County Library, http://digitalcollections.tulsalibrary.org/digital/collection/p15020coll10/id/136.
34. Tulsa Urban League, "A Concise Review of Housing Problems Affecting Negroes in Tulsa," 1958, http://digitalcollections.tulsalibrary.org/digital/collection/p16063coll1/id/5360/.
35. Joe Looney, "Greenwood Fades Away Before Advance of Expressway," *The Tulsa Tribune,* May 4, 1967.
36. Brent Cebul, "Tearing Down Black America," *Boston Review,* July 22, 2020, https://www.bostonreview.net/articles/brent-cebul-tearing-down-black-america/.
37. Gates, *They Came Searching,* 107.
38. *The Tulsa Tribune,* April 9, 1970.

* Written Testimony of Hughes Van Ellis, United States House of Representatives Subcommittee on the Constitution, Civil Rights, and Civil Liberties, Wednesday, May 19, 2021.

CHAPTER 4: THEY'LL KILL YOU IN THIS TOWN

1. The original "sooners" were outlaw settlers who illegally entered Oklahoma Territory before the official Land Rush of 1889, claiming prime land ahead of the designated starting time, violating federal rules. Unfortunately, their lawlessness and greed are celebrated in the name of my favorite football team.
2. Born in 1885 in the hill country of eastern Mississippi to formerly enslaved parents, Ellis Walker Woods spent his early years farming before heading to Rust College in Holly Springs. There, he worked his way through both secondary and collegiate studies. After graduating, he moved to Memphis in hopes of finding opportunity, but jobs were scarce. A flyer about schools in Oklahoma seeking

"colored" teachers caught his eye. Woods set out on foot and ultimately became the first principal of Booker T. Washington High School, a position he held from 1913 to 1948. Throughout his long tenure, he prioritized hiring teachers with advanced degrees, a commitment that helped the school earn accreditation from the North Central Association.

3. Preservation and Design Studio PLLC, "Report for Greenwood District, Tulsa, Tulsa County, Oklahoma," May 2020, https://www.okhistory.org/shpo/docs/ReportforGreenwoodDistrict.pdf.
4. Don Ross Associates, "Focus on Business—Holman's Jewelry," *The Oklahoma Eagle,* August 14, 1980.
5. Out of this reckoning came the legal charter of the modern Muscogee (Creek) Nation. In its second article, the 1866 treaty declared that Creeks of African descent and their descendants "shall have and enjoy all the rights and privileges of native citizens, including an equal interest in the soil and national funds." This radical promise of Black equality was negotiated and signed by Cow Tom himself.
6. My father was kicked (literally, in the behind) off his bus by the white driver because he refused to sit in the back. He and his brother and sister had to pay to ride the city bus to and from school because the school system would not have the school buses pick them up to attend Monroe Middle School and McLain High School. Aunt Edna had to fight the white students weekly due to their constant harassment. She also vigorously protested one teacher who, when he led the daily Pledge of Allegiance, would follow the line "with liberty and justice for all" by saying, "except Black people."
7. BlackPast, "(1963) George Wallace, 'Segregation Now, Segregation Forever,'" January 22, 2013, https://www.blackpast.org/african-american-history/1963-george-wallace-segregation-now-segregation-forever/.
8. "Civil Rights: The Little Rock School Integration Crisis," Dwight D. Eisenhower Presidential Library, https://www.eisenhowerlibrary.gov/research/online-documents/civil-rights-little-rock-school-integration-crisis.

* Personal letter to Professor Charles Ogletree, October 20, 2007.

CHAPTER 5: LAW IS MY MINISTRY AND JUSTICE IS MY PASSION

1. Incidentally, it was a fantastic game. Texas beat us 27–24, and De'Mond rushed for a Red River Shootout record 223 yards while future Heisman Trophy winner Ricky Williams had 241 yards.
2. A PWI is an institution of higher learning where at least 50 percent of the students are white, often established during the era of segregated education.
3. This annual gathering brings together Black student leaders and members of Black Student Governments (BSGs) from universities in and beyond the Big 12 athletic conference. The event aims to provide networking opportunities, leadership development, cultural enrichment, and conversations on issues impacting Black students in higher education.
4. Muskogee has a lot of significance to Black Creeks and Black people in general. After Oklahoma became a territory, Muskogee became a hub for Black culture and commerce, and along with Greenwood was part of a broader network of prosperous Black towns in Oklahoma. The city was also a center of activism and organization for Black communities, including advocacy for Black rights within the Muscogee (Creek) Nation.
5. *The Encyclopedia of Oklahoma History and Culture,* "Fisher, Ada Lois Sipuel (1924–1995)," Oklahoma Historical Society, https://www.okhistory.org/publications/enc/entry?entry=FI009.

6. On August 19, 1958—eighteen months before the more famous Greensboro sit-in—Clara Luper, an Oklahoma City history teacher and NAACP Youth Council adviser, led thirteen Black students, including her ten-year-old daughter, Marilyn, to stage the nation's first lunch counter sit-in at Katz Drug Store in downtown Oklahoma City. Their action helped ignite a tactic that shaped the course of the civil rights movement. See Kelsy Schlotthauer,"60 Years Later, Oklahoma's Sit-In Movement Is Remembered," *The Oklahoman,* August 12, 2018, https://www.oklahoman.com/story/business/2018/08/12/60-years-later-oklahomas-sit-in-movement-is-remembered/60508097007/.
7. Jean Pagel, "KKK Gathering Sparks Anti-Rally in Tulsa," *The Oklahoman,* May 5, 1996, https://www.oklahoman.com/story/news/1996/05/05/kkk-gathering-sparks-anti-rally-in-tulsa/62356160007/.
8. Eddie Faye Gates, *Riot on Greenwood: The Total Destruction of Black Wall Street* (Austin, TX: Eakin Press, 2003), 51–52.
9. "John Hope Franklin Timeline," Duke University Libraries, https://library.duke.edu/rubenstein/collections/creators/people/johnhopefranklin.
10. United Nations, "Basic Principles and Guidelines on the Right to a Remedy and Reparation for Victims of Gross Violations of International Human Rights Law and Serious Violations of International Humanitarian Law," OHCHR, December 16, 2005, https://www.ohchr.org/en/instruments-mechanisms/instruments/basic-principles-and-guidelines-right-remedy-and-reparation.
11. "April 16, 1862: Compensated Emancipation Act," Zinn Education Project, https://www.zinnedproject.org/news/tdih/compensated-emancipation-act/.
12. "President Gerald R. Ford's Remarks Upon Signing a Proclamation Concerning Japanese-American Internment During World War II," Gerald R. Ford Presidential Library & Museum, February 19, 1976.
13. "Japanese-American Incarceration During World War II," U.S. National Archives and Records Administration, April 10, 2017, https://www.archives.gov/education/lessons/japanese-relocation.
14. Civil Liberties Act Amendments of 1992, Pub. L. No. 102-371, https://www.congress.gov/bill/102nd-congress/house-bill/4551.
15. Cornell William Brooks and Linda Blimes, "The United States Pays Reparations Every Day—Just Not to Black America," *PolicyCast,* Harvard Kennedy School, February 3, 2022, https://www.hks.harvard.edu/faculty-research/policycast/us-pays-reparations-every-day-just-not-black-america.
16. Mark Talkington, "Council Unanimously Approves Settlement with Section 14 Group, Paving Way for Reparations," *The Palm Springs Post,* November 14, 2024, https://thepalmspringspost.com/council-unanimously-approves-settlement-with-section-14-group-paving-way-for-reparations/.
17. Michela Moscufo, "House Repairs, a Car, Grandkids: Where Evanston's Reparations Payments Are Going," NBC News, December 23, 2024, https://www.nbcnews.com/news/nbcblk/reparations-evanston-il-transforming-lives-black-residents-rcna173534.
18. Kristy Hutchings and Tyler Evains, "LA County Returns Bruce's Beach to Black Family 90-Plus Years After Manhattan Beach Took It," *Daily Breeze,* June 28, 2022.
19. Charles Hamilton Houston was the first general counsel for the NAACP and widely known as "the man who killed Jim Crow."

* Written Testimony of Mother Viola Fletcher, United States House of Representatives Subcommittee on the Constitution, Civil Rights, and Civil Liberties, Wednesday, May 19, 2021.

CHAPTER 6: WE NEVER GOT AN EVEN PLAYING FIELD

1. *Alexander v. State of Oklahoma,* Case No. 03-C-133-E, 7 (N.D. Okla. Mar. 19, 2004).
2. Daniel J. Hemel, "Ogletree Vows to Continue Lawsuit," *The Harvard Crimson,* March 25, 2004, https://www.thecrimson.com/article/2004/3/25/ogletree-vows-to-continue-lawsuit-climenko/.
3. Joel Jankowsky is an OU Law School graduate who served in the U.S. Army Judge Advocate General's Corps and was a legislative assistant in the U.S. House of Representatives and partner at the international law firm Akin.
4. *Alexander v. Oklahoma,* 391 F.3d 1155 (10th Cir. 2004).
5. Mr. Young was a longtime friend of my family. I had known him all my life, but I didn't know until these events that he was a Massacre survivor.
6. "Otis Clark," Voices of Oklahoma, Oklahoma Historical Society, https://voicesofoklahoma.com/interviews/clark-otis/.
7. Eddie Faye Gates, *Riot on Greenwood: The Total Destruction of Black Wall Street* (Austin, TX: Eakin Press, 2003), 64.
8. Gates, *Riot on Greenwood,* 64.
9. Gates, *Riot on Greenwood,* 77.
10. *John Hope Franklin Tulsa-Greenwood Race Riot Claims Accountability Act of 2007: Hearing on H.R. 1995, Before the Subcommittee on the Constitution, Civil Rights, and Civil Liberties,* 110th Cong. (2007) (testimony of Olivia Hooker, Ph.D., James B. Duke Professor Emeritus of History, Duke University School of Law), April 24, 2007, https://www.govinfo.gov/content/pkg/CHRG-110hhrg34924/html/CHRG-110hhrg34924.htm.
11. "John Hope Franklin Timeline," Duke University Libraries, https://library.duke.edu/rubenstein/collections/creators/people/johnhopefranklin.
12. One of the things I learned during my time with Uncle Don was that he once served as the executive director of an organization located in Harlem, New York, called the Harlem Commonwealth Council (HCC). Charles Rangel represented the community in Congress for more than forty years, from 1971 to 2017. Here's how the HCC describes its mission: "For 55 years, Harlem Commonwealth Council (HCC) Inc. has provided education and economic empowerment to residents and businesses in Upper Manhattan and the Bronx. Established under the 1964 Landmark Economic Opportunity Act, HCC is deeply rooted in the history of Harlem and invested in helping its people and businesses thrive." See https://www.harlemcommonwealth.org/our-story.
13. Written statement by the author.
14. Oklahoma helped launch Marshall's career toward an eventual Supreme Court seat. In 1941, Marshall, then a young NAACP lawyer, defended W. D. Lyons, a Black man accused of murder under dubious circumstances. Lyons had been brutally tortured into confessing, a common tactic used to convict Black defendants in the Jim Crow South. Though Marshall was unable to overturn the conviction, the case highlighted systemic racial injustices and strengthened his resolve to fight for civil rights. His work in such cases laid the foundation for his later Supreme Court victories.
15. "Thurgood Marshall as an Advocate," Supreme Court Historical Society, https://civics.supremecourthistory.org/article/thurgood-marshall-as-an-advocate/.
16. Thomas J. Sugrue, "Terror in the Streets," *The Washington Post,* March 10, 2002.
17. *John Hope Franklin Tulsa-Greenwood Race Riot Claims Accountability Act of 2007: Hearing on H.R. 1995, Before the Subcommittee on the Constitution, Civil Rights, and Civil Liberties* (statement of Representative Nadler).
18. *John Hope Franklin Tulsa-Greenwood Race Riot Claims Accountability Act of 2007:*

Hearing on H.R. 1995, Before the Subcommittee on the Constitution, Civil Rights, and Civil Liberties (statement of Representative Issa).

19. "Citizenship Applications Returned to Muscogee Nation for Review Tribal Judge's Ruling May Establish a Standard for Membership Claims," *The Oklahoman,* March 21, 2006, https://www.oklahoman.com/story/news/2006/03/21/citizenship-applications-returned-muscogee-tribal-judges-ruling-establish-standard-membership-claims/61895150007/.
20. Shannon Schumacher et al., "Five Facts About Black Women's Experiences in Health Care," KFF, May 7, 2024, https://www.kff.org/racial-equity-and-health-policy/issue-brief/five-facts-about-black-womens-experiences-in-health-care/. During an ER visit for a recurring reproductive health issue, Mia experienced this same kind of unfair treatment. A nurse refused to provide my college-educated, broadcast journalist wife, one of the most intelligent and well-known women in the Tulsa area, with pain medication because the nurse thought she was "pill searching."
21. Cary Funk, "Black Americans' Views About Health Disparities, Experiences with Health Care," Pew Research Center, April 7, 2022, https://www.pewresearch.org/science/2022/04/07/black-americans-views-about-health-disparities-experiences-with-health-care/.
22. Ariel Washington and Jill Randall, " 'We're Not Taken Seriously': Describing the Experiences of Perceived Discrimination in Medical Settings for Black Women," *Journal of Racial and Ethnic Health Disparities* 10, no. 2 (2023): 883–91, https://doi.org/10.1007/s40615-022-01276-9.
23. National Public Radio, "Suspects Arrested in Okla. Shootings," NPR, April 8, 2012, https://www.npr.org/2012/04/08/150247062/suspects-arrested-in-okla-shootings.
24. Here is how the institute describes its mission: "The Oklahoma Policy Institute seeks to create a more equitable Oklahoma through its nonpartisan policy research, analysis, and advocacy. OK Policy encourages critical conversations through data-driven research and outreach regarding state policy so that every Oklahoman has equitable opportunities to thrive." See https://okpolicy.org/who-we-are.
25. Dylan Goforth, "Security Guard Found with Weed When He Shot and Paralyzed Tulsa Man," *The Frontier,* May 13, 2015, https://www.readfrontier.org/stories/security-guard-found-with-weed-when-he-shot-and-paralyzed-tulsa-man/.
26. Roni Caryn Rabin, "Paralyzed by Gunfire, but Denied Care," *Well* blog, *The New York Times,* July 20, 2015, https://archive.nytimes.com/well.blogs.nytimes.com/2015/07/20/illegal-activity-fine-print-leaves-some-insured-but-uncovered/. This article reports on insurers' use of "illegal activity" exclusions to deny coverage even without convictions, highlighting the case of Monroe "Trey" Bird III, who was never charged with any crime yet was denied care after being shot and paralyzed by a white security guard. It underscores how such denials operate as systemic discrimination that disproportionately harms Black families and strips them of economic security.
27. Founded in 1903, Boley was one of the most prominent all-Black towns established during the early twentieth century and the only one remaining. Located in Okfuskee County, it thrived as a center for Black entrepreneurship, self-governance, and culture. Boley was home to banks, schools, newspapers, and businesses owned by African Americans, attracting settlers seeking economic and social independence. It gained national recognition when Booker T. Washington praised its success. Though the town declined due to the Great Depression and urban migration, it remains a symbol of Black resilience. Today, Boley hosts an annual rodeo and celebrates its rich history as a pioneering Black community.

28. "A Security Guard's Bullet Ended Monroe Bird's Life. Here's the Rest of the Story," *The Frontier,* August 21, 2017, https://www.readfrontier.org/stories/monroe-bird-was-shot-by-a-security-guard-then-he-died-in-silence/. This article details how Ricky Stone, the white security guard who shot Monroe "Trey" Bird III in the back, was allowed to walk free under Oklahoma's stand your ground law, even though he was ineligible for that protection due to his own unlawful conduct—an outcome that exemplifies how the justice system shields white perpetrators while denying Black victims accountability.
29. Former Oklahoma City police officer Daniel Holtzclaw was charged with sexually assaulting thirteen Black women while on duty, deliberately targeting those he thought would not be believed. In 2015, a jury convicted him on eighteen counts and sentenced him to 263 years in prison. I represented these women in related civil litigation alongside my fraternity brother, noted civil rights attorney Ben Crump—an experience that further elevated my national profile.
30. Tobias Salinger, "Video Released in Fatal Police Shooting of Unarmed Oklahoma Man Terence Crutcher (WARNING – GRAPHIC)," *New York Daily News,* September 19, 2016, https://www.nydailynews.com/2016/09/19/video-released-in-fatal-police-shooting-of-unarmed-oklahoma-man-terence-crutcher-warning-graphic/.
31. "Read Full Letter from Jury That Acquitted Tulsa Police Officer in Fatal Shooting of Terence Crutcher," KFOR.com, May 22, 2017, https://kfor.com/news/read-full-letter-from-jury-that-acquitted-tulsa-police-officer-in-fatal-shooting-of-terence-crutcher/.
32. PBS, "100 Years after Tulsa Race Massacre, Black Mistrust Remains," PBS News, May 29, 2021, https://www.pbs.org/newshour/nation/100-years-after-tulsa-race-massacre-black-mistrust-remains.

* Interview by Eddie Faye Gates, Chair, Oklahoma Commission to Study the Tulsa Race riot of 1921. Recorded February 2000.

CHAPTER 7: FINDING PHIL JACKSON

1. Liz Farmer, "Tulsa Struggles to Make Amends for a Massacre It Ignored for Nearly a Century," *Governing,* October 16, 2018, https://www.governing.com/archive/gov-tulsa-black-wall-street.html.
2. "Chamber Donates Meetings Minutes from 1921 to Greenwood Cultural Center, Tulsa Regional Chamber," May 28, 2019, https://tulsachamber.com/news/2019/05/28/community-development/chamber-donates-meeting-minutes-from-1921-to-greenwood-cultural-center/.
3. "Tulsa Regional Chamber Donates Minutes from 1921 to Greenwood Cultural Center," *The Black Wall Street Times,* May 28, 2019, https://theblackwallsttimes.com/2019/05/28/tulsa-regional-chamber-donates-minutes-from-1921-to-greenwood-cultural-center/.
4. *Hearings on H.R.40–116th Congress (2019–2020): Commission to Study and Develop Reparation Proposals for African-Americans Act,* June 19, 2019, https://www.congress.gov/bill/116th-congress/house-bill/40.
5. Jan Hoffman, "Johnson & Johnson Ordered to Pay $572 Million in Landmark Opioid Trial," *The New York Times,* August 26, 2019, https://www.nytimes.com/2019/08/26/health/oklahoma-opioids-johnson-and-johnson.html.
6. Oklahoma Statutes, Title 50, Nuisances, §50-2 "Public Nuisance," https://oksenate.gov/sites/default/files/2019-12/os50.pdf.
7. Oklahoma Statutes, Title 50, Nuisances, §50-1 "Nuisance Defined," https://oksenate.gov/sites/default/files/2019-12/os50.pdf.

8. Lauri Scherer, “Estimating Long-Term Effects of the 1921 Tulsa Race Massacre,” Summary of Working Paper 28985 (National Bureau of Economic Research, September 1, 2021), https://www.nber.org/digest/202109/estimating-long-term-effects-1921-tulsa-race-massacre.
9. David Blatt, Executive Director, Oklahoma Policy Institute, “Community Discussion: Resegregation of Tulsa's Schools?,” presentation to the Dan Allen Center for Social Justice, September 4, 2014.
10. Hannibal Johnson, “Greenwood District,” in *The Encyclopedia of Oklahoma History and Culture,* Oklahoma Historical Society, https://www.okhistory.org/publications/enc/entry.php?entry=GR024.
11. Andre Perry et al., “The True Costs of the Tulsa Race Massacre, 100 Years Later,” Brookings Institution, May 28, 2021, https://www.brookings.edu/articles/the-true-costs-of-the-tulsa-race-massacre-100-years-later/.
12. Hutchins Center for African & African American Research, “A Conversation Between Charisse Burden-Stelly & Orisanmi Burton,” YouTube, January 25, 2024, https://www.youtube.com/watch?v=8CE6RVLFWeo.
13. Justice for Greenwood Foundation, “Press Conference - September 1, 2020 (Tulsa) - Justice for Greenwood Foundation,” YouTube, September 2, 2020, https://www.youtube.com/watch?v=nhEISldRjs0.

* Lessie Benningfield Randle, Deposition Transcript, *Randle v. City of Tulsa,* Case No. 121502 (taken remotely, October 14, 2020).

CHAPTER 8: PRESSURE

1. Transcript: *Randle, et.al. v. City of Tulsa, et. al.,* CV-2020-1179, May 2, 2022.
2. Ibid.
3. Ibid.
4. Ibid.
5. Ibid.
6. The ruling was the number one story in America for a few hours until the United States Supreme Court leak related to the *Dobbs* decision, which would overturn *Roe v. Wade,* occurred later that day.
7. Lessie Benningfield Randle, Deposition Transcript, *Randle v. City of Tulsa,* Case No. 121502 (taken remotely, October 14, 2020).
8. Viola Fletcher, Deposition Transcript, *Randle v. City of Tulsa,* Case No. 121502 (taken at her residence, October 16, 2020).
9. Marissa Taylor, “UW Forum Hacked with Racist, Pornographic Material,” *News Letter Journal,* February 18, 2021, https://newslj.com/uw-forum-hacked-racist-pornographic-material.
10. Randy Krehbiel, “ ‘No Reconciliation Without Reparations,’ Says Race Massacre Panelist,” *Tulsa World,* June 1, 2020, https://tulsaworld.com/news/article_080d60be-bfac-5c56-a44a-0d7ce92689c7.html.
11. “Five Tulsa Police Officers Indicted in Corruption Probe,” News on 6, July 20, 2010, https://www.newson6.com/story/5e366c562f69d76f6207bd5e/five-tulsa-police-officers-indicted-in-corruption-probe.
12. Personal email sent on October 20, 2016.
13. “City of Tulsa Releases 2023 Equality Indicators Report,” 2 News Oklahoma KJRH, April 19, 2024, https://www.kjrh.com/news/local-news/city-of-tulsa-releases-2023-equality-indicators-report.
14. Kimberly Jackson, “Mayor Says Reparations Would Divide the City, Focuses on Development,” KTUL, https://ktul.com/news/local/mayor-says-reparations-would-divide-the-city-focuses-on-development.

15. Letter from the Tulsa Race Massacre Centennial Commission to Mayor G. T. Bynum, April 16, 2020.
16. Matt Trotter, "Race Massacre Centennial Commission Announces New Site for Greenwood Rising History Center," Public Radio Tulsa, April 28, 2020, https://www.publicradiotulsa.org/local-regional/2020-04-28/race-massacre-centennial-commission-announces-new-site-for-greenwood-rising-history-center.
17. Andrea Suozzo, "George Kaiser Family Foundation, Fiscal Year Ending Dec. 2023," *ProPublica,* May 9, 2013, https://projects.propublica.org/nonprofits/organizations/731574370.
18. Michael S. Schmidt and Luke Broadwater, "Officers' Injuries, Including Concussions, Show Scope of Violence at Capitol Riot," *The New York Times,* February 12, 2021, sec. U.S., https://www.nytimes.com/2021/02/11/us/politics/capitol-riot-police-officer-injuries.html.
19. Damario Solomon-Simmons, "The Power of White Supremacy," Instagram Reel audio, January 6, 2021, https://www.instagram.com/reels/audio/3231077943872966/.
20. "Sen. Lankford to Stay on Tulsa Race Massacre Commission," 2 News Oklahoma KJRH, January 25, 2021, https://www.kjrh.com/news/local-news/sen-lankford-to-stay-on-tulsa-race-massacre-commission.
21. Greenwood Rising (@GreenwoodRising), "TULSA TRIUMPHS," X (formerly Twitter), February 15, 2021, https://x.com/GreenwoodRising/status/1361380845664292865.
22. James King, "Survivors and Descendants Gather amid Growing Call for Reparations," News Channel 8 Tulsa, May 31, 2021, https://okcfox.com/news/local/survivors-and-descendants-gather-amid-growing-call-for-reparations.
23. "US: Failed Justice 100 Years After Tulsa Race Massacre," Human Rights Watch, May 21, 2021, https://www.hrw.org/news/2021/05/21/us-failed-justice-100-years-after-tulsa-race-massacre.

* Eddie Faye Gates, *Riot on Greenwood: The Total Destruction of Black Wall Street* (Austin, TX: Eakin Press, 2003), 65.

CHAPTER 9: THE POWER OF MORAL AUTHORITY

1. *Continuing Injustice: The Centennial of The Tulsa-Greenwood Race Massacre,* Before the Subcommittee on the Constitution, Civil Rights, and Civil Liberties of the Committee on the Judiciary, 117th Cong., May 19, 2021 (statement of Hughes Van Ellis).
2. *Continuing Injustice: The Centennial of The Tulsa-Greenwood Race Massacre,* Before the Subcommittee on the Constitution, Civil Rights, and Civil Liberties of the Committee on the Judiciary, 117th Cong., May 19, 2021 (statement of Lessie Benningfield Randle).
3. *Continuing Injustice: The Centennial of The Tulsa-Greenwood Race Massacre,* Before the Subcommittee on the Constitution, Civil Rights, and Civil Liberties of the Committee on the Judiciary, 117th Cong., May 19, 2021 (statement of Damario Solomon-Simmons).
4. "Congressman Johnson Announces Compensation Bill During Hearing on 'Continuing Justice: The Centennial of the Tulsa-Greenwood Massacre,'" press release, May 21, 2021, https://hankjohnson.house.gov/media-center/press-releases/congressman-johnson-announces-compensation-bill-during-hearing.
5. In Black families, titles like "Uncle" and "Auntie" go beyond bloodlines. They reflect African traditions of kinship and respect that endured through enslavement and segregation, when family often meant more than genealogy.

That's how I grew up. The title carried the respect they deserved and connotated the role they played in my life.

6. Brandy McDonnell, "'Remember + Rise' Tulsa Race Massacre Event Scrapped After 'Unexpected Circumstances,'" *The Oklahoman,* May 27, 2021, https://www.oklahoman.com/story/entertainment/2021/05/27/remember-rise-tulsa-race-massacre-Centennial-featuring-john-legend-canceled/7477836002/.
7. Cory Smith, "Chairman: Higher Financial Demands for Survivors Led to Remember & Rise Cancellation," KTUL, May 28, 2021, https://ktul.com/news/local/chairman-higher-financial-demands-for-survivors-led-to-remember-rise-cancellation.
8. Frederick Douglass, "The Significance of Emancipation in the West Indies," in *Two Speeches by Frederick Douglass, One on West India Emancipation* (Rochester, NY: O.P. Dewey, 1857), 22.
9. News 9, "A Look Back at Tulsa's Infamous 'Tower Guy,'" News on 6, August 16, 2015, https://www.newson6.com/story/5e34c378e0c96e774b34a285/a-look-back-at-tulsas-infamous-tower-guy.
10. Keisha N. Blain, "Tulsa Race Massacre Survivors Are Fighting for Reparations, 100 Years Later," MSNBC, May 31, 2021, https://www.msnbc.com/opinion/tulsa-race-massacre-survivors-are-fighting-reparations-100-years-later-n1268891.
11. Matt Trotter, "Soil Ceremony Memorializes Unnamed Victims of Tulsa Race Massacre," Public Radio Tulsa, June 2021, https://www.publicradiotulsa.org/local-regional/2021-06-01/soil-ceremony-memorializes-unnamed-victims-of-tulsa-race-massacre.
12. "Commander Apologizes for Oklahoma National Guard's Role in Tulsa Race Massacre," Public Radio Tulsa, May 31, 2021, https://www.publicradiotulsa.org/local-regional/2021-05-31/commander-apologizes-for-oklahoma-national-guards-role-in-tulsa-race-massacre.
13. Roland S. Martin, "Atty Damario Solomon-Simmons Details Demands for Restitution, 'Public Nuisance' Suit against Tulsa," YouTube, June 1, 2021, https://www.youtube.com/watch?v=nPX2-JW-Syc.
14. Ayesha Rascoe and Alana Wise, "Biden Says the Tulsa Race Massacre 'Can't Be Buried, No Matter How Hard People Try,'" NPR, June 1, 2021, https://www.npr.org/2021/06/01/1001380354/biden-to-visit-tulsa-to-mark-the-1921-race-massacre-that-wrecked-black-wall-stre.
15. Ofronama Biu et al., *The Color of Wealth in Tulsa, Oklahoma: The Destruction of Greenwood and the Legacy of Land Loss,* 2021, https://racepowerpolicy.org/wp-content/uploads/2024/01/Color-of-Wealth-Tulsa-Full-Report_December2021.pdf.
16. "The Color of Wealth: The Destruction of Greenwood & Tulsa's Legacy of Loss," hosted by Karen Hunter, Justice for Greenwood Foundation, https://www.youtube.com/watch?v=ufpXhI1_fBY.
17. "Tulsa City Council Passes Race Massacre Resolution," 2 News Oklahoma KJRH, June 3, 2021, https://www.kjrh.com/news/local-news/tulsa-city-council-passes-race-massacre-resolution.
18. "Quotes from Rev. Dr. King's Last Years: 'a Revolution of Values,'" 2017, Kairos, January 15, 2017, https://kairoscenter.org/quotes-from-rev-dr-kings-last-years/.

* Testimonial of Dr. R. T. Bridgewater in Parrish, Events of the Tulsa Disaster, 46, 120. Tulsa City Directory, 1921.

CHAPTER 10: KEEPING IT IN THE COURT

1. Carlos Chappelle was a Massacre descendant and the first Black presiding judge in Tulsa County. I knew him—he died in 2015—and he was a great gentleman

whose grandfather Peter Addison Chappelle was one of the three lawyers who represented people whose houses and businesses were destroyed during the Massacre. His father, the late Reverend Dr. T. Oscar Chappelle, Sr., was the longtime pastor of Morning Star Baptist Church, the only one of the thirteen churches that survived the Massacre that is still in operation today.

2. *Randle v. City of Tulsa,* Case No. CV-2020-1179, Transcript of Proceedings Before the Honorable Caroline Wall, Judge of the District Court, Tulsa County Courthouse, Tulsa, Oklahoma, September 28, 2021, 4. https://www.justiceforgreenwood.org/wp-content/uploads/2022/04/2021-09-28.-Hearing-Transcript.pdf.
3. *Randle v. City of Tulsa,* transcript, 12–14.
4. *Randle v. City of Tulsa,* transcript, 65.
5. Civil Rights Cold Case Records Collection Act of 2018, Pub. L. No. 115-426 (2020).
6. "Oklahoma Court Overturns $465M Opioid Ruling against J&J," AP, November 9, 2021, https://apnews.com/article/business-oklahoma-opioids-statutes-health-555d0e67459962416b251c8f15edd326.
7. *State ex rel. Att'y Gen. of Okla. v. Johnson & Johnson,* 2021 OK 54, 499 P.3d 719.
8. Kimberly Jackson, "Mayor Says Reparations Would Divide the City, Focuses on Development," KTUL, February 20, 2020, https://ktul.com/news/local/mayor-says-reparations-would-divide-the-city-focuses-on-development.
9. "Oklahoma Ex Rel. Attorney General of Oklahoma v. Johnson & Johnson," n.d., *Justia Law,* https://law.justia.com/cases/oklahoma/supreme-court/2021/118474.html.
10. "Bible Gateway Passage: Jeremiah 12:5 - New International Version," Bible Gateway, 2019, https://www.biblegateway.com/passage/?search=Jeremiah%2012%3A5&version=NIV.
11. Bryan Greene, "Created 150 Years Ago, the Justice Department's First Mission Was to Protect Black Rights," *Smithsonian Magazine,* July 1, 2020.
12. Chad Leistikow, "Attorney for 8 Black Former Iowa Football Players: Demands Are Not a 'Money Grab,'" *Hawk Central,* October 20, 2020, https://www.hawkcentral.com/story/sports/college/iowa/football/2020/10/19/attorney-8-black-former-iowa-football-players-demands-not-money-grab-statement-racial-discrimination/5983050002/.
13. "Timothy Mayo, Descendant of U. D. Emerson," Justice for Greenwood, May 2021, https://www.justiceforgreenwood.org/timothy-mayo-descendant-of-ud-emerson/.
14. Amir Vera et al., "Tulsa Race Massacre Reparations Lawsuit Survives Motion to Deny and Will Move Forward, Judge Rules," CNN, May 2, 2022, https://www.cnn.com/2022/05/02/us/tulsa-race-massacre-hearing-trial/index.html.
15. Ibid.
16. Deon Osborne, "City of Tulsa Will Stand Trial for Its Role in 1921 Tulsa Race Massacre," *The Black Wall Street Times,* May 3, 2022, https://theblackwallsttimes.com/2022/05/03/city-of-tulsa-will-stand-trial-for-its-role-in-1921-tulsa-race-massacre/.
17. DeNeen L. Brown, "Judge Allows Lawsuit by Tulsa Race Massacre Survivors to Proceed, *The Washington Post,* March 3, 2022, https://www.washingtonpost.com/history/2022/05/03/tulsa-race-massacre-lawsuit-proceed/.
18. Nicole Chavez, "Three Survivors of Tulsa Race Massacre Receive $1 Million Donation," CNN, May 19, 2022, https://www.cnn.com/2022/05/19/us/tulsa-massacre-survivors-1-million-donation/index.html.
19. "Watch: Survivors of the 1921 Tulsa Race Massacre on *The ReidOut,*" Justice for Greenwood Foundation, Inc., Facebook, https://www.facebook.com/justicefor

greenwood/videos/watch-survivors-of-the-1921-tulsa-race-massacre-on-the-reid-out/262485202894050/.

20. Associated Press, "Oklahoma Judge Throws Out a Suit Seeking Reparations for the Tulsa Race Massacre," NPR, July 9, 2023, https://www.npr.org/2023/07/09/1186690457/tulsa-race-massacre-reparations-lawsuit.
21. MoreLaw, "Re: Lessie Benningfield Randle, et Al. V. City of Tulsa, et Al," Morelaw.com, 2023, https://www.morelaw.com/verdicts/case.asp?n=CV-2020-1179&s=OK&d=173191.
22. Tamia Fowlkes, "Reparations Suit for Tulsa Race Massacre Dismissed," *The Washington Post,* July 10, 2023, https://www.washingtonpost.com/nation/2023/07/09/tulsa-race-riot-lawsuit-reparations-dismissed/.
23. April Siese, "'We Will Not Rest Until There Is Justice for Greenwood': 1921 Tulsa Race Massacre Survivors Vow to Fight Lawsuit Dismissal," *Reckon,* July 11, 2023, https://www.reckon.news/news/2023/07/we-will-not-rest-until-there-is-justice-for-greenwood-1921-tulsa-race-massacre-survivors-vow-to-fight-lawsuit-dismissal.html.

* Mary Jones Parrish, *Events of the Tulsa Disaster* (Tulsa, OK: self-published, 1922), 18–21.

CHAPTER 11: TWENTY-FIVE MINUTES

1. This is one of the ways government and big corporations crush poorer opponents who lack the necessary human and financial resources: They bury you in paperwork, often citing cases that don't help their arguments. Knowing that most opponents don't have the same time or manpower to fight back, they bank on people's inability to keep up with the endless motions or to fact-check every claim. Luckily, we did not have that problem.
2. Effective trial advocacy requires good storytelling and a deep connection with the jury. To achieve this, I often rely on thoughtfully chosen demonstrative aids. I frequently use visual tools—timelines, charts, enlarged photographs, and detailed diagrams—to translate complex information into clear, relatable images. I routinely use documents, such as contracts, receipts, or official records, to substantiate important points. Most important in today's world, I use powerful audio or video evidence to evoke an emotional response and make my arguments resonate. Together, these exhibits help me craft compelling, memorable arguments that connect deeply with jurors and even some judges.
3. You may be wondering why I used the term *justices* and not *judges*. In our nation's legal system, the title *judge* is used for those who preside over lower courts, such as trial courts or intermediate appellate courts. Judge Wall, for example, serves in this capacity. In contrast, members of the Oklahoma Supreme Court are referred to as *justices* because they sit on the state's highest court. Their role is not to oversee trials but to interpret the law and the state constitution, resolving legal questions that can have broad implications for how laws are applied across Oklahoma.
4. According to the U.S. Census Bureau, as of 2024 Owasso is 71 percent white and only 3.5 percent Black, with a total population of about forty thousand. Owasso has two hospitals and at least five urgent care facilities. In contrast, the majority of Black Tulsans, including Mia and me, live in North Tulsa. Depending on the source, the total population of North Tulsa is between fifty-five thousand and sixty-five thousand people.
5. Bryan's extraordinary advocacy has substantially influenced constitutional law as it relates to juvenile justice, the rights of individuals with mental impairments, and

the death penalty. His most significant U.S. Supreme Court cases probably are (1) *Miller v. Alabama,* 567 U.S. 460 (2012). The court ruled that mandatory life-without-parole sentences for juveniles violate the Eighth Amendment's prohibition on cruel and unusual punishments; (2) *Montgomery v. Louisiana,* 577 U.S. 190. This decision made the *Miller* ruling retroactive, allowing individuals previously sentenced as juveniles to seek new sentencing hearings; (3) *Madison v. Alabama,* 139 S. Ct. 718 (2019). The court held that executing a prisoner who cannot rationally understand the reason for their execution due to dementia may violate the Eighth Amendment; and (4) *Sullivan v. Florida,* 560 U.S. 181 (2010). Bryan argued against life-without-parole sentences for juveniles in non-homicide cases. Although the court did not issue a definitive ruling in *Sullivan,* it addressed the issue in the related case of *Graham v. Florida,* 560 U.S. 48 (2010).

6. *Randle v. City of Tulsa,* Case No. 121502, transcript of Proceedings Before the Oklahoma State Supreme Court, Oklahoma Judicial Center, Oklahoma City, Oklahoma, April 2, 2024.
7. I know that she was battling cancer and that is why she was not able to attend.

* Eddie Faye Gates, *Riot on Greenwood: The Total Destruction of Black Wall Street* (Austin, TX: Eakin Press, 2003), 66–67.

CHAPTER 12: SUSPENDING DISBELIEF

1. Associated Press, "Muscogee Nation Judge Rules in Favor of Citizenship for Slave Descendants," NPR, September 28, 2023, https://www.npr.org/2023/09/28/1202417288/muscogee-nation-freedmen-citizenship.
2. Russell Contreras, "U.S. House Members Back Freedmen Tribal Recognition Fight," *Axios,* April 25, 2024, https://www.axios.com/2024/04/25/us-house-freedmen-muscogee-creek-nation.
3. "Possible SNAP Cuts, Tulsa Race Massacre, Biden's 200th Federal Judge Confirmation, Crockett Chronicles," *#RolandMartinUnfiltered,* iHeart, May 23, 2024, https://www.tapesearch.com/episode/possible-snap-cuts-tulsa-race-massacre-biden-s-200th-federal-judge-confirmation-crockett-chronicles/EdPm37J9X2DwLZ2uDWtgRS.
4. "Oklahoma's Supreme Court Dismisses Lawsuit from Last 2 Survivors of Tulsa Race Massacre Seeking Reparations," PBS News, June 12, 2024, https://www.pbs.org/newshour/nation/oklahomas-supreme-court-dismisses-lawsuit-from-last-2-survivors-of-tulsa-race-massacre-seeking-reparations.
5. "Randle v. City of Tulsa," VLex, June 13, 2024, https://case-law.vlex.com/vid/randle-v-city-of-1039240276.
6. Clarissa Lim, "Oklahoma Supreme Court Dismisses Tulsa Race Massacre Survivors' Lawsuit," MSNBC.com, June 12, 2024, https://www.msnbc.com/top-stories/latest/tulsa-race-massacre-lawsuit-oklahoma-supreme-court-rcna156828.
7. "Michelle Obama Speaks at 2024 Democratic National Convention," PBS News Hour, YouTube, August 20, 2024, https://www.youtube.com/watch?v=YgJBFBwRXvc.
8. Adria Walker, "US Justice Department Announces Investigation into Tulsa Race Massacre," *The Guardian,* October 1, 2024, https://www.theguardian.com/us-news/2024/oct/01/tulsa-race-massacre-doj-investigation.
9. Justice for Greenwood Foundation, "Special Announcement: DOJ Announced Critical Update on Tulsa Race Massacre Case," YouTube, October 1, 2024, https://www.youtube.com/watch?v=i7gdyLjqmpQ.
10. SolomonSimmonsLaw to Barbara Kay Bosserman and Walter Henry, November 15, 2024, in possession of SolomonSimmonsLaw.

* DeNeen L. Brown and Leo Ji, "'They Was Killing Black People': A Century-Old Race Massacre Still Haunts Tulsa," *The Washington Post,* September 28, 2018, https://www.washingtonpost.com/news/local/wp/2018/09/28/feature/they-was-killing-black-people/.

CHAPTER 13: GREENWOOD IS STILL BURNING

1. "Tulsa Race Massacre Survivor Celebrates 110th Birthday," ABC News, November 11, 2024, https://abcnews.go.com/GMA/Living/video/tulsa-race-massacre-survivor-celebrates-110th-birthday-115748956.
2. Robert F. Smith's Post, LinkedIn, https://www.linkedin.com/posts/robert fredericksmith_justice-tulsaracemassacre-activity-7217537372048027648-utAZ/.
3. Damario Solomon-Simmons to Mayor Monroe Nichols, December 3, 2024, in possession of Justice for Greenwood.
4. Damario Solomon-Simmons, statement, published January 17, 2025.
5. U.S. Department of Justice, Civil Rights Division, *Review and Evaluation: Tulsa Race Massacre (Amended January 17, 2025),* https://www.justice.gov/crt/media/1383756/d.
6. Karen Attiah, "For Tulsa Victims, This 'Apology' Stings," *The Washington Post,* January 29, 2025, https://www.washingtonpost.com/opinions/2025/01/29/tulsa-greenwood-massacre-report/.
7. Deon Osborne, "'Project Greenwood' Reparations Package Gains Mayor's Support," *The Black Wall Street Times,* February 4, 2025.
8. Ben Abrams, "Tulsa Designates City Holiday Commemorating 1921 Race Massacre," Public Radio Tulsa, March 17, 2025, https://www.publicradiotulsa.org/local-regional/2025-03-17/tulsa-designates-city-holiday-commemorating-1921-race-massacre.

* Eddie Faye Gates, *They Came Searching: How Blacks Sought the Promised Land in Tulsa* (Austin, TX: Eakin Press, 1997), 43.

CHAPTER 14: WHEN WE FIGHT, WE WIN

1. Nehemiah Frank, "Road to Repair: Mayor Nichols' Full Transcript," *The Black Wall Street Times,* June 4, 2025, https://theblackwallsttimes.com/2025/06/04/road-to-repair-mayor-nichols-full-transcript/.
2. "Schulte Roth & Zabel LLP," McDermott Will & Schulte LLP - City of Tulsa Sued for Withholding Race Massacre Documents. Schulte Roth & Zabel LLP, 2021, https://www.srz.com/en/news_and_insights/firm-news/city-of-tulsa-sued-for-withholding-race-massacre-documents.
3. "Texas GOP Gerrymander, Tulsa's $105M Road to Repair, Joni Ernst & Moral Monday Arrest," #RolandMartinUnfiltered, iHeart, June 3, 2025, https://www.iheart.com/podcast/1119-rolandmartinunfiltered-43072236/episode/texas-gop-gerrymander-tulsas-105m-road-278962624/.
4. "S. 3543 | U.S. Department of the Interior," U.S. Department of the Interior, May 22, 2024, https://www.doi.gov/ocl/s-3543.
5. I disagree with Senator Lankford on most issues—often strongly—but I want to thank him for keeping the story of Greenwood alive in the Senate, for pushing this bill year after year, and for always making himself and his staff accessible on this issue.
6. Deon Osborne, "US Senate Passes Bill to Make Black Wall Street a National Monument," *The Black Wall Street Times,* May 23, 2025, https://theblack

wallsttimes.com/2025/05/23/us-senate-passes-bill-to-make-black-wall-street-a-national-monument/.

7. Deon Osborne, "Tulsa Mayor Unveils Historic $105 Million Reparations Plan for Greenwood," *The Black Wall Street Times,* June 1, 2025, https://theblackwallsttimes.com/2025/06/01/tulsa-mayor-unveils-historic-105-reparations-plan-for-greenwood/.
8. Alyse Martin, "Resurfaced Video Shows Trump Outlining Plans to Give 'Reparations' . . . but There's a Big Catch," *The Root,* November 14, 2024, https://www.theroot.com/resurfaced-video-shows-trump-outlining-plans-to-give-re-1851697450.

* Eddie Faye Gates, *Riot on Greenwood: The Total Destruction of Black Wall Street* (Austin, TX: Eakin Press, 2003), 66–67.

CHAPTER 15: THINKGREENWOOD

1. K.L. Gilbert et al., "Social Capital, Black Social Mobility, and Health Disparities," *International Journal of Environmental Research and Public Health* 19, no. 3 (2022): 1362; T. Hobson-Prater and T.G.J. Leech, "The Significance of Race for Neighborhood Social Cohesion: Perceived Difficulty of Collective Action in Majority Black Neighborhoods," *Journal of Social Service Research* 38, no. 4 (2012): 540–550.
2. Harlan Ellison, *Sleepless Nights in the Procrustean Bed* (San Bernardino, CA: Borgo Press, 1984), 197, 210.
3. "Summary of Key Data Points in Tulsa," Human Rights Watch, September 12, 2019, https://www.hrw.org/news/2019/09/12/summary-key-data-points-tulsa.
4. Tulsa Police Department, "Annual Report 2023," https://www.tulsapolice.org/_files/ugd/a38616_ab3074286d364605bff0e2bffce817ba.pdf.
5. Drew Diamond quoted in Transcript of Public Hearing on Tulsa Equality Indicators Report and Racial Disparities in Policing, NAACP Legal Defense Fund and the Terence Crutcher Foundation, March 7, 2019, 45–48, https://www.naacpldf.org/wpcontent/uploads/Tulsa-Community-Led-Public-Hearing-Transcript.pdf.
6. "50 Local Leaders Sign Letter Penned by LDF to Tulsa Officials Demanding Police Reform," 2 News Oklahoma KJRH, June 1, 2018, https://www.kjrh.com/news/50-local-leaders-sign-letter-penned-by-naacp-to-tulsa-officials-demanding-police-reform.
7. Human Rights Watch, *"Get on the Ground!" Policing, Poverty, and Racial Inequality in Tulsa, Oklahoma,* September 2019, https://www.hrw.org/sites/default/files/report_pdf/us0919_tulsa_web.pdf.
8. Carter Godwin Woodson, *The Mis-education of the Negro* (Trenton, NJ: Africa World Press, 1990), 4.
9. Peter Myers, "The Ballot or the Bullet," Teaching American History, April 3, 1964, https://teachingamericanhistory.org/document/the-ballot-or-the-bullet-2/.
10. "Dr. John Henrik Clarke - Harlem, Part 2 (1981)," Pbs.org, May 16, 2024, https://www.pbs.org/video/dr-john-henrik-clarke-harlem-part-2-tgliwn/.
11. Mohamed Younis, "As Redress for Slavery, Americans Oppose Cash Reparations," Gallup, July 29, 2019, https://news.gallup.com/poll/261722/redress-slavery-americans-oppose-cash-reparations.aspx.
12. Carrie Blazina and Kiana Cox, "Black and White Americans Are Far Apart in Their Views of Reparations for Slavery," Pew Research Center, November 28, 2022, https://www.pewresearch.org/short-reads/2022/11/28/black-and-white-americans-are-far-apart-in-their-views-of-reparations-for-slavery/.

BIBLIOGRAPHY

Appiah, Kwame Anthony, and Henry Louis Gates, Jr., eds. *Africana: The Encyclopedia of the African and African American Experience*. Oxford University Press, 1999.

Franklin, Buck Colbert, John Hope Franklin, and John Whittington Franklin. *My Life and an Era: The Autobiography of Buck Colbert Franklin*. Louisiana State University Press, 1997.

Franklin, John Hope, and Alfred A. Moss, Jr. *From Slavery to Freedom: A History of African Americans*. Alfred A. Knopf, 2000.

Gates, Eddie Faye. *Riot on Greenwood: The Total Destruction of Black Wall Street*. Eakin Press, 2003.

Gates, Eddie Faye. *They Came Searching: How Blacks Sought the Promised Land in Tulsa*. Eakin Press, 1997.

Greenberg, Jonathan. *Staking a Claim: Jake Simmons, Jr. and the Making of an African-American Oil Dynasty*. Atheneum, 1990.

Hurston, Zora Neale. *Dust Tracks on a Road: An Autobiography*. Harper Perennial Modern Classics, 2006. Originally published in 1942 by J. B. Lippincott.

Johnson, Hannibal B. *Acres of Aspiration: The All-Black Towns in Oklahoma*. Eakin Press, 2004.

Luckerson, Victor. *Built from the Fire: The Epic Story of Tulsa's Greenwood District, America's Black Wall Street*. Random House, 2023.

Madigan, Tim. *The Burning: Massacre, Destruction, and the Tulsa Race Riot of 1921*. St. Martin's Griffin, 2003.

Moreno, Carlos. *The Victory of Greenwood*. Jenkin Lloyd-Jones Press, 2021.

Oklahoma Commission to Study the Tulsa Race Riot of 1921, *Tulsa Race Riot,* 2001.

Parrish, Mary E. Jones. *Events of the Tulsa Disaster*. Self-published, 1923.

Stevenson, Bryan. *Just Mercy: A Story of Justice and Redemption*. Spiegel & Grau, 2014.

Tademy, Lalita. *Citizens Creek*. Atria, 2014.

INDEX

ABOUT STOREHOUSE VOICES

Storehouse Voices celebrates culturally rich narratives that reflect the dynamic influence of communities across the globe. Our imprint is dedicated to amplifying underrepresented and overworthy voices in fiction and nonfiction, with a focus on accessible and engaging content that honors the past, disrupts the present, and imagines new futures.

Learn more about us at storehousevoices.com.